Beyond Lament

Beyond Lament

POETS OF THE WORLD

BEARING WITNESS

TO THE HOLOCAUST

EDITED BY MARGUERITE M. STRIAR

NORTHWESTERN UNIVERSITY PRESS

EVANSTON, ILLINOIS

Northwestern University Press
Evanston, Illinois 60208-4210

Compilation and introduction copyright © 1998 by Marguerite M. Striar.
Published 1998 by Northwestern University Press. All rights reserved.

Printed in the United States of America

ISBN 0-8101-1555-7 (cloth)
ISBN 0-8101-1556-5 (paper)

Library of Congress Cataloging-in-Publication Data

Dedicated to the six million Jews and other victims
of the Nazi Holocaust, and to the U.S. Holocaust Memorial Museum
completed April 1993 in Washington, D.C.

Contents

THE NIGHTMARE BECOMES REALITY

IN MEMORIAM

THE LIBERATION

THE AFTERMATH

Acknowledgments

First, there were the voices that urged me and inspired me: voices of the dead whose unspeakable sufferings, losses, and heroism called out to me to be remembered. I called out to the poets. They heard and felt impelled, as I was, by those violated spirits to bear witness. It was the importunity of those voices that has made me persevere these last seven years without benefit of grants, subsidies, or staff.

There were many along the way whose interest, help, and guidance were invaluable. I am especially grateful to Lawrence Langer and Merrill Leffler for their careful and critical reading of early versions of the introduction and their suggestions for its direction and scope. Harry Zohn was invaluable in checking the accuracy of historical references in the introduction. His advice on any number of matters related to anthologies, translations, and important poets was superb. He, as well as Seymour Mayne, Max Ticktin, Michael Berenbaum, the late Rabbi Eugene Lipman, and Doris Vidaver were as a lamp unto my feet lighting my way to possible poets, source material, and publishers.

First to offer help with the necessary chore of condensing and shaping poets' biographies was my writer friend, Mary Coddington. Next was my brilliant young neighbor, Hannah Schneider, who willingly gave me many hours of her vacation time condensing more of these bios and alphabetizing a mass of material into neat and accessible files. To Pauline Schmookler, many thanks for helping with the organization of the book's sections, to Helene Ivey for essential early help with her computer skills, to Davi Walders for helping to address envelopes, and to Marie Maurice for her invaluable typing.

To all my friends and my family who were unstinting in their support for my persevering with this venture, my love and thanks—and especially to my daughter Diane, whose cheerful and efficient expertise with the computer made it possible for the book to meet its deadline. Most heart-warming has been the encouragement of the poets who have written, called, sought me out, all to tell me they appreciate the purpose of *Beyond Lament,* my efforts to bring it about, and are glad to be a part of it. Even if you are determined to run the race, how it helps to have a cheering section!

ACKNOWLEDGMENTS

Introduction

Those dying here, the lonely
forgotten by the world,
our tongue becomes for them
the language of an ancient
planet.
Until, when all is legend
and many years have passed,
on a new Campo dei Fiori
rage will kindle at a poet's word.

— from "Campo Dei Fiori"
(on the destruction of the Warsaw Ghetto)
— Czesław Miłosz, Warsaw, 1943

The word "Holocaust" describes that period between 1933 and 1945 when Nazi Germany, with malice aforethought and a brutal efficiency that numbs the mind, systematically slaughtered six million Jews. Also murdered were millions of others, including Catholics, Jehovah's Witnesses, trade unionists, homosexuals, Gypsies, Communists, and, in fact, anyone who didn't meet Adolf Hitler's physical, racial, ideological, and religious standards. But only the Jews of Europe were singled out (dare we use the word "chosen"?) to be totally exterminated according to a well-thought-out and efficient plan.

Since the destruction of the Temple and the fall of Jerusalem to the Romans in A.D. 70, the Jewish people have been dispersed throughout the world. Because they were strangers, wanderers, with no home of their own, their welcome was always tempered with distrust and often with contempt, leading eventually to vilification and persecution. Even when there was tolerance and appreciation for their cultural, economic, and civic contributions to the state, Jews were aware of an undercurrent of disdain that threatened the safety of their refuge. Jews learned, as best they could, to live with anti-Semitism, a word so general that it covers behaviors ranging from dislike or intolerance of Jews to violence, persecution, pogroms, and to the disaster we call the Holocaust or Shoah.

While anti-Semitic discrimination and hostility persisted in Western Europe into the twentieth century, after World War I widespread violence against Jews seemed to be diminishing. Jews in Germany achieved a high level of economic success and personal security. Assimilation into German society was on the rise; there were many reasons for those Jews who lived there to think of themselves not as German Jews but as Jewish Germans. But, as the 1920s came to an end, economic conditions in the war-impoverished country deteriorated. With the rise in unemployment came a rise in complaints, and Germans demanded explanations from their government, which promptly reached for a historical scapegoat: the Jews.

Although anti-Semitism had official approval in Germany as early as 1920, it was in 1933, when Adolf Hitler became chancellor of the German Reich, that the attacks on the civil and economic rights of Jews accelerated. In September 1935, the Nuremberg laws decreed that Jews were no longer citizens and would not enjoy the protection of the state. Not only did Jews lose their jobs, but a boycott forbade non-Jews to serve them. Signs saying "No Jews" appeared on the doors of cobbler shops, theaters, and restaurants. Jewish doctors, lawyers, and other professionals had their licenses taken away; Jewish students were removed from schools and universities; and Jewish-owned businesses, both large and small, were confiscated by force. Soon shootings, lynchings, and torture became commonplace. Although these were ominous rumblings of what was to come, most Jews refused to believe the extent of the danger and delayed escape until it was too late.

November 9, 1938. Kristallnacht, "the night of broken glass": Attacks against the Jews and their property were organized throughout Germany. For this bloody pogrom against them, the Jews had to pay one billion Reichsmarks as "reparations" and repair all damages at their own expense as well.

July 22, 1939: The Nazis began the "resettlement" of 380,000 Jews from Poland's Warsaw Ghetto. Six thousand Jews a day were sent in sealed freight cars to the nearby concentration camp at Treblinka, where they were asphyxiated by carbon monoxide.

September 1, 1939: The German Army invaded Poland, and 700,000 Jewish men, women, and children were gassed in mobile gas vans. German factories processed the corpses into fertilizer, soap, glue, and lubricants.

January 1942: At the Wannsee Conference, the Nazi high command confirmed the plan to exterminate all the Jews in Europe using Zyklon B, a poison gas. The hundred or so concentration camps in Germany and Poland were turned into extermination centers, human abattoirs. Auschwitz was the most efficient; others included Dachau, Bergen-Belsen, Buchenwald, Ravensbrück, and Treblinka. The victims were subjected systematically to the harshest treatment, so that thousands died from hunger and cold, overwork and beatings, even before the scheduled trips to the deadly gas chambers and the ovens.

"Writing poetry after Auschwitz is barbaric" is an often-quoted statement made by German-Jewish sociologist and aesthetician Theodor W. Adorno. He later modified his statement by saying that "literature must resist the cynicism such comments express." Adorno knew that, despite the inadequacy of words, language is all we have to give voice to our grief, our outrage, our kinship with those who suffered more than we can ever imagine. The only alternative when confronted by such massive violation of the human body and spirit is to be stunned into inarticulateness, because no word can be worthy of describing such suffering.

I honor and cherish Elie Wiesel, and yet I would argue with him when he says, "I firmly believe that art is not appropriate to the Holocaust. Art takes the sting out of suffering. . . . Any attempt to transform the Holocaust into art demeans the Holocaust and must result in poor art." He says, further, "there are no metaphors for Auschwitz." But Auschwitz itself has become a new metaphor for the extremes of depravity and unspeakable degradation, the hell to which some humans subjected other humans. Even Wiesel, to whom the Holocaust was "a sacred event not to be defiled" by writing novels or poetry about it, could not resist metaphor. He says in his foreword to *Voices from the Holocaust,* a collection of interviews with survivors edited by Sylvia Rothchild (New York: New American Library, 1981), "The stories they tell—I know them. It's strange how similar they are. In those days all European Jews went through the same trials. Forced to enter the kingdom of night, they discovered the same truths" (p. 1).

No poetry after Auschwitz? Tell that to the survivors who on meeting the poet Lily Brett exclaim, "How can you know what happened to me at Auschwitz? You are telling my story!" I believe it is not the poet's intention to transform the Holocaust into art, but to describe it as best he or she can, to capture and express a personal reaction to it, and to memorialize the event by creating a poem. In doing so, the poet will use metaphors and images; if the poet puts his or her heart into the task, the result will be art. The same is true whether it is a poem, a story, a speech, or an essay that is being created. Wiesel himself, though he will deny it, is guilty of committing art, and undoubtedly he will do so again. Indeed, most poets don't choose to write about the Holocaust; it chooses them.

Are there other reasons poets write about the Holocaust? Israeli poet Yehuda Amichai describes poetry as a kind of remedy or homeopathic medicine that poets use to cure themselves of the pain in their lives. Writing about the Holocaust is an attempt to exorcise the horror they feel by naming it, describing it, recounting the tales over and over again, hoping for meaning or a lesson for the future or, at least, some personal release.

For readers as well as individual poets, such release is possible and necessary. As Adrienne Rich says in *What Is Found There: Notebooks on Poetry and Politics* (New York: Norton, 1993), "I have never believed that poetry is an escape from history, and I do not think it is more, or less, necessary than food, shelter, health, education, decent working conditions. It is as necessary" (p. xiv). Poetry is not only necessary, but can be subversive in the way it poses a challenge to the status quo of ideas. Totalitarian governments have always feared open poetic expression, often reacting with suppression, censorship, and persecution.

Richard Newman, in a letter accompanying his poems, says one reason he writes about the Holocaust is

> needing to give in my life a form to the Holocaust, to my identity as a "post-Holocaust Jew" that would allow me to move beyond it, beyond the fear and the anger, and I felt that the Jewish community needed to do so as well. . . . Giving voice to survivors in a poetic form (the sonnet) that by definition achieves closure was, for me, a way of saying that, yes, I could, within the limits of my understanding, create a meaning for the Holocaust before which I did not have to tremble in uncomprehending awe, but which I could use in building a spiritually and communally Jewish life for myself free of the fear and the anger that comes from being told that such a meaning is impossible.

Newman adds that he "worries that giving coherent form to horrors popularly thought to be transcendent of the limits of human understanding would trivialize what I was trying to say about them." That was Adorno's concern. "A poem of any sort," Newman continues,

> is an imaginative attempt to create meaning, and I would say that the presumption of these sonnets toward meaning fills me with trepidation, if that didn't sound too stylized and intellectual. The fact is, they scare the hell out of me. They scared me as I was writing them, and they terrify me now that, having been written, they demand an audience. The fear of being heard is only one step removed from the fear of speaking in the first place. I have suffered too long from the latter. I refuse to give in to the former.

Some poets mention the need to fight back by letting the world know. In her poem "a jew's love for language," Chaia L. Heller writes:

> i've got a jew's love
> for language and i'm gonna write it all down
> before the next generation of amnesiacs
> comes rushing in all red-cheeked and smiling
>
> i'm gonna write how you robbed me
> of my memories. how you looted the banks

of my blood. i'm gonna tell how my family tree
has been stripped and made into coffins
you burned to keep your tea warm.

Other reasons that impelled poets to write range from the need to set the record straight, as Joan Fondell, daughter of a survivor, does in "How Can They Say It Never Happened?" to rage, as in Karl Plank's "Malediction," or to the thoughtful recording of events that touched many people's lives only peripherally, as E. Ethelbert Miller does in his poem "The Fifties."

A poem, rather than a textbook chapter, biography, or memoir, is memorized easily. Poetry has the power to force history upon us through the passion of art. Every nation has examples of poetry that help make their history memorable. Many Americans hang their knowledge of early American history on the hook of poetry they memorized in school: Ralph Waldo Emerson's "Concord Hymn" and Longfellow's "Ride of Paul Revere" are examples. We share with the British the poet Rudyard Kipling's "Recessional," in which he reminds the British Empire (and all boastful nations) of their impermanent grandeur, closing with the plea "Judge of the Nations, spare us yet / Lest we forget—lest we forget!"

Here Richard Newman's sonnet 33, written in the persona of a survivor, reports:

> *That week, a woman's skirt*
> *was found at the Ghetto gate to be lined*
> *with smuggled food . . .*
> *The officers stripped her, spread her legs and probed with knives*
> *before they let her go. She brought her shame*
> *to me and I wrote it down, including her name.*

Fourteen-year-old Pavel Friedman, a prisoner in the Terezin ghetto, wrote in 1942 about the world around him of which he would soon be forcibly deprived. He describes a butterfly, the very last: "So richly, brightly, dazzlingly yellow, / Perhaps if the sun's tears would sing against a white stone / . . . only I never saw another butterfly." Forty years later, in her poem "In the Absence of Yellow," Israeli poet Reva Sharon writes, after a visit to Pavel's birthplace in Prague and to Terezin where he died, "In only seven weeks / you grasped the universe / within these ramparts / and etched a page of sorrow with your poem."

In addition to making history memorable, poetry can also demonstrate how the creative spirit can temporarily transcend suffering, even though it may have seen some of the worst times of the Holocaust horror. Darcy Gottlieb's "Rehearsal at Terezin" is a poem based on "The Terezin Requiem," a story by Josef Bor, a survivor who writes about Raphael Schachter, a young conductor at Terezin. With the help of prisoner musicians, he succeeded against great odds in performing Verdi's *Requiem*.

> *"Play!" Our conductor yells at us. "Play, sing,*
> *rage for those you love."* . . .
>
> *The violins tremble with crescendo.*
> *We no longer hear the transports*
> *thundering across our cellar sky.*
> *The music thrusts itself beyond lament.*
> *We feel it crash,*
> *splitting our terror into fragments.*
>
> *"Bravo!" the conductor cries out*
> *wiping his glasses on his sleeve.*
> *"You have surpassed yourselves today."*

And where can we find a better example of the triumph of artistic creation than the poems of Abraham Sutzkever, who, writing under the constrictions and constant threat of death in the Vilna ghetto and, during a period of ten days when the Nazis marched into Vilna, hiding in a broken chimney of his old apartment, wrote the nine poems of *Faces in Swamps*. In the introduction to *Burnt Pearls* (Ontario: Mosaic Press, 1981), a collection of Sutzkever's ghetto poems translated by Seymour Mayne, Ruth Wisse says:

> Sutzkever's trust in the redemptive capacity of art rather than morality became the key to his artistic and physical survival. Even before the war he had determined that the failure of humanity could not alter the basic criterion of art. In the living hell that followed, the incorruptible standards of the good poem became, for Sutzkever, the touchstone of

a former, higher sanity and a psychological means of self-protection against ignominy and despair. (p. 11)

In selecting poems for this collection, I chose about 280 from more than a thousand that caught me and would not let go, poems that writers could not help writing and I could not help including. Even after dozens of readings, I am still gripped and believe other readers will be also. Although I have included such great poets of yesterday as Paul Celan and Nelly Sachs, the majority are poets writing today. Some poems have been translated from the German, Hebrew, Yiddish, Greek, and Russian.

Some poets use irony to serve their purpose most effectively, as Christopher Fahy does in "Cinema III" and Elisavietta Ritchie does in "The German Officer Writes a Letter." Tamar Rodzyner ("Again"), Herbert Kuhner ("The Class of '38"), and Georg Kreisler ("Neither Nor")—all Austrian poets—employ a subtle but bitter irony.

Many poets have probed their subconscious, their memories, or drawn from their dreams. Although there is ideological content in these poems, their primary effect is emotional, whether the poet speaks from personal experience or in the persona of someone who was there but cannot speak for him- or herself. I suspect that, in most cases, the subject determined the form and the poet merely obeyed, whether that involved following regular rhyme and metrical patterns, exploring the unboundedness of free verse, or making a poetic statement in prose. In their use of spontaneous free verse, some poets have written to the margins, as in prose, or followed Charles Olson's open field theory of line lengths, determined by the poet's breathing.

It has now been fifty-three years since the end of World War II and the Holocaust, in which three-quarters of all European Jews were slaughtered by the Nazis. Yet today there is fresh news about new acts of anti-Semitism, and neo-Nazis circulate vicious propaganda claiming that the Holocaust is a fabrication. At the same time, around the world, ethnic and religious strife threatens to wipe out whole peoples.

Speaking at a ceremony at the nearly completed U.S. Holocaust Memorial Museum, then-congressman Jack Kemp said, "Most of what we learn from history is that people do not learn from history.

That's why the Holocaust Museum is so important." And, likewise, books of poetry like this one.

The act of writing poetry about the Holocaust may be an attempt to express the inexpressible, but, for the sake of present and future generations, we must give voice to our angers, our despairs, and our aspirations. We must believe that our voices will be heard and will make a difference. All of us are challenged to break the pattern of bestiality that runs through human behavior. If all of us are to survive on this planet, we must turn from hate to love, at the very least to civility. We can never pardon the criminal perpetrators of the Holocaust, but we cannot blame their descendants and hold them responsible for the sins of their fathers. We must make sure they know and understand the causes and consequences of the Nazi evil, lest they follow in their fathers' footsteps. We and they must know about it, must hold it ever in our consciousness, so that we can recognize signs of its rebirth wherever on earth this happens.

Marguerite M. Striar

Beyond Lament

IN *Defense* OF POETRY

After Poetry

Jane Schapiro

After Auschwitz, poetry is barbaric.
— T. W. Adorno

What should we do with silence
when we feel it bristling inside

or clearing its raspy throat
in the middle of a phrase?

How should we pretend not to hear
the waterless stream, filaments of color

stirring beneath the leaf's green skin?
And suppose we could bleach words

until they crumple off their stalks, what
about their stalks? Black irises springing up

in the Negev sand? Our own barbaric blood
scribbling across the wound?

a jew's love for language

Chaia L. Heller

you convert, you expel,
you exterminate.
you said, "jew, you'll burn in hell"
you said, "jew, go live by yourself"
and just when you silenced her name,
she sang back into your world
beaming and book carrying
and wearing pearls.

then one day you said,
"jew, you are going to die.
all of you." and with gas in her mouth
she went under six million times.
and finally, you inherited a meaner world
silenced of our humor, our music,
the sound of our laughter breaking
the stiffening walls of your theaters.
no more.

and you almost won in the end.
you painted the walls of your world
with our saddest blood
till they glowed a glistening red
only to be dulled to their usual gray
when our blood washes off.

and it will wash off.
and you and your children will forget
only i won't. cause i've got a jew's love
for language and i'm gonna write it all down
before the next generation of amnesiacs
comes rushing in all red-cheeked and smiling

i'm gonna write how you robbed me
of my memories. how you looted the banks
of my blood. i'm gonna tell how my family tree
has been stripped and made into coffins
you burned to keep your tea warm

i'm gonna write letters
to all the would-be children
of all those artists, tailors, makers of poems
and ironic sayings. i'm gonna thank them
for my mother's yiddishy expressions,
for my grandmother's chutzpah
and for my own love of the power of ideas

we were the spice of the world's garden,
scattered over every land. spice you took
and ground into piles of cups and toothbrushes.
you finally sorted us out. converted us
into heaps of clothes and shoes
the fillings of our teeth into fine, gold spoons

the only monuments to our beautiful culture,
this rubble called bergen-belsen, treblinka, dachau,
and auschwitz, some horrible mecca
earnest pilgrims visit offering their bouquets
of pity, disgust, shame

but we will have learned nothing
if we do not remember the gifts of our humor,
our music, our ability to make orchards bloom
between the cracks of the world's walls.

i like to think of all those poets, storekeepers,
and yentas, gossiping and laughing
as they held up their small piece of the world.
sometimes i can hear the echo
of their rowdy songs,
the banging of books,
the clatter of pearls

The Book of Lamentations

Leo Haber

The event called Holocaust was not made for poetry,
for the rhapsodizing and the charged emotion that
we associate with the form. It was beyond form

and beyond capturing with an apt phrase and even beyond
memorializing. I never met my father's brother face to face.
He, his wife, his two children were but brownish imprints

on a photo that came to us in the thirties from a
faraway place on the back of a picture postcard.
It must have been taken in a shop that made such fine

things for America, the golden land where we struggled
in the throes of the depression. Photos do not show
height or even weight, only depth, and sometimes

the sequestered soul. My uncle must have been a little man
like my father. He was dressed in the black of believers,
black hat over furrowed brow and curled black sideburns,

black coat, black shoes. His eyes were piercing, perhaps
from all the time he spent looking deeply into holy books.
I confess that I had no interest in the figure of his wife,

but she was beautiful and young (in my mother's words)
though to me she looked like all the old ladies who
had been wearied by their own children, if not by me.

The two boys fascinated me because they seemed taller
than their father and had curled sideburns longer than his.
They would have made fine playmates with their ends of hair

flapping in the wind during touch-football season. But
they were not fated to spend their young days at play.
They ended up in furnaces struggling for breath

against the advanced science of gas, systematically,
routinely destroyed, by a master plan created by
a country of musicians and poets. This is what we

justly call "unspeakable," unworthy of words, of music,
of the art of poetry. Still, Jeremiah sang in poetic form
of ancient Jerusalem's destruction where other young cousins

of mine, playmates all, died too. He wept and proclaimed
the poetry of lamentation against the cruel triumphal song of
the destroyer. The old prophet's art prevailed as mine may —

pale consolation, dear God of poetry, of justice, of mercy,
of explanations, for the murder of little children.

Song Is a Monument

Yala Korwin

In the old country our bards
sang Jewish sorrows, joys
of the rich and poor

of tailors, peddlers, scholars
mothers, fathers, children
lovers, sages, fools

Their hearths extinguished
ancient shtetls vanished
only songs remain

of the multi-petaled world
each petal a promise
each petal a voice

Do not mourn them in graveyards
their ashes mantle the earth
billow in clouds

swirl in eddies of rivers
dwell in rustling of trees
whirl in gusts of winds

Do not enshrine them in stone
let them breathe with your breath
Time grinds stone to dust

breath is a cradle of song
song is a monument
song is forever

Letter to a Poet

Herman Taube

To Chaim Grade

Shall you ask:
How long will we continue
to bemoan our past?
Your question answers
itself: Forever!
I will write endlessly.
Pain, strife, ugliness
of war and hate,
cannot be written
by historians alone.
We are the witnesses.
Like you, I'm pulled apart
by opposing
desires; I strive for love,
happiness to share with
my wife, children, friends,
or sit and write about
the despair of our people.
I am a self-imposed
codifier of chaos,
so preoccupied with pain
that I condemned myself
to solitary exile.

My poems are my enemy;
they rob my precious days
left at the gate of life.
Writing about the past
defies all logic, sense,
I'm in a spiderweb,
entangled in images
that haunt me, hold me,
calling, demanding:
Write! You are our memory! . . .

Dedication

Czesław Miłosz

You whom I could not save
Listen to me.
Try to understand this simple speech as I would be ashamed of another.

I swear, there is in me no wizardry of words.
I speak to you with silence like a cloud or a tree.

What strengthened me, for you was lethal.
You mixed up farewell to an epoch with the beginning of a new one,
Inspiration of hatred with lyrical beauty,
Blind force with accomplished shape.

Here is the valley of shallow Polish rivers. And an immense bridge
Going into white fog. Here is a broken city,
And the wind throws screams of gulls on your grave
When I am talking with you.

What is poetry which does not save
Nations or people?
A connivance with official lies,
A song of drunkards whose throats will be cut in a moment,
Readings for sophomore girls.
That I wanted good poetry without knowing it,
That I discovered, late, its salutary aim,
In this and only this I find salvation.

They used to pour on graves millet or poppy seeds
To feed the dead who would come disguised as birds.
I put this book here for you, who once lived
So that you should visit us no more.

Warsaw, 1945

Translated by Czesław Miłosz

THE *Beginning*:

PREMONITIONS AND PROPHESIES

Where We Are

Peter Desy

I am a human being, so nothing human is alien to me.
— Terence, d. 159 B.C.

Could you imagine slaves slaughtering
your legions, smiting bone and gristle,
then 6,000 hung up like beef along
the Appian Way? Really? Even the flies?
What aristocratic and humanistic intuition!

Fog, too heavy to rise,
hunches near the gas factories,
and the commandant plays Mozart
on the Victrola and eats delicacies.
In the showers, without dalliance, children
clutching stones like hope . . . You thought
of that? People being homogenized into fat?
Did you divine all this
from an expansive sensibility you developed
writing comedies for Patricians?
Everything was accessible to you?
I'm an alien myself, parts of myself
not even introduced to the rest of me:
there are some things I'd rather
not think about. You know, a lot has happened.
Wisdom isn't what it used to be.

Certain felicities in the drama, and other
amenities are no longer possible . . .
You say you knew 6,000,000 would die in camps?

How could you know this: continents
glide, so even the dead move, slowly,
toward some convergence and upheaval.
"Terence, there's no still point, no song
or play to help us navigate. Terence,
everything's gone serious,
and we ride currents too deep to know."

A Transport of Children*

Cornel Lengyel

My greetings to all at home with thanks!
    I send you the good news at once:
I have been chosen! Yes, it's true!
    The train is pulling out, I'm on my way,
I've all the cards and passports I need,
    signed or stamped by the authorities!
So many applied, so many were rejected—
    How lucky am I to have been chosen!

My thanks to our Learned Rabbis,
    My thanks to our Loving Neighbors,
My thanks without end to Everyone!
    To you, dearest Papa and Monel,
for the copy of Birth Certificate!
    To Rabbi Mosheh for my Card of Identity!
To Rabbi Akiba for the Diploma!
    To Rabbi Todt and Company
for their Letters of Recommendation!
    To Rabbi Himmler for the Work Permit!
I can hardly believe it—
    To Rabbi Eichmann for the Passport—
How lucky am I to have been chosen!

*From Misha Mishling's letter of thanks (en route to Auschwitz, 1942).

I have all I need till the end of my journey,
    the rest they'll furnish in Auschwitz, they say.
The weather's uncertain, the work may be rough,
    but I'll do my best, you needn't worry!
I'll write again from Auschwitz as soon as I can—
    till then remember your loving son,
and praise the Almighty Lord of the Universe—
    How lucky am I to have been chosen!

Oma's Opera Fan

Rochelle Natt

Her long fingers, holding the lacquered spokes,
slowly unfold a sheen of ebony pleats.
Above this hemisphere
her brown eyes gaze.

When the young doctor looks at her,
the fan stills.
Heat rises to the top of her cheeks.
He is the music.

In German, he asks,
"May I look closely at the fan?"
He studies its scene, painted in fine detail:

> A man, rowing a boat.
> At the bow, a woman stands.
> The couple's eyes are fixed
> on the shore
> where in a copse of dark pines
> a young man hides.

Stealing the moment, Oma studies the doctor's strong body.
Pinned to the breast of his uniform—the Iron Cross.
A hero, not much taller than she.

If she were to lean against him,
her forehead would touch his cheek.
She says, "The painting is by Frau Grieg."

If he isn't too distracted
by the tremolo of her voice,
the moonwhite of her teeth,
will he forsee
the libretto of their later life?

> Their flight
> from Frankfurt to England.
> The son they'd thought was safe,
> seized, shipped east
> on a rattling train,
> those trains,
> that Crescendo,
> the Black Unfolding.

Born in Safety, 1941: a broken villanelle

Davi Walders

In the beginning was the end of innocence
Placental coat wrapped round a tiny fist
Goose steps clicked, evil licked the womb with violence.

Tear glistening, lips wailed against dawn silence
Ruby cells calling through memory mists
In the beginning was the end of innocence.

Cord clamped and cut, heart beating, life commenced
Warm white wool, a name, pink around a wrist
Goose steps clicked, evil licked the womb with violence.

Soft skull crowned by curls damp and dense
Washed, soothed, and kissed
In the beginning was the end of innocence.

Who will remember, imagine, sense,
The silent millions lost
That year, those years, a thousand years hence?

In the beginning was the end of innocence
When goose steps clicked
And evil licked the world with violence.

The Last Letter

Charles F. Streckfus

The sirens wail and
I can hear the caving in
of the neighbor's door.
I hope you are safe in
England as I write
this final note to you.
Keep me in your mind always and remember.
    Remember me after all
        acquaintances have parted.
    Remember beyond those that
        toast me in memory.
    Remember past the sobs
        of my mother and son.
    Remember past the snowdrifts
        blowing into summer fields.
    Remember when all others have
        forgotten their yesterdays
        and are tired of remembering.
And when I return to you,
you with your glistening eyes,
I shall say, "I've come home because
you remembered as no one did."

The Photograph

Mary Engel

For my grandmother

You sit in the two-room hovel you call home.
Your eyes, oasis in the wrinkled face,
replay the drama in Hitler's hippodrome.
It was, Grandma, the wrong time, the wrong place.
Your children left for the promise written in gold,
for the opportunity in a distant land.
Their letters begged you to leave. You said, "Too old
for change." Your shtetl seared with the Nazi's brand,
the house ransacked, the tombstone overturned,
you thought, "This, too, shall pass. Why follow them?"
You waited for miracles. The Nazis burned
the synagogue. Their crimes we now condemn.
Yad Vashem, Chagall,* record the date.
You waited, prayed, but then it was too late.

---

*Marc Chagall's painting *White Crucifixion* hangs in the Art Institute of Chicago. It depicts Jesus wrapped in a prayer shawl and hanging from a cross. German storm troopers are setting fire to a synagogue. Figures clutching the Torah are seen fleeing from the burning synagogue.

Hearing Him Talk

Barbara Goldberg

Eric Heymann, 1903–1957

My own father died of swine flu, spent
his days reading Talmud in the back
room while my mother ran the store,
workhorse daughter of horse thieves.
That was my stock: one foot in heaven,
the other in mud. Never forgot that.

War already brewing when I first danced
with your mother in Karlsbad, she making
eyes at the dark Hungarian who looked
like Robert Taylor, American film star.
I know she didn't think much of me, though
for a stout man I dance a mean tango.

Followed her back to Prague with clear
intentions, ended up yelling at that
chicken-brained idiot who was her best
friend's brother, he believing Hitler
wouldn't invade: too well-off to be smart.
Hand-delivered twelve long-stemmed roses.

Had to drag your mother out. The others
perished. No matter how bad things are
they can always get worse. Stay liquid.

Avoid real estate, handsome men. Choose
one like a rock. Never cheat on taxes.
This country deserves every dime.

Sometimes I have no patience with lumps
in the horseradish sauce, you girls
for refusing to practice your scales.
I go up and down with the market.
You shouldn't take it so hard.
A lot of noise. The way I am.

The Document Room at Nuremberg

Enid Shomer

The truth abounds in triplicate,
initialled with a rainbow
of ink, a color for each high
official: Keitel, Jodl,
Goering (green, I think),
and, guilty as a bloody
fingerprint, Hitler's red *A.H.*

Also on display, tangible
proof that orders were obeyed:
photo of Poles and Jews
relocated against a wall;
photo of bodies slumped
against the wall now sprayed
with the bureaucrat's ink;
photo of trucks whose only
destination was the death
their occupants breathed
as they wore ruts
in circular roads.

Where did it begin? Begin
at the beginning—in the empty
stomach of an out-of-work
paper-hanger screaming
in the streets, nothing left
to eat but the world.

Choni, The Circle Man*

Asher Torren

Before Auschwitz and the Great Loss
I went down to the beach
To talk to the fish.

Below the soft brown cliffs,
Choni, the circle man, was drawing
In the sand with his staff.

"One hundred thousand circles from
Haifa to Netanya, and millions to go;
Shelters for my children," said Choni.

While my eyes, glued to the horizon,
Waited for their arrival, the sand
Under my feet erupted.

Petroleum, cried the fish when
Every circle became a well;
One hundred thousand wells in the sand.

The waves rose high and crashed
Hard against the cliffs
Chasing us from the beach.

---

*Millions of Jews were left stranded in Nazi Europe when the British, under
Arab pressure, severely restricted the entrance of Jews into Palestine.

"My children . . . they will never come," said
Choni, the circle man,
And drew a circle around us
Atop the soft brown cliffs.

The Non-Emigrant
(My Father in Nazi Germany)

Lotte Kramer

He left the application forms
Hidden inside his desk and missed
His quota for the USA.

He thought he'd stay and wait and stare
The madness out. It could not last.
He would not emigrate, not lose

His home, his language and his ground.
Beside his armchair sat a pile
Of books; the smoke from his cigar

Fenced comfort with a yellow screen.
His daily walk was all he'd need,
He thought. Abroad was where he'd been.

On Shutting the Door

Lotte Kramer

Often, when I leave home,
I think of you,
How you'd have shut the door
That last time
They fetched you out at dawn.

What fears would prophesy,
What intimations
Could foretell the terrors
Of those plains,
The herding into ash?

Or maybe, you looked round
As if before
A holiday, leaving
No trace of dust,
No crumbs for pests, no moths

In cupboards, carpets;
Covered the chairs,
The settee from the glare
Of light and sun,
Turned off the water, gas . . .

Fugue

Lotte Kramer

There was no irony in it,
After their nightfall arrival.
She always came shadowless now.

This time she brought one in his black
Swastika uniform. They ate
As usual at the oak table.

Then, in the yellow light's comfort
The older woman's accurate
Fingers unpinned a stepping fugue.

His words cut that afterglow calm:
"I did not believe that a Jew
Could play Bach like that, I thank you."

A New Subject

Lotte Kramer

"Today we start a subject that is new
To everyone. As your new master now
I've come to tell you something of those true
Great ancestors we have. You must be proud,

You boys, our fatherland, our new decade,
Is nurtured by a giant race: red-blond,
Eyes blue, a strong physique and unafraid.
The finest ethnic heritage is ours.

Let's see the type of man we used to be—
Yes you—just there—behind that darkish head,
You in the seventh row—get up, come here!
What is your name? Ah, Heinz, ah, very good.

Now face the class. You see in this blond boy
The perfect specimen of purest race;
His bones are powerful, his hair is fair,
His eyes are blue set in an eager face.

No shameful mixture in his blood or breed.
This is your future now, our Germany!
You grin—you laugh—you too—I'll have no cheek
From anyone! What is the matter, speak?"

"Please Sir, it makes no sense, it's true, you see
      Heinz is a Jew."

The Class of '38

Herbert Kuhner

In that group photo
taken in June of '38
in the second district of Vienna,
the so-called Leopoldstadt,
also known as "Matzo Island,"
they look forward
as all graduates do.
Looking back,
we know what lay ahead.
That class
would be traveling soon
by bus, ship, plane,
but above all by rail.
They'd end up
on all four corners
of the earth,
but mostly in Polish skies.

Circus

Vera Weislitz

This will be a grand show
the announcements promise it so
I am lucky, I think,
I am the daughter of Leo
and have a seat in the first row.

The arena is spacious, the heart beats
in Berlin
the first act is pompous
the beasts
in custom-made outfits
dance their dance on twos.

They plan, they curse, set up gallows
their offspring drum the drums,
whistle the whistle, march the march,
spit in Leo's face,
new slogans are heard:
     One Country!   One Nation!   One Führer!

Jails, swelling with criminals,
open their gates,
The arena expands—
Paris, Vienna, Prague, Belgrade
Wrocław, Budapest, Stalingrad . . .

The Iron Cross glitters on their coats,
sword in hand, God's name on their lips,
the Holy Bible upside down.
Gretchens with braids
braid myrtle wreaths in elegance,
they swear allegiance and their children
to the Führer till eternity.
    Hail Caesar!   Sieg heil, sieg!

It fascinates the crowd, for a time,
makes them shout, turn into wolves,
they creep from their dens,
hunt by light of day,
under starry skies,
thirsty for blood
        Victoria!   Victoria!

In the audience, a blackout, sirens scream
Europe erupts, a volcano at Pompeii!
The pessimists talk reality, facts,
Leo—prays to God,
the blind men shriek: "See! See! the rainbow on the horizon,
the Contract's alive!"
Fata Morgana—Mirage

Six endless years—
flames, flames,
all turns to ash . . .

I was lucky,
saved by Leo from Ostrava

I can tell my children I saw a circus
more spectacular than that in ancient Rome
I had a seat in the first row.

THE *Nightmare*

BECOMES REALITY

Kristallnacht

Sue Saniel Elkind

Blackness
broken by streamers
of light from trucks
Trembling mothers
hide children
beg them "be still"
others try escape
All the time
marching feet
slam against cement
stopping only as marchers
hurl rocks
leaving shards of bone
Ramrods
Violate houses   people
lie splintered
amid slivers of glass
Their screams become one
Old and young
herded outside
prodded to run
"Jew, jew" following them
Bullets fired
shatter windows of dreams
that will become eternal
nightmares.

Last Train to Auschwitz

Lois Van Houten

After Herman Wouk

The train: long, black, rain-splattered
the bold-faced eagle feral and brazen
across the engine plate.
The train, cutting their lives in two
like a long, black fence.

The terror of heavy doors slamming open
the bare, stripped caverns inside: then—
Herded into
Brutalized into
Thrown headlong into
To be counted less than the animals
of the field, who had been here before them.
Quavering behind their yellow stars:
become the stars of infamy.

And they were human:
they bled like the other
cried, laughed, procreated
like the other.
Held their stomachs in hunger
stroked the white heads of their elders
crooned to the babes in arms.

On the second day, no food, little water
the slop pails inordinately foul . . .
they began to die.
No room for proper death: the old rehearsed
their memories while life circuited
out of them.
Some of them, stronger, tried to lay the dead
in decent rows
to allow them a certain dignity.

The train went on: mile after mile after mile.
Backwards and forwards, bells clanging
jolting their sore flesh, sending the bitter
bile against their teeth.
Nudging them from their precious space
against the wall.
Hour after damnable hour . . . a carrier from Hell.
They are rubbed raw against each other.
They had been mandated to each other.
All they have left is the other.

The doors bang open: the doors bang shut.
There is still the world out there, sunshine
blue skies—soldiers waiting with clubs
with canes, guns, dogs: their faces
more rabid than their trained beasts.
Trained to the kill: to torture, to maim
to dismember, to dispense more evil
than the world has ever known.

The train goes on: denies them their lives.
Mountains poke through barred air spaces.
Snow coats their peaks, falls over the tracks.
The temperature drops, sullen and fast.
They huddle together. They are convinced
they will live. They are convinced
they are lost.
Some lick their cracked lips for water.
Some groan from their bellies' lack.
Some topple over, defeated.

It is the third day.
They huddle together: they are all they
have left.
The train goes on. It is almost there.
They pray to God.

"The Lord Our God is One God.
If I forsake thee . . . "

I'm Chugging into France

Julia Stein

How the Jewish children sang
on the train chugging into France.
I sang like that once in *schule*.*
Songs just burst out of me
in Yiddish, Hebrew, and English.

Not in public school.
We were all Jewish children in public school at
the yearly Christmas assembly
singing only Christmas carols.
My voice began to shrink.
Once I made it into choir to diligently learn
"Oh Come All Ye Faithful" in Latin.
My stout voice narrowed into a thin tremor.

In the children's train passing through Nazi Germany
the Jewish children were silent,
silent at the French border watching
in silence the Nazi soldiers take one child off each car
to inspect them the children silently hoping
the Nazis would let them go.

---

*An after-school school to teach Jewish culture.

The children burst into a storm of songs
as soon as the train crossed into France
Listen the whole train sang with such vigor
the songs pushed the train faster into France.

I want to sing
just like they sang
crossing into France
sing as I once
sang in *schule*
sing an old song
my Hasidic ancestors
used to sing,
sing a nigun,
a wordless song,

Bim bam Bim bam Bim bam Bim bam
bin Bam bin Bam bin Bam

Heading East

Davi Walders

This land I've so long known and loved
bares somber limbs I've never seen.
Is this because I've never been
when skies are wounded breast of dove,
when rivers flow like cooling lead,
fields, cindered dust on ashen ground,
sunflowers without sun, bent, brown,
heads drooping over silent dead?
Or is this the way it looked that fall?
Trains racing east, smoking zinc, a
people shoved like beasts in a stall
never to see Paris again pink . . . a
slaughter . . . September rain . . . a pall . . .
      Bear witness . . . Remember . . . Treblinka.

France, 1991

Goethe's Tree

Annie Dawid

For Reidar Dittmann

Red triangle covers
left breast pocket.
NO for Norwegian,
no tattoo on the wrist
—numbers for Jews only.

"German intellectual material"
was Reidar, with his blue eyes
and white-blond hair. Reidar
himself says he looked like
an SS recruitment poster.

Corpse carrier at Buchenwald,
Reidar was, at 19, a veteran
of the underground resistance,
arrested for singing anti-German
songs, and later for sinking
a just-christened German ship.

In the middle of Buchenwald,
Reidar remembers an old oak
around which filed
10,000 Hungarian Jews
who arrived one day in 1945.

Reidar says "smoke poured
forth so voluminously
that daylight didn't break through."

In the final months,
Reidar and the others
carried their own skeletons
around this oak,
whose brass plaque reads:

"Under this tree
Goethe sat
and wrote some of his most
beautiful poetry."

The Synagogue of Florence

Lena L. Charney

From Michaelangelo Square I feast
upon the city spread out before me
on a serving platter
rimmed by the river Arno.
Two dishes stand out:
the red dome of the cathedral with
its eleborately carved bronze door
and the green dome of the synagogue
with its plain wooden ark door.

Inside the synagogue, the ark doors
wear shining medals of
bayonet scratches and bullet holes
inflicted by the Nazis.
The doors remained closed,
refuse to reveal their Torahs
had been removed to safety.

Hands that saved the Torahs were slaughtered
swiftly and sewed into lamp shades.
Eyes that read the Torahs
turned into earrings and pendants.

At the service yesterday
I saw the ark doors open,
display the replaced Torahs.

Perhaps a Friend of Anne Frank's

Samuel Exler

I walk in the blackout, beside the Dutch
Resistance man, with his orange armband, walking
Through a blacked-out night, while his story
Opens into late afternoon. The room is beginning
To darken. A nurse stands beside the underweight child
Whose sleeve is rolled up. The nurse swabs a spot
On the slender arm, while the doctor tests the syringe.
The child watches, life withdrawn from the dark eyes
With their long lashes, switching from her arm
To the doctor's face, as if her paralyzed look
Might stop what cannot be stopped. Or
Perhaps she speaks, saying, "Please.
"Please don't kill me." But
The nurse answers, "Don't be a baby,"
And the Nazi doctor giggles, "It won't hurt a bit."

"More Light! More Light!"

Anthony Hecht

For Heinrich Blucher and Hannah Arendt

Composed in the Tower before his execution
These moving verses, and being brought at that time
Painfully to the stake, submitted, declaring thus:
"I implore my God to witness that I have made no crime."

Nor was he forsaken of courage, but the death was horrible,
The sack of gunpowder failing to ignite.
His legs were blistered sticks on which the black sap
Bubbled and burst as he howled for the Kindly Light.

And that was but one, and by no means one of the worst;
Permitted at least his pitiful dignity;
And such as were by made prayers in the name of Christ,
That shall judge all men, for his soul's tranquillity.

We move now to outside a German wood.
Three men are there commanded to dig a hole
In which the two Jews are ordered to lie down
And be buried alive by the third, who is a Pole.

Not light from the shrine at Weimar beyond the hill
Nor light from heaven appeared. But he did refuse.
A Luger settled back deeply in its glove.
He was ordered to change places with the Jews.

Much casual death had drained away their souls.
The thick dirt mounted toward the quivering chin.
When only the head was exposed the order came
To dig him out again and to get back in.

No light, no light in the blue Polish eye.
When he finished a riding boot packed down the earth.
The Luger hovered lightly in its glove.
He was shot in the belly and in three hours bled to death.

No prayers or incense rose up in those hours
Which grew to be years, and every day came mute
Ghosts from the ovens, sifting through crisp air,
And settled upon his eyes in a black soot.

Like Butterflies

Mark Pawlak

After Charles Reznikoff; for Donna Brook

The Auschwitz "Angel of Death," Josef Mengele,
would meet the trains delivering Jews to the camp
and select out from those destined for the gas
healthy pairs of twins. These he kept alive
in crowded cages for genetic experiments
to aid him in building a master race.

He gave them chemical injections
which made many nauseous and faint, and a few
became numb when the needles were put into their spines.
Some were given transfusions of blood
from one twin to the other,
or he removed parts of the sexual organs;
yet others he sterilized by radiation.

He was especially interested in the colors of eyes.
If he noticed that twins' eyes were brown
but their mother's eyes were blue,
he might keep her alive in the cage with her children.
He would try to change their eye color
with injections of dye or with drops administered daily
that burned the eyes like acid,
and he would take blood samples from these subjects
several times each day.

One twin said she was stupefied
when ushered into Mengele's private laboratory.
There she saw an entire wall of eyes looking back at her,
human eyes of every color
mounted on the wall like butterflies.

Photo, Kraków 1939

Donna Reis

You sit in your chair
in a black dress
like an etched headstone
and think how silly
to have this picture
taken at your age.
Your square, callused hands
are out of place folded on your lap
they belong more to the bread
you knead and the weeds you pull.
Your doctor is on his way
when you didn't send for him.
Behind you, life disappears
into white stillness, overexposed.
The doctor arrives with soldiers
who don't stomp the mud
off their boots.
He gives you an injection
while your sons are lined up
on the front lawn
their backs braced against bullets.

The German Officer Writes a Letter

Elisavietta Ritchie

My dear predecessor,
these three days have proved
eventful for both of us:

I moved to a new apartment,
you had a similar
upheaval of relocation.

May I remark that although
the curtains look washed
and no dust adhered to my gloves,

carpets were littered
with bits of cloth, buttons,
a doll losing stuffing,

books foreign and torn,
tatters of scores . . .
Smashed glass cut my heel.

Vital silver was missing but
my wife found matching
forks at a pawnshop.

She had a time straightening
the rooms! At last even the dolls
on your daughter's bed are aligned.

My little girl is charmed.
My son is annoyed to find
nothing of interest for him.

But in essence, the flat
is satisfactory, and I
compliment you on the Meissen.

It's the violin, though,
I wish to discuss.
My wife insists: sell it,

our daughter is tone-deaf,
our impatient son
already snapped one string.

But my Great-Uncle Franz
played the tuba. As a child
after Sunday mass I heard

his band in the park,
often thought: how nice
to play some instrument.

My problem: procuring a teacher.
I called the conservatory,
what remains of the symphony.

A few instructors of course
went to the Front.
Others simply vanished.

My wife complains that these days
I've helped with the move
are my first leave in months.

so how dare I imagine fiddling.
And such difficult scores!
Still, when I retire. . . .

Should this letter reach you in time
would you be so kind
to recommend somebody good.

To Make Sacred

Reeve Robert Brenner

You ask what desecration means.

That the lampshade at Yad Vashem
of tawny amber parchment
torn from a torah scroll
whose skin testifies to sizzling flesh,
once illumined the thighs
of an ubermensch und frau,
once cast, unflickering,
the holy tongue upon their
compounding frames,
their frankfurt, furth and fulda,
flaying limbs,
once flung filagreed letters
of redemptive writ,
obedient hebrew script,
to march and retreat across
shifting sweaty nazi spines
as on keeled carapaces,
rippling wavy corrugated words
in shadows
enlarging with their heavings,
fleeting with each thrust,
once projected silhouetted shapes:
thou shalt
thou shalt not.

and we,
still shaken by that shade,
might make love
in the holy city
in the holy tongue
my quill stenciling torah tropes
upon your holy of holies
a wholly holy act,
and therewith
discomfit Jerusalem's profaners
and soften the sacrilege.

Doubling*

Lester Speiser

The schutzhaftlagerführer dines:

Blood-red wine glows in noon filters;
the hand lightly creases damask white,
fingers nestling crystal stemware;
the smooth sleeve . . . smooth sleeve
addresses the table . . . table,
a fork dabbling a mound of schlag.

The schutzhaftlagerführer works:

The morning song: half-liter of black
coffee, five grams of sugar;
"Not everyone is capable of digging
ditches, or cracking stones, of sinking
halfway down in water . . . of being harnessed
to carts . . . "

The song of noon: something called soup,
they played a concert, the orchestra
leader fainted, one tried to help,
he was beaten beaten in the mad-dog sun;

---

*A term used by Dr. Robert J. Lifton, a psychiatrist, to describe the formulation
of a second self, an "Auschwitz self," in order to adapt. Dr. Lifton maintains that
"doubling" enabled Nazi doctors to carry on their "work" in the camps and then
become "holistic second selves" as family men, social people, etc.

"you played a classical piece . . . you should
have played jazz . . . " he was not an oompah
oompah German.

Nightsong: soup cold soup, they called it
sleep, if you went to the latrine you lost
your place.

He signed off, the schutzhaftlagerführer
signed off, locked his desk primed
for his leave, the macaroni
and the nice cheese at the ready
for the Volk back home,
the stuffed bear at the ready
for Franz, lieber schatzi Franz.

The Death of the Partisan Girl: Russia

Tom Wayman

There must have been a time when everything to you
was clear as iron: that the kitchen of bread must pass
to the gun-cleaning rag, attics and the low sheds around farms.
Your child became a motorcycle
a stretch of road, a wire and birch trees.

And when they had you, time became German.
If someone could only have whispered
you will be held four days, raped twice
beaten for this many minutes. But no one said that.
So you could not know they would not
smash you in the face for another hour
press their bloody sperm into you in turn
all afternoon, and burn your nipples and tongue with cigarettes
every day at six o'clock for a week.

Then they killed you. Someone took a photograph
of your body. Your eyelids were swollen shut.
They put the picture in a book, and years later
in another country, a man you could not possibly know
looks at your beautiful face and becomes confused.

He believes that when you knew words were useless
you opened a knapsack and took out a terrible metal canister.
His fingers are shaking now, holding only paper.

Who can touch you? You were in agony, that your brother could say
my older sister was killed in 1943, the Nazis
tortured her, your niece could say my aunt
whom I never knew, died in the war, your parents
could say there was another daughter, but she's gone

And when it happened, your cause was lost.
Now your butchers readjust themselves on a sofa somewhere
to be interviewed by sympathetic pencils.
You, partisan, no one can forgive. You are dead.
All we can do is put a black-and-white photo of the husk of dead meat
that was you, hung from a rope, in a book and forget it.
But I intend to remember.

Even the old men's last breath

Nelly Sachs

Even the old men's last breath
That had already grazed death
You snatched away.
The empty air
Trembling
To fill the sigh of relief
That thrusts this earth away—
You have plundered the empty air!

The old men's
Parched eyes
You pressed once more
Till you reaped the salt of despair—
All that this star owns
Of the contortions of agony,
All suffering from the dungeons of worms
Gathered in heaps—

O you thieves of genuine hours of death,
Last breaths and the eyelids' Good Night
Of one thing be sure:

The angel, it gathers
What you discarded,
From the old men's premature midnight

A wind of last breaths shall arise
And drive this unloosed star
Into its Lord's hands!

Abuse

Dahlia Ravikovitch

In that place,
one of those places,
the flowers were gnawed to shreds,
devoured like prey,
dogs bared their teeth,
barked in their fury—
the flowers were gnawed to shreds.
My God,
was there beauty!

In that place,
different from all those places,
they were like sunflowers
trailing the sun—
when they lifted their heads
their fragrance followed the sun.
And hours after they were torn apart.
Even after they died,
that soul still burned in them.
My God,
was there abuse!

Translated by Chana and Ariel Bloch

At Babi Yar

Jo Nelson

they lay them to sleep
by the score in the fatal gorge
and then they shot them in
an orgy of death so deafening
the very soil stained red as each
thin layer was bedded down.
Thirty-four thousand in two days
were dispatched without remorse
though a few badly wounded managed
to crawl from the grave at night
to later tell the world.
When news from the Eastern Front
turned dark, the Nazis mobilized
the Sonderkommando to dig up the
remains of the hundred thousand
bodies and burn them so the
world would never know.
It was said the stink and ashes
sifted over Kiev for days
and months and years thereafter
though Stalin never acknowledged
it was part of Hitler's Jewish solution.

After the War

Lily Brett

After the war
it made your ears ache
your skin creep
your head swim

to see
your possessions
belonging to them

to sit
with Mrs Polski
who used to be
the caretaker

while her gangly callow son
wallowed
in your father's suit

she served you cake
on china plates
that were part of your mother's dowry

and the grand piano
standing polished and proud
was your brother's most prized possession

and you could see
mother
that Mrs Polski
was surprised
to find you still alive.

A Jewish Baby in the Warsaw Ghetto, 1941

Leatrice Lifshitz

to see her again
the little baby
    dangling
        like a doll

a little baby
but she was tossed
    away
        like a toy
            a doll

a man
who never played
    with dolls
        held her by the ankle
            in a picture book

and I saw
that the baby
    was dead
        dangling
            like a doll
                a man can

toss away
and I wanted
I wanted
so little
so much . . .

Dachau '44

Judith Berke

Jawheh sat on the floor next to my bed.
He looked strange.

What's the matter with you?
I asked (well I wasn't crazy, not only I

saw him). His hair wasn't combed.
His cheeks hung down in folds.

His teeth were broken.
Try to make the best of it,

I said. Sat with him and talked
to him as you would to a woman.

There he was, an old man
and I was the father.

I knew if I let him
he'd lay his head on my shoulder

and cry. Then he would never forgive me.
So I said, quiet. Enough now.

Then I lay down on the bed, and rested.

Unanswerable Questions, Terezin

Reva Sharon

Along the path where your light feet passed
your footsteps have been lost forever. . . .
— Haim Guri

It was here Jhirka
in that black yesterday
after your fists were torn

from your mother's shirt
and you were ripped
from her breast

. . . when your eyes were dark
and your mouth was full
of questions

You shared the hard wood bunk
of a starving man
who had no answers

for a boy of five
with no memory
of life under a wide sky

beyond this
barbed electric fortress
But he captured you

in a sketch
that survives
framed and protected under glass

Oh Jhirka . . .
do your ashes
nourish wild vermilion poppies

or eddy endlessly
in the River Ohre
Your image stays

and haunts the silence
of an unlit place
where we walk now

and cry out "why"
. . . but Jhirka
who will ask your questions

Letter to Dina

John Bradley

For Dina Mironovna Pronicheva, survivor of Babi Yar

Why does it take so long

for a body to fall, longer, say, than a long strand
of summer grain, blond as a blond soldier, longer than
the smallest cricket, a pinprick of well water clinging
to the side of his stomach wall. Why is it, even as you
fell, a voice insisted: This is the way to Palestine.
This is the way out of Kiev, down the wagon-rut scars
in the face of the Black Madonna, the way to the promised land.

No one told you

to jump, but you did, before the machine gun could feel
for your breasts, your heart, and falling, you saw geese
fleeing northeast, children on their backs, facing the wrong
way, clutching reins tied to the tail, forgetting they were
not arriving, but leaving. Perhaps it was best, you thought,
the children not having to see where they were being taken.

And for some

reason not understandable still, you forgave the icicle
scars down your flesh, the tall pines who stood watch over
those women who went with the soldiers and never emerged

THE NIGHTMARE BECOMES REALITY   79

from the woods. For how long did I soak you in kettlefuls
of hot water, before we could peel away the vest stuck
to your ribs like moss, before I could bring my lips to kiss you.

Wherever you ask

I shall kiss you, whether in front of grandmother's kitchen
icon, down in the trench grandfather dug for an air-raid
shelter, or before the notice ordering all Yids to Melnikovsky
and Dokturov, whether among the bodies, naked, hugging
each other in the ravine, or before the sentry, searching
your papers while you repeated, in Ukrainian and German,

I am not a Yid

though it made no difference in the end, for they took you
to the sand quarry, the same place your parents had gone,
who, even as they fell, prayed you were alive, Dina, so
a schoolboy, lifting a pencil, writing in his notebook
the words Babi Yar, might hear, through layers of sand
and bone and sand, what can never be muffled, the sound
the balalaika will always make you hear—a body falling

into the Yar.

See, Nadia!

P. M. Callen

Every night I dream of my husband—
how he will come for me:
he strides through the gates,
tall, alight with power;
the guards tremble;
he walks through the many-eyed brambles
of necks and arms and legs,
gazing compassion on them,
but he does not stop for them;
the kapos bow their heads
as he sweeps through barracks after barracks
looking for me.
I know that he will come.
I have told Nadia,
and she says, "Yes,
he will come
when dead Jews
find a way
to rise up
out of the pit."

She speaks this way
since they burned her child.
I do not blame her.
How could she understand
the dream is a premonition
of what is to come.

(I had such a dream before he asked me
to be his wife.)
It will come true.
She brings me soup
because I can no longer stand in the line.
This morning she held me up during roll call.
She is a good friend
even if she does not believe my premonitions.

I am shrunken on this shelf,
twig limbs unable to move,
but my heart still beats, waiting,
for him.
He will come for me,
just as I have dreamed it,
and he will lift me in his arms
and carry me out over the brambles
and through the fires
and past the guards
into the clean forest.
I will grow strong in his love
and never be sick again.
My limbs will be ivory, round and soft,
and on beds of silken pine leaves
he will delight in the fragrance of my flesh
and I will give birth to children
on the cool forest floor,
and we will grow like the flowers;
we will grow like the trees.

Ah! See, Nadia! You are wrong.
See! He comes!

Folk Art

Judith Chalmer

Just the outlines
of wings
and petals cut into the curve
of the shade, then curl
into the heat,
so from golden rooms
behind intricate carvings
on the sides of a topaz lampshade
the light can shine
brighter, more warmly
at the edges—like candles in a window,
like a fairy-tale carnival seen
from a distance. This is the way
my uncle decorated cakes
in Philadelphia, even sugar cubes,
with tiny flowers,
the way his mother peeled thousands
of potatoes thin enough
to keep her place in the kitchen,
at the end of the "Boulevard des Misères"
in the Westerbork Concentration Camp.
She was spared because she saved potatoes.
I remember my mother telling me
my father wore striped pajamas
in Dachau, near the Alps,
and was cold. I thought

it must have been dark there
all the time for him
to keep his pajamas on.
I want to know whose skin stretches over
the light to carve up an old
lampshade. I want her to know:
I leave my lights on all night long.
Still, the shadow
of their lives falls over me
like the cover on a waking bird.

Children's Dreams at Theresienstadt

Margaret DelGuercio

Esther, age eight, sketched
　　her family at the dining-room table

Celebrating Purim, my Dream

drinking merrily and offering
　　gifts of food to one another

for a few minutes her crayons
　　on lined composition paper etch

memories of Aunt Miriam and Uncle Ezra
　　sipping wine from the same
　　　　cracked crystal goblet in 1940

before 15,000 Jewish children
　　vanish from Theresienstadt

into the black hole of history

I can no longer dwell
　　on Haman and his ten sons

hanged from the gallows
　　suffering the fate he had planned
　　　　for Mordecai and the Jews

My tears have scorched my life
    I want to touch Queen Esther's scroll
    and little Esther's tableau vivant

bringing Aunt Miriam and Uncle Ezra
    to life here
        sipping wine through the same

oversized cracked goblet
    celebrating Purim
        with you, my friends

Buchenwald

Samuel Exler

I

Saturday morning, playing hide-and-seek
At the synagogue, I heard prayers,
Heard the cantor's voice
Throbbing with Hebrew syllables,
Sadness soaking a strange melodic line,
Grown men praying to a sound that says,
"We are the children of heartbreak."

II

Hatless, we played hide-and-seek,
Covered our heads with a handkerchief;
Met there on Tish'ah b'Av, in holiday clothes,
Hiding on the ground floor, running up stairs,
Bursting into a hubbub of voices,
Surrounded by sounds of prayer,
Grief in the pitch of the voice.

III

At the kitchen table I hear stories;
Inquisitors, whose cunning questions
Set thought on the edge of a knife.
In icy December my father laughed and said
He was expecting Mashiakh pretty soon.
Messiah? What's he talking about?
By the rivers of Babylon I lay down and wept.

IV

Human beings reduce to a handful of ashes.
Isn't that strange—a handful of ashes.
One handful, and another, and another,
One by one the handfuls make a pile,
One by one piles of ashes unite, grow,
Fill up a room, become a mountain,
Become mountains of ashes at Buchenwald.

V

It is April, I walk around, I carry a rifle.
Survivors beg me to go, it's on the outskirts of town.
They tell me I won't believe it, but I know
What it looks like—I could sense
From the sounds of prayer, from Messiah
And Inquisition, that Zyklon B was waiting.
It was nothing I didn't expect.

Rehearsal at Terezin

Darcy Gottlieb

Inspired by "The Terezin Requiem" by Josef Bor

Listen.
What's happening here at Terezin
will happen again and again.
It is rehearsal for leaving all we love
with no time to say good-bye.

Listen. They're taking Sonya now.
Oh Mother, I hear sea gulls in my brain.

Grieve, grieve but go on playing
as we who practice Verdi's Requiem
every day in the cellar at Terezin,
where every day someone else is missing.

One time it is the cellist, then the bassoon.
Soon the soprano's footsteps will be heard
blending with hobnailed boots overhead.

Allen tries to make us laugh with a joke:
    What ails you?
    I've got terminal.
    Terminal what?
    Terminal life.

"Play!" our conductor yells at us. "Play, sing,
rage for those you love."

The flute inhales a note,
catching a syncopated breath. Listen.
A new voice has joined us. It ridicules
the shifting, sorting winds of history
that make us random choices
in a game of molecules.

Sing, sing. Find the sweet waters
beneath the desert brine.

The violins tremble with crescendo.
We no longer hear the transports
thundering across our cellar sky.
The music thrusts itself beyond lament.
We feel it crash,
splitting our terror into fragments.

"Bravo!" the conductor cries out,
wiping his glasses on his sleeve.
"You have surpassed yourselves today."

We sit. Limp with exaltation.
Time expands. We breathe joy.
      Now we can laugh at Allen's joke.

Die Verarbeitung, Processing

Mark Pawlak

All that matters now is Treblinka.
It is our destiny.

— sung by the Jewish workcrew

In the words of SS Ünterscharführer Franz Suchomel, Treblinka was a "primitive but efficient production line of death." Operating at full capacity, the camp would receive three, sometimes four trains daily; thirty to fifty cars in each, he explains. Of the three, four, five thousand Jews packed into the cars like sardines, upon arrival, as many as a third might already be dead (because of the overcrowding and lack of food and water, or because, in despair, they had slit their wrists or taken poison). These corpses were stacked, neatly as cordwood, by the thousand on the unloading ramp at Treblinka. As for the living ... The old and feeble were separated out first, and led or carried away on stretchers to an area called the "infirmary," where a white flag painted with a red cross flew overhead. There they were "cured with a single pill," as the guards joked—a bullet in the neck; and their bodies thrown into a pit. The healthy were separated, men to the right, women to the left side of the ramp, and made to strip; their clothing collected and saved for later use by the German army. Naked, they were then driven by shouting guards wielding leather whips— *Schnell! Schnell!*—through a passage lined with barbed wire called the *Himmelweg* or "Road to Heaven" (by the guards), uphill to the open bunker doors of the gas chamber; men first, followed by the women and children. The entire operation, from arrival at Treblinka station until death, required less than three hours per trainload. This, says Ünterscharführer Suchomel, was the routine. This was how between 12,000 and 15,000 Jews were "processed" at Treblinka each day (*verarbeitet* in German); and not, he emphasizes, not the 18,000 figure cited by some Jews today.

Treblinka, 1944

T. W. Perkins

More of my people died today.
I know, because the moon is red.
"Blood on the moon"
there are legends about its cause,
but I've always found
that on those nights
a Jew has died.

The moon is red a lot over Poland.

You can tell the newcomers here—
they still pray every night for the dead.
They still say Kaddish for their mother,
for their father,
for their two-year-old daughter
and Kaddish for Uncle Jacob
and tiny Aunt Ruth who worked in the fish market.
When they've been here a few weeks
they'll know it is too much.
For a while they'll say one prayer over all the dead;
soon even that will be
too much.

My family is one of rituals.
When they came for us my father said,
"Remember, my child, who we are:

even here will we praise Him."
They robbed him of everything
but his love of God.
To the end he worshipped
with what little he had left:
the rituals of the heart.
And I said Kaddish for him.

Hope and faith are gone now.
Holidays pass, and no one worships.
Who is there foolish enough to pray
"To next year in Jerusalem"?
Who is there who still believes
they will live to see next year?

Only the strongest are still alive
even the strongest are weak now.
Too weak for hope,
too weak for prayer,
too weak for rituals;
surviving is itself a ritual:
the only one we know.

When the moon is red
the night I die
who will be left to see it?
My mother prayed over my sisters
my father over my mother.
I said Kaddish for my father.
Who will care to pray for me?

Now, as we march to our death
the ritual returns:
We say our final prayer
as we have done for ages.
Above the roaring fires
can be heard our chant:
"Hear, oh Israel, the Lord our God,
the Lord is one."

At Birkenau

T. W. Perkins

Today, I have said
Kaddish
for myself
I have evoked the Holy Name
of my Lord
Father of the universe
for my own soul
And I am not alone
Has this ever happened
before, Jews praying
Kaddish
for themselves?
Never before have they seen
what we saw here
today.

Sweet Sixteen

Vera Weislitz

Behind the wall
I wish I had wings
and could fly to the South
I wish I could stop the air-raid scream
that haunts my entity
I wish I could leave this vault
talk to the wind and oranges in bloom
touch the cobalt ribbon—the horizon
                    Oh Icarus!

In Maria Theresa's Fortress
behind the wall
I am sixteen
the age of the first ball

I dream I wear an organdy dress
a poppy in my hair
and float on the parquet floor
Rescue my heart from the needling thrill!

I dream of Alexander's Ragtime
my friend in a snowy shirt
I dream of a Kaiser roll and butter
a slice of cheese, a sparkling drink

In Maria Theresa's Fortress
behind closed gates
I am a captive
the number 434

In the Fortress I wish
I was born a sparrow,
tiny, with real wings
so I could fly away from this place
                    Oh Icarus!

In the Fortress, I am sixteen
I wish I had no sight
to see the eyes of glass
I wish I had no breath of life
did not have to drink the bitter cup
I wish I was just air and could not wear
the sign of condemnation—
                    The Yellow Star!

Children II

Lily Brett

There
were
thin children

fat children

brown-eyed
children

blue-eyed
green-eyed
wide-eyed children

you'd
think
it was harder

to
kill
the children

it
was
easy

they
were
flung in the air

for
target
practice

had
their heads
broken

against
the nearest
wall

they
bent others
across their knees

like
twigs
snapping their backs

the lucky ones
walked with their mothers
to the gas.

Invisible

Lily Brett

It was
essential

to
develop

the
skill

of
appearing
invisible

to
look
at the ground

slink
around

slide
inside

mix
in the middle

to
work

and
walk

and
sometimes
talk

as
though

you
didn't
exist.

Selection

Lily Brett

He leapt through
the line
like

a
sharp angled
soloist

a
mad
dancer

a
principal
in a private ballet

before
he'd pinched
and pinched
his cheeks

so
they sat
like red moons
in a gray sky

armed
against
accidents

he'd
emptied
himself

of
the typhoid
that dripped
from his bowels

he hurtled himself
so high
his bones

looked
like
they might

burst through
and
puncture
the performance

right
said
Mengele

and
he knew
he was
all right.

Another Selection

Lily Brett

Mengele looked
while the Kommandant
lightly whipped
the thin nipples
shriveled around
their empty bags of breast

rows and rows
of wrinkled pink tips
sitting on bowed ribs

the night sky
a romantic red
blazed with arms legs and heads

the thick air
sweet
with your mother's bones burning

the snow
clothed in
black ash
was mourning

and you stood
pushing out
what remained
of the flesh on your chest

it passed the test.

The Toilet

Lily Brett

Surprisingly
few
fell in

the
thirty feet
deep
pit

with
slippery
poles

around
the
edge

to
sit
on

those
who
were
short

had
to
dangle
their legs

above
the thick
brown sea

swelling
lightly
below

like
a
volcano

cut short
forced
to
swallow

its
own
eruption.

Possessions of the Rich

Lily Brett

The
rich

walked
everywhere

with
their
possessions

never
left
them

for
one
second

for
one
second

was
enough

for
someone
to steal them

paper
to
pad your chest

was
at
a premium

and
string
to secure

your
spoon
and bowl

underwear
was millionaire's
square

almost
unheard
of

like
matching
shoes

THE NIGHTMARE BECOMES REALITY

or
shoes
at all

and
a
coat

could
make
you

feel
like
a king

a
stump
of lipstick

priceless
for
pinking your cheeks

flushed
life
into you

saved
you
in selections

showed
them

how
well

you
were.

The Sonderkommando

Lily Brett

The Sonderkommando
those prisoners
known as
the Death Squad

merely
shuffled
death around

re-arranging
and
re-packaging
the components

they
herded
crowds
into the showers

pulled
them
out
gassed

hosed
them
to get rid of
the crap

hooked
the slippery bodies
with
thongs around the wrists

and
piled
them

into
the
elevators

for
the
ovens.

The First Job

Lily Brett

The
first
job

of
every
Sonderkommando
unit

was
to
kill

the
unit

they
were

replacing

the
unit

they
were

replacing

mostly
went

willingly.

Renya's Baby

Lily Brett

Afterwards
you
heard

that
Renya's
baby

who
could
already
smile

and
point

and
laugh
at
cats

was
sucking
quietly
on
the breast

and
missed
the
gas

when
they

untangled
the
dead

chopped
their
hair

and
mined

a
sea
of teeth

they
found
her

attached

THE NIGHTMARE BECOMES REALITY

to
the
dead breast

before
loading
the
trolley

that
serviced
the ovens

they
split
her
head

hurled
her

on
top
of

another
mother.

To the Left

Lily Brett

You knew
as soon
as you
stepped
from the train

that
the world
had gone
vanished
moved on

all
that remained
was
a giant
gray stain

striped
with ghouls
and ghosts
who'd missed
the boat

they clubbed you
to the left
to the left
was life
mother

they chopped
those large wild curls
that used to whirl
around your face
mother

shaved
your sweet head
under your arms
between your legs

plucked
of yourself
you resembled
the trembling chickens
your father bought in Łódź

for
lunch
lunch with your brothers
Szymek and Abramek
Jakob and Felek

captured
and captivated
with your
quick eyes
and wide smile

they left you naked
in a line
for two days
and two nights
under a dead sky

to the left
to the left
was life
mother

Overload

Lily Brett

When
the
numbers

overloaded
even
the
ovens

they
dug
big pits

that
could
fit

two
thousand
at a time

the Sonderkommando
learned
to lay
the fires

with
a
minimum
of fuss and fuel

the
best
burning
arrangement

they
found
crisscrossed

a
fat
man

a
thin
man

and
a
child

they
slanted
the pits

THE NIGHTMARE BECOMES REALITY

so
they
could
tip

fat
from
the
bottom

over
the
hissing
spitting

glistening
black
bodies

to
keep
them
burning

for
five
hours

the
remnants
then

filled
less
than

a third of the pit.

The Shower

Jill Bart

It will be a blessing—
the warm water—I hope
it's not cold. Although

I prefer goose bumps
to the soiled gray
of my skin.

Being naked is painful—
this sagging flesh; still,
the men, the children

seem careful not to stare,
conscious of their own
bare bodies.

At first I covered myself
with my hands, then I thought,
look old woman, you're just

one of many here. So I wait
like the rest. If the guards
want to stare let them look me

in the eye—I'm more naked there.
This line moves slowly. I'm glad
it's spring—no chill in the air.

I remember the sweet scent of the
linden trees, they should be blooming now.
Once, at home, I soaked in a

perfumed bubble bath—how the
children laughed! My skin was soft
and pink then, I smelled of tuberose;

dear Werner said, "Liebchen, you
are beautiful." I'm glad he can't
see me now—all skin and bone.

This soap they gave us,
I hope it lathers.
It feels like stone.*

---

*Stones carved to look like soap were given out at the gas chambers.

THE NIGHTMARE BECOMES REALITY

A Message from the Past for the Present

Christina Pacosz

A looming mound
of empty Zyklon B canisters
behind glass: to open death
like canned peaches.

Behind the tins:
·corporate profit.

Are there no new tales
we can tell each other?

Artifacts of the age,
the waning twentieth century
on parade, naked
and exhausted.

Each time capsule
should include
one of these.

Such eloquent
refuse.

Gas Ovens

Joanna M. Weston

We dropped cyanide leaves
on 2,000 waiting faces;
they breathed spring scents
as fragrant air to death.

We dropped them
as they stood waiting
naked against naked
in our parody of Eden.

We watched as they breathed
long gulps of cyanized air;
they thrust out their arms
to hold their bodies up:

We saw the nails then,
in their opened hands,
and the brambled crowns
on their heads.

Two thousand times,
we saw that as we did to them,
the most of all God's loves,
so we did it to His Son.

Warsaw Ghetto

Harold Black

Me'ayin yavoh ezri?*
Night has fallen.
Shall I read the psalms
by the light of the candles
at the heads of the dead?

Crags of masonry and steel.
Twisted girders hurl their points,
shapes conjured in the minds of devils.
I stand on desolation square.

Litter of stone.
Traces of houses.
Charred prayer books.
A broken fork.
A housewife's earthen pot.
The sole of a shoe.
A bill marked "Paid."

With trembling hands I gather the remnants
of half a million Jews.

---

*Hebrew: From where shall my help come?

Poland

Lily Brett

What do you want
to go to Poland for
you screamed

your golden face
frozen
and distorted

the Poles
were worse
than the Germans

small children
in the towns around
the camp

would kick us
when we walked to work
in our striped rags

grown men
would throw
a piece of bread

and
nearly die with laughter
while we fought each other

oh
those nice Poles
those good people

what do you want
to go to Poland for
you wept

they
won't let you leave
so easily

something
terrible
will happen

Liebala Liebala
please
why go

you know
after the war
there was a miracle

not
one Pole
did know

about
what happened
to us

you
could smell
the flesh

burning
for
kilometers

the sky
was red
day and night

and
the Poles
didn't notice

Liebala Liebala
please
don't go.

Home Movie of Poland

Colette Inez

For Saul

A picnic table. The family assembles.
As if in a dream you are small,
your cousin squints, his shredded hair
later deloused at Bergen-Belsen.
Grandfather swatting flies. It is summer,
gentile, undulating blond.
Grandma sews a button on.

Nearby, the house stoked with bread
warm as the bed
you and mama slept in
like a closed parenthesis
in Poland's sad, long sentence.

Elsewhere, the Führer's bloody moon
rising in Sudetenland, plans for decimation.

They were so old, Noah and Sarah,
old and thin as rain,
easy to close the valve of their lives
as he bent to the news like a birch in the wind.
Grandma seizing her only hen
for a future of eggs. Auschwitz freight.
Jerusalem, if I forget thee,

let me lose my right arm.
God has plucked you out of the disease.
The frames fade, white phlox and blood
shedding their scent in a closet of dreams.

Rescued.
That your mother and father
hunched in a room to make you come true
like a glistening egg,
that will not crack
for any Wehrmacht omelette.

Your hair fringed like Polish stars
in a telescope of nights
when the moon was removed to Bergen-Belsen
in the final solution of moons.

Do not forget Jerusalem,
my love in a western land,
America, America where we live in a film
spooling forward and back in the speed of events—
unreal as the light
that blinks in our eyes after hours of darkness.

Faces in Swamps

Abraham Sutzkever

The cycle Faces in Swamps was written in hiding during the first days of the Nazi occupation of Vilna. Subsequently, it was hidden in a ghetto cellar and discovered forty-nine years later in Vilnius. The manuscript contains nine poems with the following note in the poet's hand:

Note. I wrote the nine poems of *Faces in Swamps* in the first ten days, when the Plague marched into Vilna. Between approximately June 25 and July 5. I wrote them lying stuck in a broken chimney in my old apartment on Wilkomirska Street 14. This way I hid from the Snatchers who dragged off every Jewish male they could find.

My wife carried the poems through all the horrors and tragedies. They were with her through the first provocation, were covered with blood, in prison under Schweinenberg's whip. Miraculously, my wife fled back to the ghetto with the poems, where I no longer was—I had fled in the middle of the night, during the Roundup of the Yellow Permits. When I returned, I found my wife in the hospital where she gave birth to a baby. In her labor pains, she was clutching the poems in her hands.

A . S.
Ghetto Vilna, May 16, 1942

The text translated here is from the manuscript. The titles of the poems were added later.

1 Faces in Swamps

... And overnight our thoughts grew gray. The sun
Sowed poison salt on open wounds. We choke.
White doves turned into owls. They're poking fun,
Mocking our dream that disappeared in smoke.

Why tremor, earth? Did you crack too, in trance?
Your nostrils smelled the stench of victim's flesh?
Devour us! We were cursed by overconfidence,
Devour us with our children, with our flags so fresh!

You're thirsty, earth. We, wailing pumps, will fill
With gold of our young bodies your newly opened pits.
A spiderweb of faces in a swamp will spin to kill:
Faces in a swamp—over the sunset, over huts . . .

II

Serpents of darkness: nooses choke
My breath.
Horseradish in my eyes, I toss
In a grater dungeon—
Each toss grates my skin.
Were there anything human, familiar . . .

My hand gropes: a piece of glass, the moon
Trembles imprisoned like me in the vise
Of the iron night. I grow tense:
"This was created by a human hand!"

In the glass edge I stroke the moon:
"You want?—I give you my life as a gift!"
But life is hot and the glass is cold
And it's a shame to put it to my throat . . .

A Voice from the Heart

Abraham Sutzkever

From the heart a voice commands: believe
in that already dishonored word *justice*.
The distant heir of the lion
must rebel against his captivity.

There is a way. Its destination springs
from the wild primeval forest of memory.
There is also a microbe
that carries the toxin of a millennium.

Then if you search for suffering's meaning
become its revealer
and hear how grandfathers awaken sons
like storm axes against the bronze of bells.

There is a way. So climb, stride,
kick away the perpetual stumbling block.
Death pardons every error,
but slavery it never forgives.

Vilna, July 22, 1941

Translated from the Yiddish by Seymour Mayne

I Feel Like Saying a Prayer

Abraham Sutzkever

I feel like saying a prayer—but to whom?
He Who once used to comfort me won't hear it now.
So to whom shall I pray?
The prayer holds me like a vise.

Should I ask that star in the sky: "My faraway friend,
I have lost my speech. Come, take its place."
But that good star
also won't hear.

Yet I must say a prayer. Someone very near,
within me, tortured, demands the prayer.
Senseless, I begin to babble
until dawn.

Vilna Ghetto, January 17, 1942

Translated from the Yiddish by Seymour Mayne

Burnt Pearls

Abraham Sutzkever

It is not just because my words quiver
like broken hands grasping for aid,
or that they sharpen themselves
like teeth on the prowl in darkness,
that you, written word, substitute for my world,
flare up the coals of my anger.

It is because your sounds
glint like burnt pearls
discovered in an extinguished pyre
And no one—not even I—shredded by time
can recognize the woman drenched in flame
for all that remains of her now
are these gray pearls
smoldering in the ash—

Vilna Ghetto, July 28, 1943

Translated from the Yiddish by Seymour Mayne

I Am Lying in This Coffin

Abraham Sutzkever

I am lying in this coffin
as I would lie
in stiff wooden clothing.
This could be a small boat
on dangerous waves,
this could be a cradle.

And here,
where bodies have been taken
from time,
I call out to you, sister,
and you hear me calling
in your distance.

What is suddenly moving in this coffin—
an unexpected body?
You come.
I recognize the pupils of your eyes,
your breath,
your light.

So this is the rule:
here today,
somewhere else tomorrow,
and in this coffin now

as in stiff wooden clothing
my speech
still moves into song.

Vilna, August 30, 1941

Translated from the Yiddish by Seymour Mayne

To the Thin Vein in My Head

Abraham Sutzkever

I'm entrusting myself completely to the thin vein in my head.
My word nurtures on its crystal-cadenced dust.
And all seven wisdoms the whirlwind wants to sow
plunge away with plucked wings like hail against a pane.

I love the single-minded word that does not perjure itself—
and not the wishy-washy hybrid of dubious taste.
It's all the same whether I climb aloft on my ribs or fall—
the word's mine. In the pupil of death—a reflection of flame.

However great my generation—its smallness is greater yet.
Only the word endures, homely as it is and yet resonant.
To the thin vein in my head I entrust the last loveliness:
A wind. Grass. The night's concluding star.

1945

Translated from the Yiddish by Seymour Mayne

On the Subject of Roses

Abraham Sutzkever

All wrapped up in clouds, the powerful Demon
plants a kiss on his frozen sword and speaks:
"Lord, give the word and without a tremor I will hack away at the
earth,
cutting down women and men with this blade.

Mountains I will raze and gouge into valleys,
the tindered forests I will burn like straw,
and Your Thrones—the cliffs—I will sunder while blotting out the
dew.
Give the word—I am at Your Command. My weapon waits to
    shatter the silence."

And a Voice answers: "Yes, brave and enterprising one,
I also wish to destroy earth's habitation.
But wait, yesterday I planted a rose there—
At least, give it a chance to flower."

Translated from the Yiddish by Seymour Mayne

For a Comrade

Abraham Sutzkever

Murdered comrade
at the barbed wire—
you still press this scrap
of food to your heart.
Forgive my hunger
and forgive this daring—
I must bite into your
bloodstained bread.

Nameless comrade
now I know your name—
let this stained morsel
comfort you too.
As the healing light
sustains our people,
together with the bread
you enter me.

Silent comrade,
absorbing you I live.
Demand of the world a reckoning
through every fiber of mine.
If I fall as you fell

at the barbed wire
let another swallow my word
as I, your bread.

Vilna Ghetto, December 30, 1941

Translated from the Yiddish by Seymour Mayne

Poland

Daniel Weissbort

There were millions of us,
and millions stayed.
Of the multitude that left,
I'm one of the descendants.
I look back over those heads
to the land of our forefathers.
There, people go about their daily business,
but burdened somewhat with our fate.
It is not easy to be so Christian a people
and to bear this burden too.

I am told stories, histories.
They are not untrue, only irrelevant.
It is a babble I listen to
and my silence discourages my interlocutors.
I want to say that
even a sophisticated historical explanation
won't suffice.
I want to say that
my feeling nothing, nothing
may be a measure of the sheer enormity.
I want to say that
if, even after centuries,
our alien presence was an embarrassment,

we were still human and . . .
I want to say . . . No!
I do not want to say!
I want, rather, to take back anything I may have said,

to just nod, shrug, and continue smiling.
I do not enter into a dialogue with them.
I cannot help them.

IN *Memoriam*

Like the Flash of a Bird's Wing

Marguerite M. Striar

I've seen the Washington Monument from near and far
and from the top been awed by the vista,
exhilarated by the air.
Today, I go to another monument nearby,
The U.S. Holocaust Memorial Museum
to see a monument within a monument:

The Ejsyszyszki Tower

I stand in the center of a narrow corridor
in an intimate surround of four high walls
completely covered by closely placed photographs. Very neat.
Six thousand portraits
collected by a survivor of, this, her lost community
"In Lithuania," the guard says, "but it *used* to be Poland."
They press in on me, these images of a happy past.

I crane my neck to the vanishing point forty feet up,
where faces escape through a skylight
just big enough to climb through or fly.
"Why is the light so dim?" I ask.
"To protect from light damage."
It matches the mood.

It's very strange, these paper squares and rectangles
of varying size and tone
are all that remain of the little girl
with sweetly shy smile or
the happy parents, the teenage sons, daughter
and dimpled infant,
the proud burgher, the bearded, learned rabbi,
the students, birthday celebrant,
smiling couple posing in the snow.

These are clearly seen
Those at the tower's top I can only surmise.
All that remains of a lost community
rich with fruits of the past
and hopes for a future harvest
that was not to be.
As I turn from wall to wall, from face to face,
I sense they are trying to say something to me

And to each other.

In this narrow tower where no birds fly
the soft chatter of a gathering of birds
And toward the skylight and its sudden sun
A movement, like the flash of a bird's bright wing.

The Holocaust Museum in Washington

Leo Haber

The quotations below are from the sonnet "Als mich Dein Wandeln an den tod verzukte" ("When Your Life Enraptured Me Unto Death") by Franz Werfel and from a poem "Vereinsamt" ("Lonesome") by Friedrich Nietzsche, both translated from the German by Patrick Bridgwater.

Withering wintry shades at table attend
Like unwanted guests; slivers of pain,
Phylacteried, purple the walls. Whose loss, whose gain,
Whose attic, whose basement? My heart, O God, mend

Before its descent. To the hod carriers send
Messages of love. Build this house, stain
The stairways with the blood of millions, do not refrain
From vaulted obsequies. With darkness blend.

Werfel wrote: "While I was filled with you
To the point of being carried away, there were so
Many who were tramping along in depression." I know,

My beloved. The thought, preying, burns my soul.
"Woe betide who has no home," Nietzsche knew.
I light my lamp beside the black sinkhole.

The Sky Was Not a Friendly Place

Patricia D'Alessandro

Kitty Felix Hart
walks slowly down the road
and speaks of days she spent at Auschwitz
to her son:

"They brought us here in cattle cars
when I was seventeen
and liberation clanged against a wild and wooden dream,
a bit of bread is all we're fed,
there was no water here,
I bathed in urine to be clean
and slept on planks
stacked high in rows of threes
where just beyond and triple-decked
were slats of wood with holes the size of moons
where lucky ones relieved themselves;
when they could not—
uniforms absorbed the warmth of urine down the leg.

"We ate the snow and stole the rations from the dead
and hid among the thousands brought to die
with millions dead.
We slept in darkness where the stench was stinging
to my nostrils, never calm.
My mother saved my life by stacking bodies over mine.
Typhus deafened me; the commandant had pierced my ears
to make me hear.

"I still had eyes and saw black smoke
spew above the crematorium
and curl in daily swirls from bodies burned
where millions died.

"A gypsy in the camp read my palm
and told me I would live to tell of Auschwitz
to my son. The next day
she was dead."

Kitty Felix Hart
now falters as she speaks
her gloved hands spread across her face
she holds her head
is silent
when emotions overwhelm
and tears flow free.

Kitty Felix Hart
now walks in shadows from tall birch
that whisper as she speaks
of days she spent at Auschwitz
to her son. He holds a stick
and pokes the ashes of remains they see
but cannot comprehend this pile of human bones
once brothers
sisters
friends.

Kitty Felix Hart
has lived
now walks and talks of Auschwitz with her son
so he will tell his children
and we must tell our own
that she SURVIVED
and by surviving
adds a humble sense of grace to our humanity
so we can grow with hope
that Auschwitz smoke
can never spew again.

Kol Nidre

Elayne Goldman Clift

Kol Nidre.*
I enter the temple,
find my place,
open a prayer book.

Kol Nidre.
My eyes spill over
at the first
eternal, sorrowful chant.

Kol Nidre.
And I stand beside the Jews
in the Warsaw Ghetto,
and in the concentration camps.

Kol Nidre, and I am with
the Jews of the pogroms,
and the Jews of petitions.
I am beside the Jews
who pioneered Israel,
of Hester Street,
of the factories,

*Literally, all vows; a prayer chanted on the evening of Yom Kippur in which
one asks God to cancel all resolutions between the individual and God that were
not fulfilled during the year and to be given another chance to renew them in
the new year.

the Jews of Williamsburg
and the unnamed Jewish girls
in the Triangle factory fire.
I am next to my Uncle Leo
in his beloved temple in Toronto,
and near my mother long ago
in the tiny synagogue
of my growing up.

Kol Nidre,
and I am with the children
of my children,
and the progeny of all Judaism.

Kol Nidre.
In every corner of the globe,
a Jew is standing, swaying, weeping,
praying with me.

Eternal, mournful chant,
sung to remind me
of my soul,

and the pain
of Abraham's people
through the millennia.

Kol Nidre.

Yahrzeit

Miriam Kessler

Your memory is leashed into my life,
lashed about me.
It strangles
like a morning-glory vine.
Six Million muffled cries
smothered in the hiss of Zyklon B.

Today I will be joyful
for no good reason:
only because you were denied joy.
I live what you had a right to.
My presumption is your gift,
my debt inexhaustible,
though you were not.
My candle is not Yahrzeit enough.
I burn it anyway.

When day blinks down through gray shutters
and cardinals begin their red cantata;
when leaves curl away from rain,
you will not know it.
My voice,
my sobbing,
will not shake you
from your Six Million sleeps.

What you might have been or done
I have not the ego to suppose.
My obligation starts
in the stink of Auschwitz.
It churns through the chimneys,
a gray chorus, crying Live!

Bronze Drama

Yala Korwin

*In 1984 a bronze sculpture ["The Holocaust"] was placed on
its permanent site in Lincoln Park overlooking the Golden
Gate Bridge. . . . [George] Segal used his hallmark technique
of casting live models directly in plaster. . . . The man poised
by the fence . . . is modeled from . . . a survivor of the camp.*

— From the *Jewish Museum Catalog*

Star shaped pile
nude corpses
from perfect bodies

One   arms outstretched
crucifixion style
boy Isaac   wrists bound
his dead father
clean-limbed Eve
half-eaten apple

And more
nine deaths in all
well posed   good cast
now get up
take your pay
free to go

But you   lone one
standing there in tatters
are free to carry
that wire fence
in your eyes
wherever you go

Zalman

Seymour Mayne

The name was curiously given.
Both families agreed the firstborn's
would be chosen from the mother's side.
Her father's name? No, he may still be alive—
May '44—if the Nazis hadn't killed him yet.
Who knew of his end then?
       But the mother's mother,
Zlateh—she who had married twice
and amassed money and means—
a boy named after a woman? Was it a forbidden thing?
And the name rooted from the Marranos
and hidden observance: Zalman;
Suleiman—did they know of the Turkish origins?
Not drawn from the Pentateuch,
no, a name of the orient, the eastern diaspora
and linked in the beginning, the first consonant,
with a grandmother whose only lasting image:
the block of stone carved with Hebrew
in Białystok's cemetery and her youngest son,
the uncle, standing there in the photo
just weeks before Poland fell—
the rest of her brood caught in a burning synagogue
before they could buy passage to New Jersey or Montreal.

She was dead then, her ears stopped
with that terrible silence marking its way
from the din of outrage—the flames licked the night
and the Polish and German murderers
prepared for a Saturday night off, the air incensed
with smoke of scrolls and flesh.
Enough, we begin again, the father said, name him.
She will live.
       —On their lips and in my face.

I Mourn My Death

Pauline K. Schmookler

I mourn my death
   and prepare
   with the foods I love
   for my memory's sake.

I move among the others
   and love them
   for crying at my death.

I lick at their grief
   taste it and join them
   sitting shivah
   in that comforting communal
   group grief.

Shoes off
   I try to hide the holes
   I did not make.

They say things about me
   that I pluck from the air
   and tuck among my remembrances
   in the communal coffin.

I mourn my death
    for I died in Belsen
    and again in Buchenwald
    and later in Dachau
    and again . . . . . .
    and again . . . . . .

I weep as I die once more.

Memorial Day: The Viet Nam Memorial

Cynthia Pinkus Russell

Objects of devotion have been placed against the wall,
a rose, a helmet, a scribbled note
   starting with "Dear Doc"
   ending "I miss you so"
Death shines off the black, polished, surface.

Volunteers hold books of names of the fallen
and the places they are chiseled along the wall.
   Children, open-mouthed, look up,
   khaki and hippie-clad vets
Even now stand here and whisper among themselves.

Growing up, conscienceless, I tiptoed over stepping stones.
One, the Depression, just behind me
   where parents split a five-cent Necco candy for dessert
   and wondered if they dared to have a child, with empty pockets,
That was the stone on which my sister arrived.

My stone was the Second World War
dirty sneakers threading their way through radio broadcasts
   Translux movie newsreels showing important men
   climbing off gigantic ships and planes
ration tickets determined what we'd eat; news reports when a
child could speak.

I met British children sent to safety from the Blitz
heard about Dutch children starving, eating tulip bulbs
    I grew up and married
    and along came Viet Nam
Husbands, friends, all deferred from the draft; safe inside
their college bunkers.

No bullets for me and mine, no Holocaust, no hiding.
Pain all over the world and no one had told me
    Yet deep inside a part of me always knew,
    always felt,
How the lions within us tear apart their meat.

The ranger picks up a boot and wraps it in plastic,
carefully numbered, his white gloves so delicate in touch
    as if he were a priest at the altar,
    There are the rituals of our devotions
Thousands, gathering in the sunlit May morning, to strike
back at war with our caring.

October Flowers in Prague

Rodney Pybus

i.m. Doris Weisserova 7.5.1932–4.10.1944
   Margit Koretzova 8.4.1935–4.10.1944 Theresienstadt

Here, in the heartland of Europe, I have seen pictures
   that come right at you like kids
out on a free afternoon: whiter than any old paper,
   clouds hanging in a sky of young cobalt,
a few wild spring flowers standing with imaginary
   leaves for all the things that wild
spring flowers stand for—these awkward pretty
   marks of pink and yellow, and one red
bright rose. I want to steal them all, God knows,
   holding my breath at the butterflies above
not so much caught in flight as always flying still
   on patchy wings as delicate as what
a child might think a soul to be, above tenderly right
   and unhurt grass. Not by years only do they transform
continuously the nature of design, these flowers,
   the undecaying art of wings, here under glass
in the old Jewish quarter. Fifty years have passed
   since these two girls watered their colors
in wooden dormitories. I was a child then, too,
   chasing peacocks with a jar in a long garden.
Night was a heavy dark that pressed my open eyes
   till they hurt. But that was all.

I have come to this now by the scenic route,
　　down the mountain road from Dresden and Teplice
through the quick scent of pines after rain;
　　I have driven myself through the streets they knew,
the leafy avenues of Terezin where heavy
　　garrison walls of golden stucco
are showing their age in the falling baroque
　　of an August evening. But on the banks and slopes
that were platforms at the terminus I see it is only their
　　art that can tell the brightness in the grass.

To Gisi Fleischmann

Joan Campion

Heroine of the Holocaust
Courage in battle is an easy thing
Compared to your gift—
You, who never would bow down
To your tormentors, and whose hand
Was always quick to save:
Though surely you endured
    a million secret deaths
Before your own turn came,
Dying with those you could not
    help.

Imagining you, I see your spirit
Burning as faithful as a candle
Whose flame is buffeted
But never quite put out.
For long and blood-drenched years
    that candle gleamed:
For multitudes, the only light
    there was.

Those who will not bend
End by being broken,
And you were. Yet they could do
    no more

Than murder you. The radiance
    that was yours
Will glow forever in the hearts
Of those who cherish righteousness.

And even if the memory of your name
Should fade at last, forgotten, into time,
Wherever there is love, there you will live.

Learning the Part of Otto Frank
in *The Diary of Anne Frank*

Mark Cannaday

Anne's father is played . . . by Mark Cannaday, an Episcopal priest. His portrayal of the learned Mr. Frank is strikingly subdued. Cannaday will not overact and lends to the whole production its sober and careful tone.

—From "Frank about Frank,"
San Antonio *Current*, November 24, 1988

What good to wail these sad moments?
Pinch history and blood will flow
every time, every place
along the way, gray
and shadows appear.

You can find
no one cheerful moment
sustained.

But those days when the Reich
Eagle flew and the great anger
sustained itself over the innocent,
those days of burial,
of burying burial,
they were supreme
with blood.

Oh Anna, how surely your haunted
face haunts me. How clearly
I see you seeing the barbed
wire strung, stretched
to serve, unveil
tortured creatures born
in the writhing
womb of madness.

Oh my gladness strung up,
my voice caved in,
my eyes stripped and heart
never, never free to pass
by these pages without
Deus, Deus meus.

I was forsaken by your execution
and I can never forget,
never forget.

To Rosa Cavalieri, who was taken to the camps

Grace Cavalieri

I learned you were a nurse,
a young girl who loved to visit the mountains.
Everywhere you went, you met someone
you liked and you were not afraid.

Perhaps that's why you helped the pregnant Jew.
She was about your age.
They say she even looked like you,
black hair with light that shined,
and you always thought you'd move
nearer her when the baby came
for you'd be all she had
and the baby would be named for you . . . Rosa.

After they found her and took her from you
you thought there might be
others you could love as much.
You were not afraid that
they'd take that from you too.

And on the day when there
was snow and rain everywhere
you were dressed in your best to answer the door.

When they came to get you
you purposely wore the blouse with
wide sleeves, her blood in the seams
which never washed clean. Or you dreamed
it was her blood. You no longer remembered.

That year summer came and you didn't notice it
nor the next one nor the next
until finally there was no summer left for you at all.

I heard the baby lived and she called herself Rosa.
She loved the mountains and went there
every summer.
They say her hair was dark with light
and that she was a strong child and was not afraid.

Personal to Kaplan

Judith Chalmer

Kaplan, I saw your name
carved into the top bunk, the only scar
in the smooth white wood, the only
whiff of rotten flesh in the sweet incense
of fresh sawdust that lingers in the corners
of the reconstructed barracks at Dachau.

Only it's 1990 and the framed signs
remind us to be respectful
of the careful display, keep our breath
out of the bunks, and use quiet voices
while we tour the exhibit, as if we'd be
joking around like we were waiting
in line for the Tunnel of Love.

But I tell you, Kaplan, I left my blood
that sprung like a poppy out of a trench,
when I gouged my finger with a point
of reconstructed barbed wire on the way in
to this place, then smeared it on the wall
like the amputated stories my father
couldn't tell. Right where you leaned
yours, friend, I leaned my impious head,
stroked my finger down the rough side

of my father's drawn cheek in the picture
I held, sitting on the bottom bunk, looking up
at your name under the empty bowl
that hung from its hook.

And I can see you smiling, after all,
clapping for me as I doubled over
the empty foundation of Barrack #9,
slamming my Papa's "No!"
against the concrete echo in the arid
roll-call square, spitting curses
over the caps of the cheerful
postcard concessionaires.

Kaplan, wherever you are, I'm carving
this message for you in the clean
smooth side of God's unflinching sky:
We are here, you and I! Our coats on,
ready to go, our cheeks full and hot
against all that was planned. We're passing
notes across the tracks, through the fence,
bearing good hot food—big chunks of potato,
thick cream, fresh dill—steaming from the fire.

Female Jewish History: Aunt Anka

Jean Colonomos

REMEMBER:
Your defiant Aunt Anka
who crossed Occupied Austria
without papers
to bring francs to her fugitive husband.

REMEMBER:
Your courageous Aunt Anka
who, crossing the Pyrenees,
nearly killed her son.
He had whooping cough
and
to protect the escape party
from a Nazi bicycling by,
she buried his head in the earth.

Female Jewish History: Aunt Tanya

Jean Colonomos

She thought she had it all
when she stared at her diamond engagement ring
and caught it winking back.

She thought she had it all
when she married him under the *chupa*
and moved from Poland to Belgium,
to begin a better life.

She thought she had it all
till she heard the Nazis shot her family
the day she left them behind.

For Janusz Korczak

Charles Fishman

It is a fine murder of landscape,
Korczak Ziolkowski, to persist
against a mountain, to shape
from the torque of epochs
a monument to Crazy Horse;
but to enter the chamber of death
with no tool but your will,
with no power but your rage
to be human—
                    Janusz, to die
with your orphans, one moment
the work of a life! Your choice
carved a space in the air
over Europe that will endure
when Giza is dust and the Great
Wall is rubble and Michelangelo's
chapel gapes with the true heaven.

Isolde, Dead in Vichy France

Jean Hollander

I had no time for love
or breaking faith.
A quick magnolia bloom
I burst too soon
into a frozen world.
Before I was thirteen
before I could
feel blood between my legs
my flesh was blasted
from my bones.

Into the moment
when their guns were up
and father raised his hands
to beg reprieve
I grew to woman
in my grief.

Buddha and Me

Barry Ivker

Buddha sat at Auschwitz
On the roof of the shower house
Where he could hear
What he couldn't see
A rotund figure
In yellow robes
He rested in lotus position
His upturned palms
Upon his lap.
What he saw
He saw through half-closed lids
And he never lost
That quiet smile
That slight upturning
Of the very corners
Of his lips.
There is no difference here
He said from what I
Saw in India
or China or Malaysia
Men dying
Together or alone
Preoccupied with self
Each frail existence
Screeching to a close
Sinking

In spite of all its protests
Into all-embracing
Unity.
Unity of victims and executioners
Unity of the dogs
That sniff the edge of burial troughs
And the very earth they stand upon
Unity of Bo tree and oak
If men would stop a while
And Think.
I sat with Buddha on the shower house
And heard the movement
Of bodies toward the door
Shaved bodies
Stripped bodies
The sound of scraping on the walls inside.
They did not look so different
When the living
Stacked their bodies up
For burning—
A few teeth more or less
A strip of skin missing on one or two.
Did not that mole
Under that left breast
Belong to a girl named
Tessie who used to
Write sentimental nature
Poetry and like
Her coffee strong?
The fire unified the
Bodies of the victims

And I paced the roof
While Buddha sat,
And muttered angry promises
While Buddha meditated.
I will remember Tessie's
Poetry I said
Bad though it was
And the mole beneath her breast
I will remember the hands
That placed her on the pyre
The name of the inventor
Of the burning process
And the post he holds now
in the new republic.
My eyes strained open
My mouth gaped in an
Ugly grimace
And the gasp that
Escaped me was not
Euphonious or
Buddha-calm.
I do not know where Buddha sits today
Or what he sees or hears.
I think I am the only one
Who still remembers Tessie's poetry
The smell of her
As she joined the others
In essential unity.
My eyes still refuse
To close halfway.
My joints are now

Too stiff to form a lotus.
Just recently
I found another Tessie
In Bangladesh
Buddha's old stomping ground
If I remember history correctly.
And near the corpse I found
Some pebbles
Transparent
But slightly murky
Buddha's tears they call
Them in this region.
This Tessie
After all
Was Indian.

Kristallnacht '88

Marta Knobloch

On this night of shattered glass,
I honor you, Primo Levi.
Reluctant Lazarus doomed to accost
The wedding guest with the tale
Of the Kiddush cup ground under the boot.
A Fibonacci sequence gone mad
Where the spirals of the sunflower*
Record the murder of six million.

Never the straight back;
The boulder careening downhill
Awake, asleep, the awful knowledge
The burning blue numbers
What quarter turn cracks the joints,
Tumbles a boneless rag into the void?

On this night of shattered glass,
I honor you, Primo Levi.
Stern ghost, could you rest
if we learned to haunt ourselves?

---

*Sunflowers were planted on the graves of German soldiers during World War II.

For Mirjam Lenka

Born 1/15/1935, Prague
Died 1/6/1944, Auschwitz

Barbara Lefcowitz

What was I doing when you died in the ovens,
not quite nine, the two of us born
the exact same day;
    were my eyes covered
with a rag, the hide 'n' seek "It" girl, or
was I learning that 9 x 9 = 81,
    precisely,
fixed in every language and catalogue
of laws, fixed long after your name, incised
on the vault of the
    Pinkas Synagogue in Prague,
is but a small stone wound that cannot
be felt or seen.

    And lashed by these lines to your
vast, nearly anonymous death, my own name
once again a tiny scar on the planet's
tough old skin,
    a scar that will never
heal, replace, or even protect you. Come, Mirjam,

come let's play. My house, your house,
the schoolyard. I twist your hair into braids,
lest it fly off with you,

dress you in a peasant blouse, your eyes the same shade
as mine, snapshot gray-green.
    No need for fear, Mirjam,
I'll let you go,
or need our play be morbid,
    each rope a noose
and all the dolls dead,
their slung heads swaying from the horse-chestnut tree.

Laughing and glossy red,
we uncross our legs,
    stuff secret rags and gourds
in our skirts, deliver them under the porch.
We feed them seeds and kernels,
    pink milk-buds,
peel open their swaddled bodies. For hours we
make them obey our private biology,
the cleft between our legs still hairless
and bloodless, we ourselves a pair of planes
free from the tugging moon,
the solid geometry of gestation.

    With crayons and paper
you show me your curve of a papa,
tangential to the right-angle chair, his top hat
floating above the bread, the cut flowers,
your mamma bearing precarious bowls,
    or are they birds perhaps,
birds that took flight from the fringed piano shawl,
its French-knot branches and ripe bushes
of bright cotton berries.

You bid me enter, snap on
a tasseled lamp, play the same flutter of rush-notes
as I would,
    a gutted Schubert sonatina, all
gapped walls and rickety steps, its real music
locked in the piano's brain, too rich and complex
for our nine-year fingers.
Later you walk me across the Charles Bridge,
its gloomy black statues looming all the way
to Mala Strana,
    each separate and rigid
as a tombstone, never to sway,
meet, much less touch.

    Mirjam, let me tell you
about the concert: the Stalin, Hitler,
Roosevelt, Chamberlain string quartet,
their instruments glittering mid-bridge,
hands held on the haft of a knife
    so sharp your country's heart
lifts like scooped fruit they split

and spit out in the Moldau. Other news
as well I tell you, how the pictures
you made at Terezin were rescued,
like very old tools and bone, spectacles,
shoes, and gold teeth;
    how I myself fast
reached ten, eleven, twenty, middle age,
multiplied and learned at last to live with fractions,
an occasional equation

or even a whole that seemed, I said seemed,
to be more than the sum of its parts.

Back, Mirjam, to you, my twin with no marker,
guilt-twin, occasional dreammate,
ashes to feed Polish weeds,
    bodiless name,
the grief that grounds all art: to claim,
to fill with flesh and blood, add, multiply,
divide, to make once more a body.

But your loss so vast and monstrous
who am I to do more
than make a shoddy pact with grief.

    Subtract. Hollow with scalpels.
A scaffold with nothing inside, not a brick,
not Prague's bronze astronomical clock,
its hourly display of death and disciples
disrupted for repair when I joined the crowd
in Rathaus Square.
    Here, right here,
you must have swung your schoolbag, the books
filled with penmanship and sums.

How can it be,
I say as I look for you
one last time,
how can it be that $9 + 9 = $ zero?
Even if I make it $9 + 9 - 9$,

still you come out zero,
come out zero,
come out zero long before your time
to come out zero.

Raoul Wallenberg Slept Well Last Night

Jim Ignatius Mills

Raoul Wallenberg established an elaborate resistance to save Hungarian Jews from the Holocaust. At the end of the war he was imprisoned in the Gulag. Rumors circulate that he is still alive. In winter he can be seen each morning exercising, then bathing in the new snow.

I

It always snows this time of year.
The chill spreads routinely.
Old men stay inside playing chess by the stove:
Pawn to King-four. The guards don't mind.
And only history watches,
wondering if there might not be a better move.

II

"Look," Piotr says, "it happens again this morning.
The old Swede taking his morning exercise,
washing himself with snow,
too dumb to know when to die."

"In his memory he is saving Jews," Alexis says.
"Over one hundred thousand Jews!
Who knows? Perhaps the old man is thinking
he is thirty again and saving Jews."

III

To suffer another's pain, to feel the club and taste the blood—
as from a distance one watches while brothers are led away.
Helpless. Poor men. And their faces are always so moonlike.
Even now you can see them.
They rise like light and rush to fill the darkness,
buoyant light filled with memories
rising from the depths of a shoreless ocean,
like a wounded beast waiting on a murky bottom
for the sun to set too near the sea.

IV

All around him now the camp is still and quiet.
He thinks: "This place," stripping himself down to old skin,
then letting his hands fall quickly beneath the snow.
And suddenly it's all there, tangible as longing:
frightened children, brave mothers, old men in black suits.

V

"Pawn to King-four," Piotr says, "and do you notice?
Raoul Wallenberg is so tranquil,
as if everything is all right,
as if everything is perfect."

Mystery My History

Victor Mingovits

Clip my curls
scissor my licorice
render me naked then
split my lip

bruise my nose
swollen my colon
concrete my feet over
ledge of a bridge

stretch on my flesh
the give of my skin
mystery my history &
who now my me

splinter the winter wood
horse whips and sticks
raper the paper with
purple black pricks

ermine the german
fur-line the coats
well-tailored
voluptuous silence
violence

whisper the reaper

this is for the men who were whipped with
horsewhips
this is for the men
who were cut up in so-called medical experiments
this is for the men who were shot with American weapons
to give German medics practice
in treating such wounds
this is for the men who stood barefoot in the rain
this is for the men
who stood dripping cold with winter water,
body lice aching on body ice
Jetzt sehen wir wie das dich aufkuhlen wird,
warmer bruder.
Let's see how this cools you off,
flaming faggot.

this is for the men whose records were burned
this is for the men whose bodies piled anonymously in group
graves
this is for the men
who traveled as boys
on the bus from Minnesota to
Grand Central Station, NY
this is for the men
who did sexual favors for the campos*
for a little extra bread
this is for the men

---

*Campos is Mingovits's variation on the word "kapos."

who stood beaten while their "straight" campo lovers
looked on, speechless
with long shit in their throat

this is for the men
without mothers, brothers, or lovers
to remember them
this is for the men
whose neighbors whispered nasty about them
once they returned
this is for the men
who were set free but who were never set free
this is for the few
men who keep talking about it saying don't forget
saying don't forget
saying don't forget
this is for the men who can't talk about it anymore

this is for the men who broke windows at Stonewall
this is for ACT UP
this is for QUEER NATION
this is for GAY AND LESBIAN ALLIANCE
        AGAINST DEFAMATION

this is for the men who meet after work
in porn booths on 42nd Street
before going home to
wife & children

this is for the men who are never set free

Poem Beginning with
a Line by Fitzgerald/Hemingway

Alicia Ostriker

The very rich are different from us, they
Have more money, fewer scruples. The very

Attractive have more lovers, the very sensitive
Go mad more easily, and the very brave

Distress a coward like myself, so listen
Scott, listen Ernest, and you also can

Listen, Walt Whitman. I understand the large
Language of rhetoricians, but not the large

Hearts of the heroes. I am reading up.
I want someone to tell me what solvent saves

Their cardiac chambers from sediment, what is
The shovel that cuts the sluice

Straight from the obvious mottos such as *Love
Your neighbor as yourself*, or *I am human, therefore*

Nothing human is alien, to the physical arm
In the immaculate ambassadorial shirtsleeves

—We are in Budapest, '44—that waves
Off the muddy Gestapo in the railroad yard

With an imperious, an impatient flourish,
And is handing Swedish passports to anonymous

Yellow-starred arms reaching from the very boxcars
That are packed and ready to glide with a shrill

Whistle and grate on steel, out of the town,
Like God's biceps and triceps gesturing

Across the void to Adam: Live. In Kraków
A drinking, wenching German businessman

Bribes and cajoles, laughs and negotiates
Over the workers, spends several times a fortune,

Saves a few thousand Jews, including one
He wins at a card game, and sets to work

In his kitchenware factory. A summer twilight
Soaks a plateau in southern France, the mountains

Mildly visible, and beyond them Switzerland,
As the policeman climbs from the khaki bus

To Le Chambon Square, where the tall pastor
Refuses to give names of refugees;

Meanwhile young men slip through the plotted streets,
Fan out to the farms—it is '42—

IN MEMORIAM

So that the houses empty and the cool woods fill
With Jews and their false papers, so that the morning

Search finds no soul to arrest. It happens
Over and over, but how? The handsome Swede

Was rich, was bored, one might have said. The pastor
Had his habit of hugging and kissing, and was good

At organizing peasants, intellectuals
And Bible students. The profiteer intended

To amass wealth. He did, lived steep, and ended
Penniless, though the day the war ended,

The day they heard, over the whistling wireless,
The distant voice of Churchill barking victory

As the Russians advanced, his *Schindlerjuden*
Still in the plant, still safe, as he moved to flee,

Made him a small present. Jerets provided
His mouth's gold bridgework, Licht melted it down,

Engraved the circle of the ring with what
One reads in Talmud: *Who saves a single life,*

It is as if he saved the universe; and Schindler
The German took it, he wears it in his grave;

I am reading up on this. I did not know
Life had undone so many deaths. *Now go*

And do likewise, snaps every repercussion
Of my embarrassed heart, which is like a child

Alone in a classroom full of strangers, thinking
She would like to run away. Let me repeat,

Though I do not forget ovens or guns,
Their names: Raoul Wallenberg, Oskar Schindler,

André Trocmè. Europe was full of others
As empty space is full of burning suns;

Not equally massive or luminous,
Creating heat, nevertheless, and light,

Creating what we may plausibly write
Up as the sky, a that without which nothing;

We cannot guess how many, only that they
Were subject to arrest each bloody day

And managed. Maybe it's like the muse, incalculable,
What you can pray in private for. Or a man

You distantly adore, who may someday love you
In the very cave of loneliness. We are afraid—

Yet as no pregnant woman knows beforehand
If she will go through labor strong, undrugged,

Unscreaming, and no shivering soldier knows
During precombat terror who will retreat,

Who stand and fight, so we cannot predict
Who among us will risk the fat that clings

Sweetly to our own bones—
None sweeter, Whitman promises—

Our life, to save doomed lives, and none of us
Can know before the very day arrives.

Martyr

Elizabeth Rees

In memory of Etty Hillesum

Weeks before they called your name,
you turned your body in. The guard
was only too happy to show you
to your train, such a law-
abiding citizen as you, a pity
your mother was such a Jew.
Suddenly, birds sounded so close,
you had to stop. Innocence sung!
The guard jabbed you only once
with the butt of his gun.

Even he heard the birds,
heard autumn's fast hiss—
but not because of you.
He was counting in his head
what year this was and whether
the locusts would be back.
As your cattle car clacked
out of the station,
you were already a ghost.
The leaves leapt and broke.

You offered to go with the first transport
because you accepted a common fate.
Not an interruption of your life,

you would sing in letters to your friends.
Because if God didn't help you
to go on, you should have to help God.
Yesterday your heart
was a sparrow, caught
in a vice. Today, tucked away
in a protective hand, the still bird waits.

In Der Nacht (In the Night)

Curtis Robbins

Rose Rosman

You have come a distance to speak
Your heart of a life no man or woman would
Ever, should never, relive. It's like day
And night. But, you see only Darkness
Where no light can ever guide you—
Rosa, Rosa, *in der Nacht,*
The darkness is brighter than the flame.

A Nazi soldier was gathering your deaf friends,
Guiding them, with his kindly, assuring hands,
To the trains of a certain destiny.
Rosa, Rosa, *in der Nacht,*
The darkness is brighter than the flame.

You were such an impeccable child—
Watching them come to take your family,
Acquiescent as silent drums.
Rosa, Rosa, *in der Nacht,*
The darkness is brighter than the flame.

The moon outshone by a distant fire
Glowing by night with kindlings of hearts—
Who knows where they went to witness the blackening sun.
Rosa, Rosa, *in der Nacht,*
The darkness is brighter than the flame.

Ner Tamid. Ner Tamid,
The eternal flame, has never dimmed.
The joys and smiles are never forgotten.
A new life reminisces the bitterness *in der Nacht*,
When the darkness was brighter than the flame.
Rosa, Rosa, *in der Nacht*,
The darkness is brighter than the flame.

Pesach, 1988

The Beginning of the Lies

Diana Rubin

For Siegbert Kindermann, murdered March 13, 1933 by Nazis

Before they beat his head senseless into pulp
Threw him with brutishness from the window
    of the Stormtroops barracks in Berlin
They fastidiously carved a substantial swastika
    into his tortured chest—
The foul anger of the Aryan fiends, it seems,
had festered with the putridity of an open sore
and it was revenge, they alleged, that they sought.
As he fell, they uttered his singular crime
    in harsh, guttural contempt: "Jude!"
To others, he was known as a baker's apprentice
who, having been previously attacked by Nazi punks,
had once sought justice and had had them convicted.

But this was not the story they would ever tell
to their children or to their children's children.
Instead, in future years, when asked about
    the Kristallnacht, the Holy Ark for the Scroll
    of the Law of Moses, the smashed woodwork,
heaps of stone, the scorched parchment, the horrific screams
of German Jewry witnessing the terror of legalized torture
    unfurl with skulls crushed, eyes purged, torn out
They were unable to meet one's shocked gaze
And it became apparent that, quite conveniently,

A protective amnesia had set in—
As they spoke quickly, ardently, merely
    of how horrible things had been for them during the war.
The rest, abhorrent and ruthless, seemed irrelevant—
    A painstakingly forgotten perverse monstrosity.
For murderers, you see, lies are always easier.

Kaddish for Felix Nussbaum (1904–1944)

Willa Schneberg

I

Strapped in my life,
like breasts in a brassiere,
I couldn't get to you
although I tried. But the
Women's Army Auxiliary Corps
said I was too young to go overseas,
so they sent me to Fort Benning
to stand under the merciless sun
in attention saluting, until I
toppled over like a dreidel.

So sorry for myself,
while you were behind electrified
barbed wire in St. Cyprien,
either sweltering in the hot barracks
or scorched, the sun never
ceasing its beating,
you sleeping on sand and straw,
your plate a tin can. But somehow you kept painting
tallised men entering a makeshift synagogue,
their backs to the horror and yourself
surrounded by walls impossible to climb,
wearing the yellow star on your coat
and holding a Jewish identity card.
So I could go to Chattanooga on leave,

dance the lindy with *sheigitz* boys,
eat a B.L.T. for the first time
and visit a plastic surgeon
to have my nose made non-Jewish,
small and turned-up.

II

Yes, you and Felka hid together
in Brussels at Rue Archimede,
but you never loved her.
You saw her through the eyes
in the back of your head and heard her
only faintly over the din behind
whatever you spoke or thought,
the stomping up the stairs,
the fist pounding the door.
If you were with me
you wouldn't have painted the vase
with the stem bent in half,
or you two in a stiff embrace
as if chained together.
In my body you would have returned
to your summers in Norderney
and afterwards we would be
a small blue boat slightly rocking.

III

If I could have taken you back
to my old neighborhood in Brooklyn,
where Uncle Dave had the only car
and we all piled in, you probably

wouldn't have become a painter
who spoke for an entire generation
of artists who were exiled, hunted,
banned or imprisoned, and I would
have never seen you in a museum
and fallen in love
with your taut, determined face.
At best, you might have become a fine arts
professor remaining unextraordinary,
painting your mother solid
in a flowered dress and yourself
at the easel in a pink-lit
country road near Osnabruck,
where you were young and at worst,
which really isn't so bad,
you might have given up painting altogether
and taken a desk job like my Irving,
who went with me and the kids
every Sunday, July and August
to the beach at Coney Island to hear
transistors blaring, the ice-cream man
chanting, "Dixie cups, popsicles."

Ursula Goetze*

Gary Sea

Born March 29, 1883

I find it very strange—
Those words
    pronounced with paralyzing finality
sent surges of life
        through me
        as if I were reborn.
My senses began probing with intense curiosity,
    as if emerging from long hibernation,
        intoxicated
by the scent of humanness
    which filled me
        like a breath of wind
from my heart.
I discovered my self,
    buried treasures
    never ever imagined,
becoming ecstatic with my riches.

---

*Ursula Goetze studied philosophy in Berlin. With other students she took up collections for political prisoners and racially persecuted peoples. She listened to French radio broadcasts, passing information along to French prisoners. She was arrested and condemned to death on January 18, 1943, and was hanged on August 5. This poem was adapted from a letter to her parents.

And slowly, gracefully
    with astonishing little effort
all the holes torn in my life by fate
    were filled by something new and beautiful—

a knowledge, a peace,
    wisdom,
        the greatest wisdom of all—

It is never too late to live!

Erika von Brockdorff*

Gary Sea

Born April 29, 1911

Promise
you will not long mourn for me,
disturbing my peace
which I shall need
when passing through the dark gate.

Mourning is not necessary
   for those
who give of themselves gladly,
     and with Goethe's Egmont
       I say—
"If my blood can flow for the many,
     to bring my people peace,
then let it flow."

     For those
who give of themselves gladly
sing a song of joy;

*Erika von Brockdorff was the daughter of a postman. An underground radio station operated from her apartment. She was arrested in September 1942, and on December 19, 1942, was sentenced to ten years' imprisonment. In January 1943, the sentence was revised, and she was condemned to death. She died on the guillotine on May 13, 1943, at the age of thirty-two. The first and last stanzas are her own words, translated from letters.

look on us not as martyrs
        but as prophets
of better times to come.
I shall live those times through you.

And no one can say of me, without lying,
that I cried and clung to life,
        or trembled.
Laughing! I will end my life
        as I loved life the best, laughing!
and love it still.

Ottilie Pohl*

Gary Sea

Born November 14, 1867

If you think age makes this woman weak
    you are wrong.
Like the resilient olive,
    eons polished by wind—
your ravings only brighten my luster.

And my soul—
    how dare you think you can touch my soul!
My gnarled fist—at which you laugh—
    will slough off its mottled skin
    and rise
an avenging phoenix
    to grasp
you in its beak
    and fling you
    into your own hate-filled flame.

....

*Ottilie Pohl was a Jewish dressmaker and went to Berlin to further her career. She first joined the Socialists, then the Spartakus-Bund. She actively worked against war and fought against the Nazis in 1933. After the Nazi takeover, she helped collect monies for victims of the Nazi terror, care for their relatives, and hide Resistance leaders in her apartment. She was arrested in 1940, held in Berlin's women's prison, and then transported to the concentration camp at Theresienstadt. She died in the gas chambers at Auschwitz sometime in 1943, at the age of seventy-six.

Motele the Incongruous*

Lester Speiser

Your violin shattered stars;
call yourself a nice Jewish
boy?
        "Play nice
        Don't fight."

Were you the fiddler ratat
tatting on the roof . . .
another canvas, another
show?
        A little
        match. Bang!
        Gottcha.

Was your mouth tight, grim
and pressed; did you wear
a cap or a yarmulke;
did you wrap phylacteries
around the arm?

---

*Motele, whose parents and sister had been killed by the Nazis, was a twelve-year-old member of a Jewish partisan group in Poland during World War II. A fiddler, he was able to earn his keep by playing for Nazi troops in a restaurant called Soldiers Home. Utilizing his regular access to this place, Motele was able to smuggle forty pounds of explosives into the cellar in his violin case. One night, when the place was full of SS officers, he lit the fuse and blew up the restaurant. He was eventually killed in battle a few days before the liberation.

"You're dead!
Fall down!"

Were you cheerful helpful
friendly brave clean reverent?
Little scout, did you pee
in your pants?
             "Fall down play
             fair play nice
             don't fight."

Your violin exploded,
no pomegranates there,
A Song of Songs
unrecorded in the
Book of Life.
             Without a doubt,
             your mother
             called you Mottie
             did she not?

Was your name O'Toole, Johnson,
Esterhazy, Werner von Braun?
Are you in the Yellow Pages,
yellow like the Star,
like the Yellow Submarine?
(Yeah-Yeah-Yeah)
             "Yo, Bro!
             What book
             are you in?"

Hey, you got to fire
a real gun and stay
up; no clock watchers
in your life.
                    So what.
                    You never ate
Chinese, you
never saw the Met
Chagalls, you never
watched Ninja,
you never went
to Lincoln Center,
you never read
the *New York Times*.

You never even saw *Fiddler*. . . .

Martyrs of Israel

Bradley R. Strahan

When I think of you
I think of stars
of sand. Black waves
swallow the shining.

Beneath the ages
you wait, to thrust off,
to break open
the chains of darkness.

You wait to gather
your strength. Ember-
eyes burning, bone
sockets still charred

from an older fire.
Flaming hands knock
at our doors, demanding
the bones still hidden
                    in our flesh.

The March of the Orphans—August 5, 1942

Rich Michelson

*All residents of the Korczak Children's Home
will report to the Gdansk Rail Station for
resettlement.*

— Posted Notice

*I assert with joy that with few exceptions, man
is a creature of goodness and understanding.*

— Janusz Korczak, *How to Love a Child*

How simply my children, like newborn pups,
jostle each other, barking for stories,
words tossed their way like coins
to a blind man who rattles his cup
more for sound than for money.

I tell them of young Dmitry Tolstoy, sighing
over his mother's grave; his brother Leo
scribbling notes. Suddenly the guests arrive.
Dmitry straightens himself, wipes his eyes.
Leo pounds the earth and weeps.

The lessons I teach, I teach myself.
These children desire to change
their world. If I cry for them now,
it's to keep the world from changing me.
Read, they beg, chapters from your life's work,

how the famed Dr. Korczak, physician and poet,
self-proclaimed father of all orphans,
took us in and gave us hope.
But my voice sounds strange to me,
weak, even foolish. Reminiscence

makes the saddest literature,
my Stefa scolds. How old she looks
among the scrubbed, expectant children.
It is harder to live one day with honor,
she tells them, than to write a book

as great as any the world has known.
She calls me mad. I've no response
except more words. This morning,
Stefa by my side, I'll lead
along Krochmalna Street, two hundred

of our sons and daughters. Proudly
clad in Sabbath clothes, we'll line up
four abreast and sing so loudly all Warsaw
will hear our joyous song. I'll kiss Stefa
and if there's time, recite some poems,

before, like wild dogs, we're slaughtered.

Two Boys 1940–44

Lotte Kramer

Two boys played on a farm in France.
Quite ordinary boys. "No harm
Will touch them," so the farmer priced
His promise for a bar of gold.
He stored and fathered orphaned lives.

Before their bones had stretched full size
Their minds were strung with adult ache.
In earnest they played blindman's buff
Or hide-and-seek. They knew the ways
Of tunneled moles and fumbling bats.

Their growing pains had hostile names.
Their town-hands learned to crumble soil,
To master trees, to sweat with fear.
We thought them safely caged in barns.
What made him break their padlocked years?

To let the hunter grab his prey
And shunt them on an eastern train
In cattle-trucks to nameless graves
Where fathers never heard them groan:
Amen—for their dumb growing pains.

How did he plow his land and reap
With children's ghosts, their splintered nails,
How did he clean his grubby skin
From their cold questions in its cracks
And shrug away his ailing sin?

Jankel

André Heller

Jankel
Has anyone seen Jankel?
Jankel with the black hat.
Did he lie down to sleep
among ashes and embers?
Is he looking for Myriam again?
Smoke following smoke.
Are lilies or gorse
growing out of his heart?
Mazel tov, mazel tov Jankele
You could use a bit of luck.

Last Rites for Bert Brecht

Mimi Grossberg

Although they call me a Jew, that's not what I am.
But since so many have been gassed and beaten to death,
perhaps there'd be a need for one.
I'll volunteer in the hope that I'll be accepted.

— Bert Brecht

You owed it to yourself
and now after your death
you've had your last rites
and received what's due

Resurrection has been bestowed
with no lack of valor—
your grave has been desecrated
and now you're a Jew.

Welcome to the club!

Biography

Stella Rotenberg

Born
in wartime
in Vienna,
died
in wartime
marching towards Minsk,
bludgeoned by an SS man
who hailed from Vienna
because she marched
too slowly.
She left
no name,
no bones,
nothing
but a low scream.

In the Absence of Yellow

Reva Sharon

The last, the very last,
So richly, brightly, dazzlingly yellow,
Perhaps if the sun's tears would sing
against a white stone . . .
. . . only I never saw another butterfly.

— Pavel Friedmann, June 4, 1942, Theresienstadt

It is summer and it is quiet
where I am standing in the yard
several feet from the wall
scarred by executions
It is quiet now . . .
more than forty years have passed
since you arrived that spring
late in April—Pavel
how long did you live
here . . . In only seven weeks
you grasped the universe
within these ramparts
and etched a page of sorrow
with your poem

Pavel—I have just come
from your city . . .
the glorious buildings of Prague
are unscathed by the war

In the narrow winding streets
of the Jewish Quarter
where you were born
centuries-old synagogues
are museums . . .
One thousand only
of your people live there now
On a wall in Pinkas Synagogue
your name is inscribed
with nearly 80,000 others

in remembrance
Pavel—the light
is tarnished with ashes
and every stone is stained
Here in Terezin
wings the color of rust
are fluttering

Shoshana

Reva Sharon

For Shoshana Shreiber, who bears number A-25415 on her arm

Leaning on her cane   and into
the wind of two continents
that lifts the leaves of Jerusalem
and sweeps by her in
the streets of New York
wisps of blond hair
straying from under
an elegant hat
she listens
as the wind carries
the refrain
> *Shoshi Shoshi*
> *you will survive*

At end of day she removes
hairpins   and as she brushes
remembers a scarf
long lost   white and crimson
rescued from a heap
of abandoned clothes
and stuffed   (verboten)
in the toe of her shoe
as she passed (otherwise
innocent   naked and shorn)

the armed guards of Auschwitz
Shoshi Shoshi
you will survive

On her high hard bunk
she tied the scarf
securely around her head
Crimson and white   in a sea of sick gray
caught the eye of the kapo
who selected her for
work in the kitchen
where in addition   to thin soup rations
she ate what she could scrape
and wondered   why with a scarcity of bread
the stacks always smoke at the bakery ovens
Shoshi Shoshi
you will survive

She remembers   The hands of her mother
And the eyes of her father
and recalls the clatter
of wheels on tracks
And the voice of her brother
in the cavedark of the boxcar
"Shoshi Shoshi
you will survive"
The faces   their faces   she remembers
the last time she glimpsed them
when she gazes into
her grandchildren's faces
(eight in New York   thirteen in Jerusalem)

And she leans
into the wind of two continents
which rises
under a stone heavy sky
bypasses Europe
lifts the leaves
and shifts

THE *Liberation*

The Last Day

Lily Brett

The last days
in
this

slaughter
theater

were
even
worse

perversely
the
prisoners

missed
the
security

the
certainty
of the enemy

most
were
half-dead

no one
was
wholly alive

the
muddy yellow
water

had
run
out

people
scraped
the remaining

gray
spots
of
snow

drank
their
own
piss

slept
in
their
shit

on
the
last
day

a
man
cooked

his
friend's
liver.

This Broken Silence

Bruce V. J. Curley

It was the silence that most terrified us.
The silence at night
The silence at dawn
The silence of day.

We'd lay down, pained
At night . . . forbidden to cry out
Our pain to each other.

So . . . Silently, so silently,
Each second of the night passed,
Silently, for five years.

Steinberg screamed once.
Screamed, "You Nazi scum!!!
We'll pay you back someday!!!
Your Reich will last a few years!!!
We've been around millenniums!!!
We'll see who survives who!!!"

Steinberg screamed this out
In the silence of night

He was executed in the silence of dawn.

We learned the lesson quickly.
Every execution from that day on
We viewed in silence
Cold, black-steel silence
Cold, gray-dawn silence.

Sister Anne prayed once.
Prayed out loud. Prayed, "Dear sweet, sweet Jesus!!!
Forgive them all!!! They don't
Know what they are doing to you!!!"

Prayed it again and again
While a group of old Hasidim
Like a flock of battered sheep
Who were shorn of their wool locks
In frosted dead of winter
Were pushed by the dreaded overseers
Headlong into the concrete ovens.

The Commandant had the ovens opened mid-burn
And Sister Anne was told
To view the Jewish sheep
Now charred and black
Before being thrown in with them.

She was executed in the silence of day.

We learned the lesson quickly.

Every murder we witnessed
From that day on
We prayed, those of us who still prayed,
In silence.

Cold, ebony-dazed silence.

The Pole was silent once.
But only once.
Commandant screamed, "Give me an answer, swine!
Give me an answer
Or you'll die!"

The Pole remained silent.

Stared, eagle-eyed, determined and strong,
Commandant screamed into the Pole's mouth,

"TALK!!! WHO DID IT?!"

BAAABBBBAAABBBAAAWWWHIRZZZAABAD-
DDDDACHUHH

GI commando's carbine plug
Found the Commandant's head.
Silence cracked all over.
Cracked by bullets of life.
Cracked by guns of love.
Cracked by voices gruff with fatigue,
GI voices of Pennsylvania,
Georgia, California, Montana.

Nervously viewing our gaunt bodies
and death eyes
They tried to crack the silence
With their foreign talk.

"FREUND!!! AMERIKANISHER!!! SEEE!!! FREUND!!!
"How's about a candy bar, buddy?
Hershey's chocolate!
Real good stuff!
Here, have one, man!!!

"Who here needs a plug a tobacco?

"Watcha'll doin' standin' aroun' quiet for???
Ya'll free!!! Free, ya hear!!???"

Then these strange tongues
Of liberation, of life, of love
Asked us to state the abuses
Of our tormentors for the record.

But all we did
Was stare back in silence

The silence of Steinberg.
The silence of Sister Anne.
The silence of the Pole.
The silence of the Commandant,
The silence of five years
under the Commandant's rule
Who, dead and bleeding before us,
Even now, made sure the nightmare continued.

Seven years later,
In a synagogue in Philadelphia
I took an American wife
Because she knew nothing of the silence.

Even today
Her incessant American chatter
Is like life itself to me.

And silence,
Like loneliness and pain
Lies buried with the Commandant.

But I know, now, how to speak
With a voice bold and ecstatic
Of life and love
This moment of present,
This moment of future
To my children.

My voice shouts to them
To honor Steinberg,
Sister Anne, the Pole,
And the American GI.

It has been resurrected
From our crucifixions,
And from the Chosen voices
Of millennia past.

Twilight of the World

Jacob Glatstein

In a darkening world
sits the mad law-carver
gouging out new commandments.
All of our cherished thou-shalt-nots,
everything that was forbidden to us,
everything that was destined for us,
and everything denied us,
bombers have obliterated.
The madman's chisel
cancels good and evil.

Meanwhile we exist
on laws of the in-between.

Translated by Doris Vidaver

A New Command

Jo Nelson

The Allied commander's first order
as he gazed uncomprehending at
living cordwood stacked with dead;
skeletal figures barely able to walk;
was that they assemble for a memorial
to the free world's tragic news
that Roosevelt had died.
He asked them to liberate thoughts
of vengeance; to reply to
barbarism with understanding
as though the skulls were baseballs
and the losers could shake hands.

The Shower

Tsipi Keller

Bergen-Belsen, April 1945

With such care she moves her hand
Over her skin, her bare breasts,
White and heavy in the cold sun,
Her nipples, a mother's nipples,
Like small towers defy the wire.
With such care she spreads lather
Between her breasts, moves her hand
As though her body weren't hers.

       Habitual motions, yes,
Yet forgotten, now slowly retaking shape
With water splashing, drops sliding
Forever on her skin.

       No matter that
She is in the open for all to see;
These men are soldiers who fought for her,
In a way, only for her. These men,
She knows, would understand
The simple fact of water,
The warmth in a hand.

THE *Aftermath*

Anonymous Recollection

Robert Anbian

the precise incision of the shadows
on the bleached ground
the wretched ex-guards, arms
hanging in their sleeves,
the good bourgeois huddled like crow

the ex-inmates crushed openly by their feelings,
our sentry, his slouching posture,
angle of his rifle barrel, all he didn't do with it

the frozen single frame of it,
baffling eternity

not even the pit with its trellised mass of ivory torsos,
its sphere of shriveled limbs, sexless faces
imprinted on the soil

5,000 at their feet in a single pit!

yet
the precise incision
of the 13 shadows
on the blanched earth—

Auschwitz, August 1988

Linda Ashear

I

My travel agent said,
Why do you want to go there?

II

Silence cracks the world wide open.
A crow shrieks.

III

No one screams in the cement room.
I fix my eye on the door,
remind myself that Zyklon B
is something that happened to somebody else.

IV

I follow tracks to the horizon.
Black sandals leave their mark
in fine gray dust.
Gravel crunches, waking sleeping ghosts.
Three white moths circle my head.

V

In the women's section, Israeli tourists
enter Barracks 26. One old woman
wanders through rows of wooden bunks,
stops, stares, points . . .
This was my bed.

VI

At the ruined crematorium our guide
bends to pick up something from the earth.
Open your hand, she says.
What is it?
Bone, she says.
A stone grows in my throat.
After Auschwitz, words, like lungs, collapse.

Kristallnacht, 1991

Crystal V. Bacon

Night of glass, Germany is broken.
Brothers of the new order pledge against foreigners.
Break the glass, burn the synagogues.
Whatever they think, they sniff
out of the German air. Berlin or Munich,
ashes of the not forgotten dead. This is their Fatherland.
This their ethnic purity. They eat the bread of bones.
Drink the wine of blood. This is the feast of fear.
The orgy of panic. The church of slash and burn.

Train wheels echo across the German landscape.
Treblinka, they hum. Dachau, comes the refrain.
Auschwitz, I am thinking, and liberation.
In Tutzing, my grandfather pledged himself
to the Voice of America, itself no small feat.
In Munich, Hitler himself held my mother
up on the running board of his parade car:
the stories I know about "the war."
Sixty years later, I am cut loose in America
with this past, a vast space where history
bares its teeth like the silent face of death.

The Tattoo

Judith Berke

The artist said we shouldn't detract
from the one on my arm, so I said All right,
just the back then. I could hear a noise
as he worked, an insect ticking,
huge, metallic—the instrument,
I suppose. Day after day to keep from feeling
the pain, I studied the sketch I'd made him.
The maiden would start at the lower part
of my back and look up at the dragon,
whose head would look down from the blade
of my right shoulder. I did not look
in the glass till it was almost finished.
Moved my shoulders alternately
forward and back, as I'd moved different
parts of me in the camp, to keep the muscles
from dying. First the dragon
would look more alive to me, and then
the woman—in fact if I flexed the muscles
a certain way, the flames would appear
to come from her mouth. Claws
she had, talons, though I'd never
sketched that. Good,
I thought, let everything be its opposite,
and I said to the artist, more flames,
more ashes, and he got on with it.

Inscribed

Lisa Bernstein

As in the Bible,
where one massacre precedes another,
she was born with her father's war
in her body.
There in the damp, clayey flesh:
a yellow field of grain
where the men lie bleeding.

Her father recognized
the yielding piece of land
he had walked on after the bombing,
stepping carefully through the wheat sheaves,
the dismembered
as slick as newborns.

He held her body
in his arms. When she was wet,
sometimes he thought she was bleeding
from the killing he saw.

He tilted the warm bottle
into her mouth.

Displabed

Lily Brett

I was born
in a displaced person's camp
and have often felt displaced

Although
I don't think
you could tell

When I put
my perfectly symmetrical face
in place

they say
I look like a madonna
or the Mona Lisa

I don't know
if madonnas despair
or gasp for air

in strange locations
in spaces that are
too big too small
too dark too tall

do madonnas
check their front door
four times before being assured
it is shut

and do they
after securing the handbrake and gear stick
rush back to the car believing
it will slip downhill

I wonder if madonnas
have to hide
when their children
climb tall slides in the park

or can madonnas
walk in the dark
without imagining
packs of attackers

I comfort myself
maybe the Mona Lisa
wasn't always at ease.

I Have Never Known

Lily Brett

Mother I have never known
where you ended

I have worn us blended
for forty years

I have walked through Melbourne
as though it were Warsaw

on guard for the Gestapo
in fear of informers

alert
to any menace in the air

and I have bought boxes
of eggs and potatoes and bread

and cheese and cherries
and pickled cucumber and herrings

to put aside
for leaner times

and I have had my nightmares too
of what I might not have been able to do

and I know how every event
a knock at the door a burst of rain

a child's complaint
a husband's breakfast

is always a question
of life and death

and I measure myself mother
against imagined obstacles

and am left
lacking.

The Immigration Man

Lily Brett

I look at my feet
and feel myself spin
when the immigration man

taps his blue biro
violently
asking me
my nationality

Australian I say
he's holding
my passport
and why should he ask

he taps faster
and I feel
I might faint

could he be
one of the
Poles
who pointed you out

mother
who called back the Nazis
to say
you've missed one in this house
take her she's Jewish.

The Cake

Lily Brett

On the fifth of December
before dawn

in the blackness
of Palacowa Street

your mother arrived
with a surprise

it was
your eighteenth birthday mother

you were living
a married life

with your husband
his mother and father and brother

in one room
in the ghetto

Rooshka Rooshka
she whispered loudly

in the
still curfewed air

I have baked you
a cake

my
darling daughter

I sold
my blue woolen dress

with the mink trim
the one I wore to your brother's bar mitzvah

to Mrs Zimmerman
for thirty-six saccharin

and a kilo
of thick potato peels

from the kitchen
that peels with a knife not a peeler

I minced the clean peels
and added

two cups of chopped
turnip and beetroot tops

some baking soda
salt saccharin and washed coffee grounds

for
extra texture

the mixture
fitted beautifully

in
my baking dish

with
a bit of water

oh
Rooshka Rooshka

my
beloved daughter

I have baked you
a cake.

An Die Musik (Schubert)

Ruth Daigon

Cultural event

Our season tickets stamped on our wrists,
we sit among the perfumed furs and patent leather
in our striped uniforms   waiting.

She appears.
Opening chords lift off
like birds flying backwards.
Long skeins of sound
wrap loosely around listeners.

Himmler nods
applauding
from his private Berlin box.

She spins music from its dark cocoon.
Phrases glow brighter than
searchlights on prison towers.
High notes strict as flames in burning synagogues
singe us in our seats.

Her burnished voice
her tempo   locked in marrow,
the even rhythm of her breath
moves us toward the showers.

She sings of spring melting shards of winter,
of summer burning along branches,
of seeds spiraling to earth
as light as babies falling in slow
motion into soft beds of soil.

The texture of her voice
rubbed smooth by each new season,
ours grown thin as parchment.

Now, she carves sound out of
a country of bare surfaces
where we pound rocks into pebbles
paving roads to Treblinka, Auschwitz,
Bergen-Belsen, Buchenwald.

And when she sings of love
hidden circuits warm our bodies
packed in vats of ice.

The audience rises with applause,
the stage buried in bouquets.
She bows. But from somewhere in the wings,
a voice hums lullabies of barbed wire
and the string quartet rests between numbers
waxing their bows.

The Death Mazurka

Charles Fishman

It was late—late in the silence—
yet a mangled tune still rose
as if from a needle trapped
in a warped and spinning groove:
an inarticulate moan
fragmented out of sense
but insistent it be known.

Footfalls turned me around:
a troupe of dancers spun
and kicked and dipped as one—
three score minus one,
and that *one* danced alone.
I watched them skip and prance
but followed only her.

And yes, the drum was swift
and kept a lively beat,
and violins sang sweet
then stridently meowed—
a mocking sliding note.
She alone danced on
uncoupled, incomplete.

But the trumpets shrilled their tongues
and the saxophones crooned deep
and cymbals scoured the night

to a clashing brassy gleam.
How the women's earrings shone
like sparks from a whirling fire
that never would be ash.

Then the men whisked off their hats
and bowed to the slide trombone
as though it sat enshrined.
But still *she* danced alone
at the edge of the wheeling ring:
I could feel the horizon tilt
when she veered close to me.

Then she turned   then I   then the night
blew back forty years:
I stood in a desolate place,
a reservoir of death
—I could kneel anywhere and drink!
Yes, here was the shul in its bones
and here Judenrein* Square

and here a few scorched teeth
from some martyred, unknown saint.
The sky was a scroll of pain
—each star a sacred name!
I saw through time in that light.
But I turned and blood rained down
and I turned and dipped and drank

---

*Cleaned of Jews.

and could not take my fill:
I yearned to find *her* there.
And I turned toward darkness again
where dancers in masks like skulls
twirled in smoke and fire,
whirled in fire and smoke.
Now! screamed the violins.

And she was near as my heart
as we clasped each other and turned.
And *Now!* they shrieked. And *Now!*

The Children

Charles Fishman

I thought my poems were finished
— the dance of death I was called to —
but your pain, your tears for the children
and for the mothers who could not bear
and for the mothers who had to quiet their young
forever . . . your tears woke the words in me
again where they had slept, where my thoughts
had withdrawn from the pain of so much death.

Dear wife, I have you to blame for this yielding
to memory, this warfare of the spirit. I have you
to thank: you, and your wise heart that will not retreat
to the safety of ignorance. You have called me again
to witness and be maimed, to name and remember, and to not
be healed.

Train to Munich

D. Dina Friedman

Once thousands of us were on this track, shivering like fish stacked on ice. Large men reached into our teeth for gold. Now, as we cross the border, three large men enter our dark compartment. We reach into our sleeping bags for ID. Grass turns yellow, flattens under the tracks. All of the passengers are thirsty.

The trees have arthritis. Their limbs are as knotted as my grandmother's. She must think about each step and breathe as heavily as a train engine. You and I are so close there is no air between us. I choke on your insistence that genetic engineering is the only way to change human nature. If I visit the memorial, I will be able to see the soap made from the fat of my ancestors, but you will not let me go. You curse because my bar of Ivory has flaked onto your toothbrush.

If I visit the memorial, you tell me, you will not be there for my return. You will go instead to cavort in Bavarian cafés. But we will meet at the glockenspiel and there I will tell you that I have seen the scrub brushes made from the curly dark hair of my people. We will listen to bells that are electronic and out of tune, watch the crowd applaud as one knight knocks the other off a golden horse.

I think about each crossbar as the train crawls along the track, trying not to remember how blond and pale you are. Yet, I have long ago given up the hope of color, of blood. I only want you to continue to fade into the white, white wall. I only want to cross another border.

This Week

Roberta Gould

The defendant, Juozas Kungys, is accused of lying about his past when
he entered U.S. in 1948 and became a citizen in 1954.

    — *New York Daily News*, March 1983

I never give up on the dead
and if I forget them for a day
it doesn't prove I'm consumed by my carpet
or the promise of a decent pension
but that I'm human

Still, I'm not a bad egg
This week I phoned my personal Nazi
saying I was the "Keidainia Memorial Society"
saying I was the "Jewish Women of Mount Tremper"
He answered the phone with true joy,
his voice sunny and rich

Friends,
        don't cut off your wrists as Jim did
        don't go mad every year like Renée
        don't slice off your finger like Tanya
        don't lie in bed afraid of morning
        don't smoke yourselves to death
        like Daido and Lorraine
        don't go sexually dead
        obeying the message,

"Work for death
you handcuffed slave
you pest!"

When I got his number from information
after the *News* printed the story
of how he worked for a dentist in Clifton
of how he'd forced 2,000 Jews from their homes
marched them to a ghetto in Keidan*
marched them to a horse farm
ordered them to remove their clothes
had them shot into the ditch
I remembered El Salvador
thought how this is the model of history
I went to the telephone then
half my friends have unlisted numbers
afraid of obscene callers
afraid of their mothers, their shadows
Juozas' number is listed
Here it is
Jot it down:
201-779-8888
Show your love for the dead and the future
speak for them, call him tonight when you awake to urinate
or to drink your glass of water
Proud as any fine neighbor
he sleeps deeply, suffers no insomnia
The hacked corpses in Guatemala are his latest version

*In Lithuania.

He doesn't think of them
when he skates on Fridays with his grandson
who thinks he's Saint Francis
That I never get busy signals when I call
disturbs me
Am I the only only one who has thought of the obvious
who isn't merely ideas, but someone who acts?
Does everyone feel powerless in Metropolis?
May I revive the sense of community through this!

Don't worship privacy, friends,
pick up your phones and call him
He'll hear your first syllable

Enter history as an angel
Be his dreams

Being Seemingly Unscathed

Israel Halpern

To my communards at Little Sur and Misgav Am

We were singing
Blessed is the Holy Name   Barooche Ha-Shem

Celebrating the betrothal of our canyon companions
Seated at long tables over bowls of hummus and cholent
We were happy!
The drunken fiancée stood up, swaying, agreeing to say a few
words
Admitting to being a little spaced out
The soon-to-be-bridegroom spoke these words:
   "As I have wandered, I have become aware of a responsibility
   first held by our spiritual foreparent, Avrooahm Avaynu.
   Being a *Shomer* and a *Misgav*, Hebrew for guardian
   Exactly what befell our people before we were born,
   recurred in each generation, and will occur with us,
   in our generation"
We . . . who had been celebrating, stopped,
         we knew that toast quite well.
All around that room, filled with people on benches
Scanned each other's eyes
We knew what had been
We knew the phrase "DO-ER V'DOER. AYLLEH TOLDOS"
"GENERATION TO GENERATION. THESE GENERA-
TIONS"
         This Generation

Knowing Majdanek. Theresienstadt. Auschwitz. Buchenwald.
We know we are the seemingly unscathed generation.
We stopped singing to look around
Wondering about ourselves celebrating Ha-Shem.*

*Literally, the name; the word substituted for "God," which Orthodox Jews
are not supposed to mention.

The Chosen

Jean Hollander

For Primo Levi

I try to tell them how it feels
to be chosen for death

how a child accepts
the policeman no longer friend,
that men, in and out of uniform
are looking for you—

how you've been prepared:
"Jud!" "Jude!" "Judin!"
with snowballs that didn't respect
even your parents. Streets were not safe,
gangs waiting at the last corner
each way home from school
how terror softens you
like tenderizer on tough meat,
how laws anoint you
for your bitter fate

It is so hard to explain
how Jews accepted their heredity
as tigers obey their stripes—
yellow armbands, each child
a Star of David to the fire

how having been
in the jaws of that beast and spat out
does not make you kind,
how you bite back at the innocent
instead of the brute offender

how it has taken you a lifetime to shut
the pages of that bestiary,
to stop fearing
footsteps on the stairs

how you cannot find
a reason to have been spared

Bone Songs

Barry Ivker

They were naught but
Skin and
Bones
What flesh was left to them wavered between
Death and
Life
And each day they practiced
Verdi
Prepared to sing for
The steel-eyed ones
A Mass for the Dead
For the not quite dead
To remind these men of stone of the
Glories of the Europe that had come to
This
And as they marched to the showerhouses
One last time
Five minutes before the gas began to flow
Before anguish and panic and
Hunger for life would set them
Clawing
Soft, brittle nails
Scarring
Concrete walls for
An eternity
They sang

Old songs and
New
About a millennium that they would never see
They sang
From their bones they sang—
And that is all that is left of them—
Piles of bones
(I see them
Still)
And songs
Lingering over the empty barracks of the earth
Songs
Infusing themselves in the well-furnished rooms of the
Full-fleshed ones
We who whisper doubt to
Mirrored images of unspoken longing
Who assiduously turn mystery into
Routine
Who mouth words that once shook grown men to
Tears
That once carried women and children on eagle wings to
Mountains at the very center of the world—
And David danced before the Lord
Wildly
Danced
While his barren wife
Fumed
David took out his harp
He sang bone songs
(I hear him still)
His voice blending with the gaunt songs of

Theresienstadt
Bone songs
As I dance
As I paste pieces of plastic on paper to celebrate
The color that is in the world
The form
The harmony
As children in Jerusalem paint flowers on gas masks and
Greet the spring
As I search for words
To choreograph wisps of
Collective memory
To fill the space through which I move
Dancing
Always
To the faint notes of my own
Bone songs

Family Tree

Alvin M. Laster

It is all here,
a chronicle in black
and white, its branches
spreading like a shower of
arrows to pin time in place like
the hands of Papa's silent pocket watch.
It is a compaction . . . life bled white and desiccated,
substance minimalized and ordered, whys and hows unanswered.
Names and dates straddle its limbs like witches riding
broomsticks in a cartoon drawing, but I can resurrect
the familiar and make them speak by breathing my own life into them.
Soft as a memory, the first entry whispers from the past.
"I am Great Grandma Fanny,
Eve of the line. matriarch. fountain of branches.
singer of sweet swaddling songs."
In my fertile dreams, I have seen Great Grandma Fanny,
and I have heard the lost lullabies. I have created her
eyes, nose, and smiling mouth from the nearer lines
of mother and sister; seen her reflection
in the burnished glow of her Sabbath candlesticks,
and I have savored her art in the
benediction of Mama's chicken paprikash.
Where have you gone, Great Grandma Fanny?
Did the blue-eyed boys lead you
gently to the undressing room? Did you
go in shamed silence, wrinkled and
naked, into the hissing showers?
Did you die for the sins of
all non-Aryans?
My sins?
My sisters?
The sins of
all of our
children?
I lift
this
page
to my
Jewish
nose
and
I can smell your smoke.

Rebecca

Toby Lorber

Mother and father hush us

"no questions, no staring, no talking, go play in your
room," whenever Rebecca the fruit & vegetable lady came to
visit, to drink tea from a glass with a spoon in it, taking
bites of sugar cube between sips of steaming tea.

We would stare anyway, my sister and I, "we couldn't help
it, maa . . ." We couldn't. Rebecca had little blue numbers
stamped into the flesh of her arm.

Mother, now alert, gives us "the look" and we know,
Adrianne and I, that it's time to go to our room and play
holding questions we dare not ask at any civilized kitchen table.

Grown now, my sister lives in New York City. She paints
paintings filled with wonder, filled with colors that take
your breath away like so many multifaceted bits and pieces
of what I'm sure must be God, or parts thereof.

I sit in classrooms at Nassau which are filled with wonder, too.
I watch a film,
I've seen such films before yet
Mind says "do not watch." I watch.
I force myself to watch. Why?

Something in me says "you have to watch, it's time."
It's time and time again
pinch inside of palm and watch.

Eyes riveted to screen.   "But I have seen these films before!"
Just watch.
Watch!   You have to watch.   "no questions, no talking"

And I do and I hurt and I bleed. Now parts of me will be
buried with all of them.

Branded into cells of my brain are faces, bodies,
bits and pieces of
once glorious chunks of humanity.

Is this the hell we could not mention at any civilized
kitchen table?

how many times have I wondered,
how many times have I put myself into
their bodies, minds, souls,
just to "see" what it was like.

I have been that mother, arms outstretched
reaching toward uniformed and shiny product
of a madman yanking my newborn from my arms.
I have stood squashed one against the other
in cattle cars of trains riding tracks
leading deep, deeper, deeper still into
the deepest circles of hell,
More than can be imagined.

Do madmen dream up new hells as they go along?
Is each hell an original?
Did Hitler say, "Hey, I can do it for you wholesale!"

Does it matter
How or Why?

I have been that mother, many times
knowing all the while
It could (easily, so easily) have been my baby
taken, my husband, mother, father, sister torn
from me.

It could have been *me* left standing soulflesh
Shattered, left to . . . what?
What determines who will live and who will die
Who will survive the hells of our creation
Who decides?
What and Who decides which mind/spirit
will come out at all
never intact never whole again.

Kozinski says, "War defines us . . . " (our spirits, our
    characters)

Perhaps. Perhaps.

Living in my house in Massapequa,
in my house with *two* bathrooms,
I have imagined standing crushed together,
bodies, smells, having to "go to the bathroom"
and going.

There, crushed together
in cattle cars.

                  "inconceivable"
             "it never really happened"
Imagining still
and still connected
bound, like it or not,
between two points in time
by some mystical cord   (but are we? Am I?)
to *that* time
to those faces, those bodies, those separated mountains
of human hair
and human skin of lampshades.

Once, when sick with flu, shivering cold,
I used my (mere) discomfort
to imagine how it was for them.

I do not, however, allow myself to go
so far as imagining the showers or
the ovens.
Yet, always wondered while getting under our shower
"what must it have been like . . . ?"
I stop myself!
Be logical
Be reasonable
rational
That happened so many years ago, another time,
another place
having absolutely nothing
to do with you.

THE AFTERMATH

When Marilyn and I go to the Y for a swim
we hesitate to enter the steam room.
Along white-tiled starkness of walls
hanging from the ceiling in the corner
is a showerhead with chain attached.
Unspoken, the secret is shared. My friend's
eyes dart, look toward my own
and we know. It reminds us.
It reminds us, and we are (crazy as it sounds) back there
with all the others, back to that time, that place
trying, daring *not* to be there, not to look too often
or stay too long.

we must try to be brave
we must try to forget

        is forgetting courage or
          is remembering . . . ?

    Rebecca, fruit & vegetable lady, where are you now
mystery of my child years,
    where the hell *are* you now?
and why didn't you tell us?

I would have hugged and kissed you
instead of staring at your arm.

or would I?

Traveling to Der Bad

Arlene Maass

Today from Canada a copy of the family tree
arrived from your grandpa and I traced
centuries of Jews in Germany:
Seligman/Alexander/Maass/Elsbach/Weinberg/Cohen/Beer
and as far as I can read from this chart,
it all comes down to you, Aaron—
crawling on an imitation Oriental rug
in Skokie, Illinois
a Chicago-hugging village
where some 7,000 Holocaust survivors live.

In Borholzhausen from 1695 through the 1920s
came a steady line of horse dealers, textile traders,
a village butcher named Frankenstein
and a distant cousin named Oppenheimer—
yeah, *him.*
Despite all the Allied bombing,
Grandpa's former house still stands in Hamburg.
Maybe you'll want to see it someday,
you know, view it from afar.
Like maybe from Israel?

Aaron, before you were born,
Dada and I traveled to Germany with your auntie
and we lodged with a relative in a dinky bath town,
Bad Salzuflen.

A pilgrim procession converges there
from all over Deutschland.
Germans line up at *der bad*
seeking miracle waters
to wash away the indelible.
What do they seek, eternal life,
or just a thousand-year reign?

It was creepy strolling in forests
where posted signs warned in brittle German
to watch for stray hounds;
It was creepy wandering down a skimpy street
called Jews Alley
on our way to the café for coffee and cake;
It was creepy ordering Wiener schnitzel
seated among elderly German men.
When would they casually stand up,
annihilate us,
and then pray for their meals?

It was tempting to spit on a German war memorial
we discovered in the woods.
But I forced myself to think about God's vengeance.
He will do more than expectorate from heaven.
There's a cache of retribution
stored inside God's terrifying white throne.
He scares me more than a unified Germany.

When we finally left by train for Amsterdam,
we waved to our aunt remaining on the platform.
I noticed a swastika scratched on the station wall.
She never saw it and kept smiling
and kept waving.

Celia Dances

Stanley Nelson

Of all the children,
You are the harshest.

In the night,
Your cries filled us with terror.

Even when I held you
There was a shudder
Of one who had been greatly wronged.

Perhaps in some former life
Your heart was struck
By the evil of suffering faces.

Perhaps your eyes closed with anguish
On the train to the crematorium.

How good to see you,
Near the curtains,

With patient swirls,
And your quick child's body,

Dancing the dance of perfect joy.

Recognition, On My Child's Face

Betty Renshaw

You came in from playing one summer afternoon
when you were five,
to ask:
"Mamma, what does 'hate' mean?"
Startled to hear you speak a word
so far outside ourselves,
I did not have an answer,
either in the abstract or
by some concrete example.
"That's a hard one, son. Let me
think about it and I'll
try to tell you later" was
all that I could manage.
You went back to play, and I
(conveniently) forgot.

That fall
you went one afternoon with playmates
to the concrete War Memorial
beyond the Marketplace—
where I had told you not to go,
in the little town we lived in then,
in the little duchy of Luxembourg.

The anguish endured
by that little town in that little duchy
in the Second Great World War

was all recorded there
in artifacts
and horror photographs,
old wounds and bitternesses
kept alive and new.

You came home
bewildered, terrified,
all guilt from disobedience
entirely canceled out.
Full of questions, you
described, and asked and asked.
It was then your earlier question
echoed in my head.

"Son, do you remember when you asked me
     what 'hate' meant?"

And in that moment
all childhood innocence was lost:
I saw you
understand.

I thought: "I know he has to know
—But can I bear the memory of
understanding, recognition, on
my child's face?"

The Man with the Monocle

Layle Silbert

On a shimmering day in July
I went to see
"The Shop on Main Street"
in a movie house on Fourteenth
how else would I ever know
about the Holocaust?
what was a Polish actress
doing in a Czech movie?
what were the Germans
doing in Czechoslovakia?
it's only a movie
I didn't own a shop
wasn't old, my hair wasn't white
& I didn't live in Prague

the movie ended
I had to leave the darkness
I ran out
into a blinding light
a Nazi soldier, monocle dangling,
ran out after me
I said no no
I still want to be a ballet dancer
& learn Russian
you'll never learn, not you he said

he melted into the light
I stopped running
as the day began to darken

Grandmother Lost

Esther Crystal

They turned her into ashes
Before I ever knew her.
A puff of acrid smoke.

Your blue eyes, my father says,
Are just like hers.
Your golden hair, my father says,
Is just like hers.

But when I look into
The mirror of my history,
There is no reflection
In the looking-glass.

Taking the Holocaust to Bed

Annie Dawid

Metzger Trial, Portland 1990

First Amendment freedom
allows proud fascists
their placards: NO GAYS NO JEWS
and the city pays three hundred
thousand of your tax dollars
for somebody's security.
"There were no incidents."

What can you say
when your Jewish lesbian lover,
daughter of survivors, tells you
she takes the Holocaust with her
to bed every night? When every
nightmare yields the rap
on the door, door that yields
despite a thousand locks to men
in black, with chalk-colored flesh
and armbands like the ones you saw
that afternoon at the courthouse?
Pink triangles, yellow stars
tattoo invisible indelible scars.

Her family myths include hidden cousins,
sweating through 7 layers of clothing
stitched together in case of being
"found" in Bucharest: You can only
grab one thing if discovered.
They were saved.
Until later, Cousin Ernst locked
five years in prison by the Communists;
surely he must have been a collaborator
to have survived the Nazi years.

You tell her
you can't go to bed with the Holocaust.
You're only twenty-five, an Episcopalian
from Ohio, ancestors traced
to the Pilgrims. You can't compete
with history's slaughters,
its scarlet letters.
She says: Mulugeta Seraw
and quotes the newspaper:
Pacific Northwest Congenial Home
for White Aryan Nation, Skinheads,
not far from your bedroom door.

Stateless Person

Annie Dawid

"Why should I have lived?
And all the others died?"

Suddenly, at eighty, long-denied,
long delayed survivor's guilt
knocks him over, like a tidal wave,
the wave which bore him first
to China, cresting a man alone,
stateless, to a new continent.
His family of German intellectuals
called Heinz gloomy, a pessimist,
and refused to leave their home;
forty-one relatives burning
while in Shanghai, Heinz's suit
of marriage to the lovely Greek girl
refused, her parents disapproved
of Jews.

Next wave, 1949, frothed and foamed
to California, U.S.A. ("I didn't
escape the Nazis to live under
Communism.") Middle-aged man now
a student, again, alone, with baggage
of two emigrations, too many lost
lives to count; he marries a Brooklyn
gal too young to have lived

those sorrows. Together they launch
a family, fast, children like lilypads
floating atop the China Sea,
salt water stinging in wounds.

Decades of 12-hour days,
incessant work to stop the waves
from crashing, filling his ears,
demanding their own life, his voice.
When he says, "I shouldn't have lived,"
I see myself disappear, never existing.

He can't hear my calls;
the roar of the incoming tide
deafens him now, drowns him now
in the silence of the flood.

The History of Night

Dina Elenbogen

Yehuda Leib was shot by Cossacks
in broad daylight
in front of his wife, simply
for being a Jew.
Saul was a Socialist, in prison
then working in the fields
and in the book.
Angry and aimless he came and stayed
in America, but failed
to pray like his father.

My father carries his father's demons
from sleepless rooms
to glasses of brandy to hot baths
to dusk-filled streets
on his white bicycle, alone
at 65, his wife asleep
until sunup.

My father's fathers' words kept him
from being lonely in the war.
I have prayed to words and to water.
I don't know what words to give my father.
I don't know who the fighters are
in his war. We cycle sometimes
in silence through fields.

Ten years ago I wrote the words
"I am tired because
he has not slept."

While sleeping in his house
I dreamt him walking circles
through black rooms.
I stepped out into what I thought
was his darkness
but instead I walked into my own
reflection in the mirror.

The terror of my own self
coming toward me
was a deep scream that awakened
my father, it came from the deepest part
of my throat.

It said
I don't know how to keep us
from being lonely

It said
I don't know how to live
with our demons or our dreams

It said
I don't know how to keep us
still

It said
I am living in stillness
with my demons and my dreams

It said
I love you through three
generations and six lifetimes

It said
I will never lose this terror
and I will never lose this love.

Survivor

Elizabeth Rees

My lungs are glass bowls
stained from that smoke.
Tonight I will scream that
I am guilty of squander,
I will spin my piece of pain.
Tonight I shall organize
my lab for the test and
lay out every instrument.

To study the inside of a scream,
I experiment on glass bowls.
The first bowl breaks
in boiling water, the next
I whip until it cracks.
The last breaks perfectly —
I hurl it at the ghosts
clogging up the sky.

Late at night screams collide.
Their edges snap, they break
into jagged continents.
The map of the world
absorbs the change,
as it always does.
Falling glass gathers speed,
but screams cannot shatter.

Sealed

Bina Goldfield

The unopened package moved around
from place to place, as though
finding the right place
will enable me to open

it, an ordinary 11 x 15 parcel,
coarse tan paper sealed by
two parallel rows of metal staples
glinting at me as I approach, read the date
in the postmark's perfect circle
now five weeks old.
Plastic padding will briefly crackle
if I remove the contents, a thin book
described by the sender, my brother.

I have not seen the title,
Names and Fates of the Jews of Kassel—1933–1945
in German script elegant as Gothic architecture.
Not studied the names and places in this book of lists,
orderly and thorough as this sort can be.
Not sought out my name
my brother said is misspelled, but
other than this detail, accurate.
The blank space beside my name indicates I survived.

Not searched for my grandmother's name on page 127,

not read the precise facts:
1942—Deported to Theresienstadt—
1944—Shipped to Treblinka—
1944—Presumed gassed.

One day, I will have to unseal it.
Today, I found another place.

Household Rules.
Farwell Avenue, Chicago 1946

Lisa Ress

I

She turns onions into zeroes on the cutting board,
lines up the sheets at the edges of the linen cupboard shelves.
At four o'clock exactly she is marching X's with her needle
uniformed in thread along the borders of a tablecloth.
She shows me how to get up the stairs, how to come down,
how to lie in bed so no one can find me.
The knock on the door of this house in this country
is that of the milkman.
But I know I must ask myself
what is milk, what is coal, what do they mean
saying "Good morning, Lisa," as I cross the street.

II

She papers the kitchen with pictures of bodies
tangled like insects in ditches.
This could be you, she tells me.
I am a child, I say. I am not
supposed to know this, knowing anyway
that soon, or yesterday, I will be one of them, I am.
Drink your milk, she says, but it is white
elixir that will make me live too long.
At school the kids push me flat against the chain-link fence.
How shall I keep them from knowing
how far it is all right for them to go?

Tattoo

Gregg Shapiro

My father won't talk about the numbers
3-7-8-2-5 between the wrist and elbow
Blue as blood on his left forearm
Instead he spreads himself over me, spilling
protection, like acid, on me until it burns
I wear him like a cloak, sweat under the weight

There are stories in the lines on his face
the nervous blue flash in his eyes
his bone-crushing hugs
I am drowning in his silence
trying to stay afloat on curiosity
Questions choke me and I swallow hard

We don't breathe the same air
speak the same language
live in the same universe
We are continents, worlds apart
I am sorry my life has remained unscathed
His scars still bleed, his bruises don't fade

If I could trade places with him
I would pad the rest of his days
wrap him in gauze and velvet
absorb the shocks and treat his wounds
I would scrub the numbers from his flesh
extinguish the fire and give him back his life.

Portraits of the Shadows in the Flames

Leslie What

The pictures in the books are black and white
portraits of the shadows in the flames.
Freeze frames, captured stillness,
that allow us to think
it happened long ago and far away
to someone else.
When shadows turned gray
and bodies were offered up as ashes.

I have a photograph of the aunt I named my daughter for.
The picture is in black and white.
My aunt was three when the picture was taken;
she was six when she was taken to her death.
My mother was at work in the ghetto.
She came back and saw the van drive away.
She thinks she saw her sister's face
pressed against the blackened window.

It is a picture burned deep within her memory.
My mother saved those photographs she could.
In one, a child stands beside her mother
who rests a hand upon the little daughter's shoulder.
The girl, clutching her stuffed toy dog,
watches the camera, eyes burning with a child's curiosity.
When the photograph was taken,
she did not know she would become a shadow.

I want that picture to be black and white.
I want to think that it happened long ago and far away
to someone else.
But, though the likeness was captured
when darkness burned and light turned gray,
what I see is more vivid than a history book.
I see blood frozen like garnets in the snow.
I see a child, shivering, without a winter coat.
I see a world ablaze with color, and I hear a child's cry.

Paper burns more readily than flesh,
and yet, the image of one child, one captive shadow
is all that has survived the flames.
I will picture her always as she stood only once.
When my daughter was three,
I could not look upon her
face without weeping.

Trapped in Mea Shearim

Shel Krakofsky

They follow the multitude of generals
in their murky cauldron of armies
and daily scorn those who serve
without black uniforms
whose spilled blood has saved
these dark, hunched, shuffling old men
their eyes swollen and burning
to wander in this,
their living Olam Habah.*

Zaida, alevashalom,† had
no such protection and fled
the Polish shtetl in Sanok,
donned street clothes in America,
kept his head covered
and with a flowing white beard
found it proper every day to thank
their God and his government.

Obediently fertile wives and daughters
are hardly seen on the narrow, gray paths
the sons without being fruitful
have multiplied like black rabbits

*World to come.
†Grandfather, of blessed memory.

congregate as street gangs in wild debate
angry, boyish faces on ancient bodies
ready to judge, ready to stone.

With a knitted yarmulke
I am anomaly, they see only
a yiddishe toque on my goyishe kop.

Still, I am back with Zaida in his shtetl
and like the ovens of Europe, I can never
escape some places I have never been.

Where Jackals Run and Vultures Fly

Thomas R. Verny

After a day of skiing
the snowy mountains,
We rest in our comfortable beds,
enveloped by our love for each other.
Over morning coffee
we retrace our adventures in dreamland:
Sherlock Holmes and Watson
in hot pursuit of psychic mysteries.

You will tell me of your dreams
of missing trains and failing exams,
I, too, have dreams of trains and exams,
trains headed for the camps,
exams to select for the gas chambers.

God, how I envy people like you
who can take a shower
and not think of Auschwitz;
who can dance
to the strings of the Blue Danube,
and not hear machine-gun fire
from the banks of the bloody Danube.

Who can enjoy a walk through forests
such as these
and not see the jackals

filling dark pits ten deep
with the bodies of dead
and the near dead.

To you a distant ski chalet
with its smoking chimney
brings forth pictures of couples
sipping brandy and exchanging sweet kisses
while I see vultures
circling smoke stacks
and smell the nauseating stench
of burning human flesh.

God, how I envy people like you,
who can play with their dogs merrily
and not hear German shepherds
barking and snarling viciously.

I envy you
your blond, hard-muscled father
and your cute, freckle-faced mother
who could walk to church
with their heads erect
in their Sunday best,
prayer books under their arms,
protected by an invisible shield
from the jackals and the vultures
that would jeer and taunt,
throw stones at me,
and call me dirty Jew.

Can you see with
your clear green eyes
why mine are dark and clouded
from having watched
for two thousand years
the jackals and the vultures
devour their prey,
the dove and the deer?

A Ballad for Tourists

Larry Rubin

Kindele, kindele,* where have you been?
I've been on a trip in my drip-dries so thin.

Kindele, kindele, what have you seen?
I've seen that thick country whose woods are so green.

Kindele, kindele, what did you buy?
A porcelain beer stein; the price was not high.

Kindele, kindele, why do you moan?
I thought I saw blood on the lip of the stone.

Kindele, kindele, how will you pray?
In a shawl fringed like Father's, I'll stand and I'll sway.

Kindele, kindele, what friends did you seek?
Some students who pointed to scars on their cheeks.

Kindele, kindele, what scene was the best?
I liked the deep forests and elves laid to rest.

Kindele, kindele, what do you dream?
I dream of the castles beside that broad stream.

---

*Pronounced kin-de-le: Yiddish term of endearment for a small child; a word a Yiddish grandmother might use.

Kindele, kindele, why do you stare?
I thought I saw ovens, and you lying there.

Collectible

Anna Bart

at the wrecking company's outdoor sale
I searched the world of old cast-off materials
looking for additions to my store
of timeworn tools and objects of ephemera

uneven piles of trash from other lives:
a broken box of crosses, heaps of radios,
crockery, machinery's spilled insides
        a torn quilt on the ground

framed a tan straw suitcase   its leather
corners gray with scuff   the handle
firmly shaped   stained dark from sweat
of anxious hands
        so light—I lifted it like air

and heard the soft fall of things inside:
two yellow stars roughly stamped
in black on cotton canvas   edges frayed
in being ripped from someone's sleeve

Because No One Said "No!"

Roseline Intrater

Because no one said "No!"
dark stinking clouds of flesh-filled smoke
black greasy clouds of bone and fat
billowed into the air of Europe
day after day, year after year

and Nazi "supermen" breathed in
their former neighbors and compatriots
and washed them down gemutlichly
with ersatz coffee
and slept guilt-free
for they were thirsty from the smoke
and weary from their labors.
It was tedious work
as tedious as any other
though they labored
for the glory of the Fatherland.

Did they sing and whistle as they worked
shoveling human beings
into furnaces and out?
And did no nightmares
haunt them as they slept?
Nightmares
of all those
millions of men and women

young and old
simple and gifted
defiant, frightened, bewildered.
(How could they believe
that hideous truth?)

And there were the children
hundreds of thousands of children
with delicate limbs and pouting lips.
On their cheeks the curve of babyhood
in their eyes the dream of growing up.

But the ovens were waiting for them
to make sure they never grew up—
those thousands of Hansels and Gretels
and Jacobs and Ruths and Marushkas and Jans—
stuffed into those ovens
day after day, year after year
those ovens built so efficiently.
Were they fired by wood
from the beautiful Black Forest
birthplace of operas and fairy tales?

From that terrible smoke came forth
no fairy tales, no songs.
As it drifted over the world
did it carry the sounds
of prayers and screams?
Did anyone hear
and look up
and cry out
and say, "No!"?

THE AFTERMATH

Out of those ovens
came no gingerbread.
No magic spell
could turn those ashes
back into boys and girls.
This was no happy-ending fairy tale.
Because no one said "No!"

Do the dark flesh-particles
float over us still
indestructible
in the ever-circling air
around and around the world
day after day
year after year
filtering into our lungs
drifting before our eyes
darkening the multi-layered
cosmic atmosphere
for all time to come?

Will the air ever again be pure?
Can the world ever be as it was before?
Do the prayers and screams still echo?
If we listen, can we hear?

Has anyone learned
to say "No!"?

Judische Friedhof: Kaiserslautern

Emily Carolyn Joyce

Who, in the still sweet mist
of Sonntag morgen
lays wreaths of daisies
on the graves of Jewish children
forgotten, mouths dumb
tiny limbs, fragile bodies?
I recall their stones
as I kneel praying
remembering how we walked,
found them, pitied them,
cherished them.

How, in the delicate lace
of sunlight and birches,
we knelt to cover them
with wild flowers,
forming Stars of David
with fresh straw,
cradling them with our hearts
as once their mothers did
in tender arms.

You were so small
like them
yellow hair,
green eyes full of mystery.

I like to think
another mother and daughter
go to them now
as we did then.

After Visiting Dachau

Rita Kiefer

The head in the mirror is not mine
it is much livelier
the eyes dark as olives
its skin much smoother
under the lash there is no fold
and the lids stay open
some days the mouth is missing
at other times it gapes
as if the German artist's hand
memorized a cry and
strands of chestnut singed
as from a flame
cover the brow follow the bend of the neck.

And now she is a heron
great and blue
meant for flying above
barbed wire, sirens, ovens
meeting the feathers of
another figure that is
beginning.

Ilse's Poem

Rita Kiefer

One red berry all day
at the bottom
of her prison pocket.
She brought it back to me.
In Dachau we'd learned
priorities.

The next night she died
on the bunk beside mine, soaked
red from her hemorrhaging.
Promise to survive
one more week.
I held her and
promised.

A week to the day: Liberation

This is a true story.

Each year on that day
I pick berries.

Daughter, A Gift of Red Shoes

Kendall LeCompte

We had the Germans broken—
rode unchallenged through spring-green forests.
Shot the empty woods from hips like cowboys.
Just no resistance, when we saw them
they flung arms down and up; wanted food,
wanted just to have the front go past.
Those weeks weren't like war at all.
And then one morning, stomachs full, we found the camp.
Remember, I was only 20, your aunt was still a child.

At first we thought them twigs.
Birch limbs, stacked to dry, white, dusty—
you could have burned them in an instant.
Then I saw red shoes sticking past the tarpaulin.
I saw the red, the knot of rocky ankles,
the clear, parchment skin like powder waiting wind.
All that day we piled, and retched, and buried;
all that night.

So daughter this is why I pass on strudel,
won't hear Bach, have no maps of Germany.
It is why I offer you my judgment of revenge
along with new red shoes.
It might be time to wear them; maybe not.

Springtime Near Munich

Merrill Leffler

Ich bin du

— Primo Levi, *If This Is a Man*

On the 20th Anniversary of the Allies' liberation
of Dachau, 1945–1965

I

It is a beautiful April morning.
The walk is banked
with purple crocuses
and the grass green
in the glare of sun. The
sunlight is almost shafting through the leaves.
The land is not rolling. There are no trees.
There are shiny spigots. They work
efficiently. As does the generator. And the traffic of bodies
peek-a-booing into corners, the clean ovens, the showers
dry. There are arms pinned with cut black ribbons—
they signify mourning. But there are gay
ribbons as well: it is the beginning of warmth once more.
Dressed for spring weather, the women's dresses
are printed with flowers; the men's faces are ashen. Somber.
Yellow armbands hang on invisible
arms limp like week-old game. And
there are announcements tacked to walls: *Achtung!*

Prege, prege! Respectez
le silence. It is Sunday and church bells
splash through the breeze and the young girls
their hair ironed straight, silky black, blown
back gently like the flags of nations. This
is the desert the mind says. Deluxe black.
A cane comes click click-
ing mildly drunk, comic. Nails white, fingers scrubbed
palms surgical and red clapping
out teeth (thank you, may I have more sir) and others are
counting the gold. The barbers come with a flourish
of sirens. Four and twenty crows all
in a row. The air healthy and robust smelling of freshly cut green.
No monument to heroes, a skeleton only
draped stupidly in folds of cement stands,
the memorial. (To what exactly?) And swaying beautifully
like a full-grown linden, the Hebrew wafts into the breeze
Adonai Eloheynu Adonai Echud
and the audience breaks bread,
flashbulbs light up and crack, serious lips blister
in the glare of heat. Pour wine now and eat the body of
remembrance. It is reported they
screamed themselves into silence, fouled themselves
and each other. And in each corner pieces
of flesh stick, stubbornly, to the wall. Corralled,
donkeys bray. The fleshy buttocks sweat, crowd
against the limp pricks; more buttocks
press helpless harder. Bellies soak.
Piss makes the floor slippery.
Ammonia stings the eyes. The screams are too loud
to hear. There is nowhere to fall

but up. There is the voyeur here? The
tongue hanging sitting in
the front row jamming tits in my
mouth. Leering into the showers. Showers. He runs his
finger down a wet crotch opens the
oven door and dives
into a ditch. Comes the click clicking. Clown.
The plow pushing bodies
steadily down the walk. Awaken. This is a trip.
You were not there. *Ich bin du.**

            You are.

2

Then is not now
And now, sitting here,
is only a poem. Related they are
but how? Brothers? Father and son? The older
died each instant, the younger
lives on, more quietly,
as insufficient memory, as envelopes of facts,
as words which give voice to some
thing. Some anguish. A memory I was a visitor to only.

So what can it mean now
that almost fifteen years ago I entered
unknowingly into a carnival of mourning
(and was it unknowingly)?

---

*I am you.

What was it but some hours
in my life, hardly a moment
in the life of my children, and absurdly less
in that abstraction we call the earth's revolutions?
What can it mean
for my children who may never read
these lines, who, even if they do, may die
in ignorance, having grown up into the abstraction of America?

1965, 1980

Bernard Mikofsky

And that year
When the fires ceased
And the ovens were finally cool
A strange wind moved out
In slow, grief-laden eddies
And sooty swirls
Across Europe—
And even beyond.

And those with conscience
(And even those without)
Heard faint sounds from afar,
Echoes from an age-old abyss.
And sometimes these seemed to come
From inside one's ear—
So tiny and yet so persistent.
Echoes of the anonymous cries
Of numbered millions.

And far from the ovens,
Far from the funeral fires,
This wind still carried
Wraiths of soot

Too fine to water the eye
Yet searing the heart
Of those with conscience
(And even those without).

That year the strange wind
Moved slowly across Europe—
And even beyond,
Now and then pausing
To eddy into the deepest corners
Of men's minds
To remind them,
To stir them for an instant
From their dream of well-being.

Cambodian Holocaust

Bernard Mikofsky

As in 1945,
Another year brings
A new grief-laden wind
That touches distant hearts
A little . . .
Another nation is dying.

All the years between, they came,
So many winds of grief.

And this year again,
Another shuddering wind
Moves again from land to land
Bearing a million souls
So light, so heavy.

The Fifties

E. Ethelbert Miller

I was born after the Holocaust.
I grew up in the Bronx on Longwood Avenue.
The neighborhood was always changing. My mother
told this to my father, in whispers that came
from the next room. I was new to the world and
accepted it as it was. The stores on Longwood
sold food and clothes and were run by Jewish
people with stars hanging over their doors. My
mother enjoyed shopping in the early morning
hours. She pulled me along as she exchanged
friendly conversations, laughter and wise sayings
with the people who gave us fish and vegetables,
sweaters in the winter. I can remember my mother
talking to a woman about the war and Germany
and a man named Hitler. She never mentioned the
word Holocaust. She only talked about the camps,
the suffering, the children who were reduced to
bones. Once I saw my mother sitting in a chair
holding nothing but her own black hands. Those
hands worked in a military factory during the
war.

Malediction

Karl Plank

Ha-ish attah

— 2 Sam. 12:7

*To the scrawler of Swastikas on a Jewish poster outside
the Religion Department*

You drew a cursed sign and penned words
    that have killed.
May this be your fate:

May the tool that marred carve emblems of shame
    on your face and in your mind.
May you sicken at the sight of your own image,
    frozen in that instant you took
    pen to hand to destroy and deface.

You failed to sign your name.
May your name now abandon you, remain unspoken,
    unheard.
May your name be borne by no one.
May no other parent bear its burden, no child its legacy.

You have wrought murderous words from letters.
When you lie in the ground, may you hear
    the words of Abel's cry

six million times
echoing from unmarked, mass graves.
May no letters combine to console you.
May this be your alphabet:

Auschwitz
Babi Yar
Chełmno
Dora
Ebensee
Ferramonti di Tarsia
Grodno
Horodenka
Iaşi
Janowska
Kovno
Łódź
Matthausen
Nesvizh
Opole Lubelskie
Plaszow
Ravensbrück
Sobibor
Treblinka
Uzligorod
Vaivara
Warsaw
Xanthe
Yanovka Forest
Zamość

Ash Wednesday

Karl Plank

For Filip Muller, survivor of the Sonderkommando

At Birkenau
the glass-eyed Cyclops
ordered pits to be dug
near Crematorium V.

Then bodies burned
behind a wall of wattle screens.

The Greek Jews could not see
the spring meadow nearby
as they entered the gray mist
with shovels

for the hot ash of kinsmen
rained down on their faces
and into their eyes,
blinding.

O priest!

You smudge my forehead
in Lenten gesture
of mortality,
unknowing.

The ash we bear
is not our own,
but those the flames
made dust.

It is again
the char of kinsmen
that burns and scars
the open face,

that sears now
our darkened cross.

One More Holocaust Poem

Elliot Richman

The poet uses "blood" and "stars" and "martyrs teeth
In the mud." He reads well, though,
And his sport jacket is nice. Of course,
He wasn't there. Hearing "Ravensbrück"
Incantated one more time, I rub Pat's thigh,
Feeling slightly guilty because I am Jewish
And should be moved by all this. So I become
An old horse in one of those towns in Poland.
I'm wearing a discarded hat and swatting flies with my tail.
Bored German soldiers in uniforms that don't fit are walking
Beside a bunch of Jews. It isn't even raining, just
Any particular day. It seems like nothing
Is happening. I'm pretty thirsty, though.
I dip my head in the trough. The water's terrific.
It is right there. When I look up the Jews are gone.

Rage Before Pardon:
An Interview with Elie Wiesel

Marguerite M. Striar

The Berlin Wall has fallen and
Elie Wiesel is interviewed on TV.
The survivor of Auschwitz and Buchenwald,
who lives to bear witness
to Europe's murdered Jews,
is asked for his reactions.
The flames of memory, licking
his troubled searching face,
he searches for a way to be happy
for the German people, says,
"How can one not be happy
when freedom is gaining space?"

Germans will remember
the ninth of November, 1989,
when the Berlin Wall
began to shatter and fall.
Will Germans remember
the ninth of November, 1938,
when their civilized nation
began to shatter and fall
in the shattering glass
of Kristallnacht?

Can they ever expect the world's pardon for that
until they sit on a mourner's bench
with the Jewish people?
meet an obligation not yet met
to teach their young the *whole*
truth of their history,
teach them to rage against it
and never, ever to forget?

The Children's Museum
at the Holocaust Memorial, Jerusalem

Joanne Seltzer

Tiny starlike souls
flicker in the darkness
of this internal sky
as we grope
toward the unthinkable,
the unimaginable.

One by one, stumbling,
we weep because we can't
unwrite the history
that is our birthright
nor can we block our ears
against sad music,

or perhaps it is the wail
of babies we hear
and ourselves as children
crying out, Mommy,
where are you? Daddy,
where are you? God,

one and a half small million!
But only a few names
and a few photographs

rub against our spines
like pieces of candy
thrown at a bride

as we continue
our struggle with the guilt
of knowing we will reach
the redemptive,
the inevitable
exit door.

Dachau 1968

Joan I. Siegel

First I heard sparrows
in the linden trees,
I heard them drop to the grass
and peck.

Then I heard the grass
giving the air a green
sweet smell.

Then I heard the air.

I looked up
looking for the fiery sky,
the black smoke,
the smell of the black smoke.

I looked at the ground
under my feet,
looking for rivers of ash
mountains
of hair
of shoes
of teeth

looking for mountains of faces
looking at me.

I closed my eyes
and listened a long while.

Finally I heard the dead
say Kaddish.

Anne Frank

John Foster West

Like a small, brilliant spark
chipped incidentally off life's steel
anvil, momentarily in barbaric dark
flashing—but long to feel
my brother Aryan's egotistic curse,
and see a crucifixion put to shame
by universal murder so much worse
than cross or simple flame
that ages may not circumvent such loss!
Like so came Anne,
oh, such a little child to bear the cross
which holds the writhing corpse of modern man.

The Suitcase

Evelyn Wexler

For Lukacs Denes

When he was nine
and on the run,
his mother gave him
a small maroon
leather suitcase.
He carried it with him
to all the places.
Taped inside the lid,
a cellophane envelope
of cyanide, in case
they caught him alive.

He lived through the war.
Cannot tell how. He's
a doctor now. Married.
Owns a yellowing
hand-crocheted tablecloth
and grandmother's hollow
bone prayer book
that survived Auschwitz.
Keeps the old suitcase
in his bedroom,
inside a waiting closet.
Just in case.

Tourist at Dachau

Evelyn Wexler

I arrive too late for the English version,
go instead with a class of German students
to view the camp movie. Part of the curriculum.
Familiar black and white flesh flashes on the screen.
German narrator intones indignation as the film ends. Stunned to
    silence,
the children shuffle out, history shackled to their ankles.

    In the next hall, Prussian efficiency
    on display, color-coded triangular patches:
    red for politicals, green for criminals,
    black for Gypsies, violet for Jehovah's Witnesses
    pink for homosexuals and yellow for Jews.

In a barracks for shelved people, a teacher tells.
Words hang themselves in the air, like bodies on meathooks.
Then swim slowly into sound waves drowning childhood.

    Row upon row of criminal poplars muffle the ovens
    Tended, fat begonias nestle memorial tablets.
    Coverings blossom prettily.

Outside the show barracks, a boy with Aryan hair,
barely thirteen, sits on a curb, hunched over.
Skinny in the knob-kneed way of boys,
all wrist and leg bones, weeping into his hands

his Germanness bulldozed away forever into the blaze of day.
I try to reach, touch shuddering shoulders.
Stillness the color of smoke rises thick between us.

When I can't sleep at night I count denuded dead
lying in uniform bones   No skin to call their own
All the same   The same   Later
I dream I wear a coat of many colors
red and green and black and violet and pink
on a field of yellow

Badge

Michele Wolf

A hard yellow badge is carved
In my forehead: *Jude,*
As plain as Asian eyes, as
African color and hair,
As plain as a mouth
Of the earth
Accepting a tumble
Of bones, bodies
Shrunken to bones,
Crushing bones, a tangle
Of two hundred corpses
Kissing in a mouth,
My mouth. My forehead,
A heritage, a tombstone lit
By six points of fire.

In the Kibbutz Laundry

Elaine Starkman

For Rivke Cooper

The number on her arm
appears as I rest
in the dead heat
of the noon sun
no longer a nightmare
of storybook horror
that I read in America
twenty years ago

She's lived somehow—God knows
is here now working
in the kibbutz laundry
her hands move in an act of love

When the day ends
and night winds blow
I search out her clear blue eyes
but they reveal nothing

Yet engraved on her arm
lives a page of history
that all the soap
and all the rubbing
can never wash away

Degania Beit, 1969

The Burden of Memory

Kenny Fries

they tell us   remember
six million Jews   killed
and I remember

my father told me   remember
and I tried
to tell him

the pink triangle
lower than
the yellow star

and I tried to tell him
my legs are not
perfect   I would have been

undesirable
they tell us   remember
six million Jews   murdered

and I remember
in *The Village Voice*
a historian in California knows

six million Jews alive
hiding beneath
the New York City subway

they tell us   remember
six million Jews   exterminated
and in movies   trains

symbols of walking
to death
and they cannot

imagine a happy ending

they tell us   remember
and I remember
outside Yad Vashem

the Holocaust museum
in Jerusalem
there is a boat

Denmark sailed seven thousand Jews

to safety
and a garden
planted by survivors

to remember
those who saved them
(Yad Vashem   the hand of God)

and I remember my father
praying to this God
but I cannot believe

an imperfect God
who lets his chosen people
die   an imperfect God

who made my legs imperfect
I remember
Chasidic Jews in Borough Park

listening to the radio
and waiting for the Messiah
FDR did not

bomb Auschwitz but
the Americans did liberate
the concentration camps

my father told me   remember
six million Jews killed
but not of a distant cousin

hid
on a farm in Southern France
Christians saved him

and though we can find
our saviors
we still remember

the stars, the trains,
hear the lies
yes

I remember
six million Jews   killed
and others saved

and they tell us
this could not happen
here   I remember

bombs not dropped
words not spoken
action not taken

and ask   who
will save us

and who will save
my Jewish lover

and know
saving was not enough
and if saving is not enough

what is

tell me the answer
I will remember

What Is Required

Jacob Gusewelle

You must write about your family, he said. You don't. That's
required. And your children. Every poet worthy of the name writes
about his children, he said, pouring tea in delicate cups. And don't
forget the death of your father. That has to be written about if you're
a poet, he said. Don't forget the death of your father. Doesn't that
get awfully boring? I said, awfully trite?—words heavy with futility.
Of course, he said, but that's what is required—words thermal with
conviction. And what if I don't have a family? I said. And what if I
don't have children? That's what is required if you're a poet, he said,
brushing crumbs from his beard, watching cat tracks in new snow.
All poets do it, he said. It's boring as hell, and self-indulgent, I said.
It's required, he said. I don't think you understand, I said, mindless-
ly sponging the countertop. I don't have a family to write about. You
don't have to like them, he said. My God it's cold in here! Just write
about them. I don't think you understand, I said. I don't have a fam-
ily to write about, I said, lighting a cigarette with a lit cigarette.
Don't be absurd. Everybody has a family to write about, he said.
Not me, I said. Mine died during the Holocaust, in Poland, at the
Auschwitz concentration camp, I said. I don't even remember them.
I just remember living there for a while—in Poland, at Auschwitz.
Now that's trite and boring, he said. Don't write about the
Holocaust. People will think you're a coarse-textured unrepentant
Jew. Here, he said, have a piece of fruit.

Roots

Helene Hoffman

My Gentile friend,
flew off to Europe
and, in two weeks,
visited 40+ relatives
in 7 villages,
drank umpteen bottles of slivovitz,
and heard all their stories
(too many times—she said)
and returned,
satiated and safe.

I
   will
      carefully
         go to Czechoslovakia
to visit a few shtetls,
my parents' map in my hands,
and, know, after 3 days,
that I am walking on graveyards
hearing the voices of my *mishpoche**
in every empty shul,
seeing only those faces from my parents' old photos—
  (always on the dresser in their bedroom)
their big eyes fill up my heart, and I
  come back
empty

*Relatives.

Hello

Mitchell Waldman

A man called
(I think it was a man)
he said:
Happy Holocaust you
hook-nosed bloodsucking
Jew worm.
All I could think to say back
was, Hi.
And he replied:
May your children's children
rot in the cold earth like you
you slimy carcass carrion
you diseased treacherous vermin.
You have a nice day too, I said
and hung up the phone gently
refreshed by such a meaningful communication
with an intelligent sensitive member
of our species genus time.
Yes dear God he's ours
and yours forever.
Let the wind whip a chill
down heaven's spine.

Yom Hashoah, Never Again

Shel Krakofsky

Never again?
still unsure,
the ever diminishing group
pledges
and mourns
yet another year,
still not comforted
by their own words.

Once again;
the press bulbs
flash
fewer children
lighting
flickering candles;
old news,
a forced march
to the back pages.

Never again?
Once again,
only the living
not there
believe the words—

safe
they mightily claim,
    freed from remembering
    freed from reminding
    freed from gasping
    another Kaddish.
Never again.

Danger: No Explosives

Shel Krakofsky

To Elie Wiesel

Lay the Prize
on the tracks,
a hollow wreath
from those
fawning
tuxedoed
selektors
who now buy their Peace
with his profits
and didn't sully their
gloved hands
decades ago
to have given instead
from Alfred Nobel
to Elie Wiesel
his dynamite sticks
to have blown to hell
the tracks to
Auschwitz.

My Jewish Husband

Sandra Collier Verny

My Jewish husband listens to another
heartbreaking story of the Holocaust. Two
women speak, with a quiet, understated
dignity. In calm, gentle voices they describe
acts of unbearable cruelty. Delicate and
precious flowers pulled to shreds and shat upon
by grinning demons.

My husband withdraws, he becomes quiet, he
goes somewhere far inside himself.
He will not share his pain. Would he, if I were
also Jewish?
Does he withdraw because in that moment I
have become the "Other" — one of "them" — the
enemy?

This is the Nazis' cruelest legacy: after the
terror, the terror remains. Innocence becomes
a waiting monster.
Love cannot be trusted.

He sits in his chair, silent, brooding, dark. I
kneel at the side of his chair and touch his leg.
I feel a tight, hard throbbing in his leg. What is
this leg saying?
Does it want to kick me? Suddenly, I am
afraid.

We go to sleep. My husband will not, cannot,
speak to me. He had gone to a distant land.
There is no bridge to this land. Even love
cannot enter here.

I lie awake beside my husband, in the darkness.
I wonder, would it be different if I were Jewish?

No More Mozart

Dannie Abse

High to the right a hill of trees,
a fuselage of branches,
reflects German moonlight
like dull armor.
Sieg heil!

Higher still, one moon migrates deathward,
a white temper between clouds.
To the left, the other slides
undulating on the black
oiled, rippling reservoir.

Can't sleep for Mozart,
and on the winter glass
a shilling's worth of glitter.

The German streets tonight
are soaped in moonlight.
The streets of Germany are clean
like the hands of Lady Macbeth.

Back in bed the eyes close, do not sleep.
Achtung! Achtung!
Someone is breathing nearby,
someone not accounted for.

Now, of course, no more Mozart.
With eyes closed still
the body touches itself, takes stock.
Above the hands the thin wrists
attached to them; and on the wrists
the lampshade material.
Also the little hairs that can be pulled.

The eyes open:
the German earth is made of helmets;
the wind seeps through a deep
frost hole that is somewhere else
carrying the far Jew-sounds of railway trucks.

Nothing is annulled:
the blood vow, the undecorated cry,
someone robbed of his name,
then silence again.

Afterward:
the needle rests on a record
with nothing on that record turning,
neither sound nor silence,
for it is sleep at last.

There, the fugitive body has arrived
at the stink of nothing.
And twelve million eyes
in six million heads
stare in the same direction.

Role Reversal

Anne Kind

Gisela, you were a leader in the Hitler Youth
You didn't see much wrong in him
Were told to hate
And meekly you obeyed.

But that was forty years ago
You, dear, and I were children then,
Come let us talk, you said.

Sit over here, gemütlicher, nicht wahr?
It's cosy in that corner, let's begin.

At that point
I recalled the poisoned showers,
You'd never heard of them.

Why did you leave the Fatherland? you ask
Insensitive, I thought,
Shan't drop my mask
The situation is grotesque
If any of my kinsfolk saw me here
They'd feel betrayed
Though you appear sincere.

Poor Gisela,
You wanted a response from me.
I cannot even hate you, dear.

Two Poems

Walter Bauer

Guilt becomes extinct
With the guilty and the guiltless,
With victims and hangmen
With yea-sayers and nay-sayers.
Desecration dries up
When the desecrators and the desecrated are gone.
The "No" spoken with closed lips becomes inaudible;
The blackness of injustice
Turns into a muted gray.
The sons still remember
But are no longer moved.
Grandchildren read about it in their history books;
The ghastly interment becomes an academic assignment.
The sleepless nights,
The years of eating one's heart out
Are not mentioned in the texts.
The terror shrinks to a few lines;
The executions are described by the word "considerable."
The historians grade people according to their points of view.
The giant smoke clouds over the camps
Become a small bit of ash on white paper
Which is easily blown away
Or the mute question of a reader:
That many? How did they do that?

Whereupon he goes on reading.
The insights which should have rung out
Like words of the Last Judgment
Are never given voice again.

Translated from the German by Harry Zohn

Traveling to the Capitals

Walter Bauer

It's been quite long
That I have been with the dead.
It's been years, long years,
Every day, but more often at night—
Not just as a visitor.
But as a fellow resident.

I haven't been to London;
I have been in Belsen.
I didn't go to Paris;
They call Rome the Eternal City,
But I went to Theresienstadt instead.
I went to Auschwitz.
I grew familiar with
The real capitals of Germany.
I became a ghost among ghosts;
My own life escaped me.
I became a night traveler.

Oh, if I could only travel
Like other people,
Enjoying the sights
Of charming cities and beauty spots.

But my assignment has been
To explore thoroughly
The real capitals of Germany

Translated from the German by Harry Zohn

Free from Shame

Neil C. Scott

These feelings of guilt
that so long have oppressed me,
a dormant infection,
I was able to suppress
if I cared
Until an American would ask,
"Are you German?"
and it flared.

My home is America, now
But my strength comes from Carmen Hubener,
my grandmother, and from my mother
Gradually, they showed me how
to overcome the pain.

Finally, it is Christ's love and salvation
that teaches me to accept my shame
and understand
I have not sinned by Hitler's murder of the Jews;
but I am responsible
as are we all
to never let it happen again.

The Victims of the "Victims"

Peter Daniel

At the 50th anniversary of the Anschluss
an Austrian politician proclaimed:
"Austria was the first victim of Nazi Germany,
and the Jews were the victims of the victims."
In other words:
The Germans were the perpetrators
and the Austrians—who were "victims"—
were called upon
to sacrifice
the Jews.

But the politician
failed to mention
how willingly
that "sacrifice" was made.

Again

Tamar Radzyner

I bore children again
as if I didn't know
how easy it is
to crush
a child's skull.

I built a house again
as if I didn't know
that one can suffocate
under its ruins.

I let myself enter new relationships
as if I didn't know
how they can be
severed.

I haven't learned anything.
I still nurture hope
under the rubble of the time.

The Gardens

David Curzon

Melbourne's Botanic Gardens! where I came
to walk along the bordered paths with him,
and pose in short pants for the photos placed
into this album I'm now leafing through,
and eat my sandwiches beside the lake,
and cast my bread on the water for the swans.
And later, when we met on Sundays, we
went off to European movies, then
to his small room where we played chess. He cut
his dense black bread held close up to his chest.
One afternoon we passed the synagogue
and saw some litter scattered on its steps
including lobster shells. He said, "This is
deliberate desecration. They must know
lobster isn't kosher." "Daddy, it's not that,
it's an Australian picnic. Not cleaned up."
I thought it was absurd he didn't know.
This must have been round nineteen fifty-five.
A mere ten years had passed. And in four years
he'd suicide, and I would read the documents
he kept inside their envelopes in a wood box—
certificates of immigration, change
of name, degrees, but mainly photographs
and letters from his parents and his friends.
And then I found a letter he had sent
to Poland. The final one. It said, "I wish

I could protect you from the sadists" and was stamped
"Unable to deliver." Somehow I
was not aware. He never talked of it.
And now I try to visualize what happened to
his parents and those smiling friends of his,
and try to understand how it would feel
orphaned, divorced, recalling, to walk in
the gardens of Babylon, and not weep.

Remembrance

Bruce Bennett

The eminent writer, who recently
committed suicide, discourses on the
Holocaust, which he survived.

As he speaks, slowly, precisely,
the camera plays back the familiar
scenes: anguished faces; soft piles
of hair; naked bodies pushed into
the pit by bulldozers.

He is riding a bus, being interviewed
as he passes from one camp to another.
He is sensitive, and low-key. Intelligence
shines from his refined face; his
lucidity and dispassion reflect his
training in science.

It is spring as he suffers this
journey. The scenery, serving as backdrop
through the bus window, is lovely,
starting to be lush, and the segments
that depict him, having been shot
in color, richly contrast with the
grainy quality of the old footage.

Seriatim

Robert Frauenglas

Nazis
and friends
in drab olive green
in verdant green countryside
stoke red-hot furnaces
while ashes of my family
cloud the sky.

Names
and histories
long, intricate and involved
are destroyed, forgotten,
tossed away as deadwood
on the already
clutter-filled path
of history.

Nazis
and friends
in drab olive green
in verdant green countryside
stoke red-hot furnaces
fire smoking machine guns
drive trainloads of cattle cars
while ashes of my
family fly across the sky.

But,
Wiesenthal says wait—
they are not all destroyed.
He knows my name,
a German-Jewish name
and my family,
from Zbaraz?
Yes!

He
worked with my cousin
on reparations
from the country and
the people
who can't buy
innocence with money—but try.

Nazis
and friends
in drab olive green
in verdant green countryside
stoke red-hot furnaces
trying to destroy
all signs of my family.

Yet,
we still live,
we still breathe,
we become engaged,
we marry,
we have children . . .

THE AFTERMATH

still peopling
all the nations of the world,
and now . . . our own.

My family continues . . .

But,
Nazis
and friends
in drab olive green
in verdant green countryside
still strive
to survive.

Overlooking Jena

Paul Cummins

For Herbert

Here we were
surrounded by a forest,
there were even trees
inside the walls.
Between the kitchen
and laundry
stood the Goethe Oak.
Its inscription:
"Above all the treetops
there is peace."
Yet as though they knew
this was no place for them—
there were no birds,
not a one,
in Buchenwald.

Survivor

Barbara Goldberg

They say I should feed you,
child with the gift of tongues.
But darting through woods of dark pine
hounds chase the scent of sandals.

Days spent under cover
in a field of eiderdown,
my fingers search for traces
of my own lost mother.

At night, when the bulb shines through
the parchment, and I scrub
my body down with soap,
I think of her parting lace curtains
looking for Father to round the corner.

A small patch of pine presses against the north
side of this house. Here, by Union Turnpike,
a car is parked in the driveway.
We'd all fit in, all, if we had
to make a quick journey.
I keep a bar of gold under my pillow.

They bring you to me, my locket
clasped in your fist. I want
to feed you.

It's those spiked needles that scrape
against the glass, those shadows
that won't sleep behind the drapes.
It's that woodsman walking
through this forest
swinging his ax.

The Shop

Elliot Richman

During the day she worked in a Nazi sweatshop.
Instead of blouses, she stitched
machine-pistols together.

A kapo gave her soap to smell good.
She scrubbed with water and etched
a poem on the soap. When
the poem was completed,
she memorized it,
and washed the soap clean.

Of course, she did not know
her "notebook" was manufactured
from Jewish fat.

When the kapo held her over the side of the bed
and fucked her like she was a boy,
she repeated the poems to herself.

One night she was burned up like a rag
on the floor of the Triangle Shirtwaist Factory.

These Ultimate Survivors

Marguerite M. Striar

Say you're in the mood for a four-star horror show,
forget *Dracula* or *Wait Until Dark*.
Tune in to history . . . or the daily news.
Choose your video:
Slaughter of the Incas,
the slaying of the "infidel" by crusading horsemen,
torches blazing as they rode,
Spain's Inquisition,
Stalin purging whole forests of his people, and of Poles,
Serbian slaughter, starvation in Angola.

Then, the truly innovative atrocities of our day:
The Nazi Holocaust!
Systematic elimination
of six million Jews, and others,
its bloody harvest of ash-fertilized real estate.
(Nineteen forty-two, the bloodiest winter.)

All through time,
fired by an Olympic manic hate,
Man races to exterminate.
Watch History's screen:
It's hardly news a constant target, through the years,
has been the Jews.

Switch channels now:
A firestorm, the summer of 1988,
(driest in U.S. history)
one hundred million acres of Yellowstone Park
destroyed, before the last flames
flickered "farewell" at Wolf Lake.

The documentary continues:
Nine months later new grass,
like green throw rugs scattered,
tiny yellow flowers and tender leaves sprouting.
Scientists dig down through blackened earth to brown,
discover roots, still strong,
eagerly reaching for the sun again.
The ashes, rich with calcium, potassium, phosphorus,
the building blocks of life.

We'll never forget the cost.
Aspen groves, dead above the ground
but deep below, roots still alive.
The large-cone pine, needles crisped by burning heat,
scatters its seeds.
New trees will grow.
The Jews survive.

The Daughter of Survivors

Hilary Tham (Goldberg)

For Elaine, Helen, Myra

She is screaming again.
You stand at your bedroom door.
Her dream claws her sleep to shreds.
Shivering, you will her to stop, will it
to go away. Your father's voice
rises and falls with the burden of her name.

She is awake. You hear her voice cling
to his, as a shipwrecked cat
digs its claws into a floating spar.
You hear the creak of bedsprings as they rise.

Soon, the kettle whistles in the kitchen.
When you peer in, they are huddled together
over the kitchen table. Her pale hands clenched
around the teacup, she whispers her dream.
He has heard it six million times,
but he listens, his arm clamped around her
to contain her shudders.
He, too, has bad dreams, different faces,
the same sequence of events.

You are afraid of this trembling woman
who replaces your mother each night.
You want the daylight woman
who bakes honeycake, and brushes your hair
smiling, as if you are her good dream.

Your father does not change at night.
He, too, fears the knock on the door.
He makes you learn street maps
by heart, sends you out alone
on the New York subway so that
if you should come home from school
and find them missing, you would
know how and where to run.

33 Union Square West

David Gershator

Thirty-three Union Square West
Mother's workplace
narrow building
ornate masonry facade
nine stories high
full of inventors and artists
seeking that gust of inspiration
but who invented sudden death
radio said gale-force winds
body sprawled on the sidewalk
big chunks of masonry scattered about
police couldn't identify him
head smashed by a cornice
no wallet no papers no next of kin
they said he had blue numbers on his arm
it meant he survived
it meant he was guilty of survival
it meant his number was up
it meant a cornice was loose and waiting
for the right moment
and the landlord of 33 Union Square West
should be sued but who was going to sue
it meant no next of kin
but death itself tattooed
on the dead man's arm
it meant oh God!

THE AFTERMATH

it meant crazy grief
calling out Kaddish after Kaddish for the unknown
but all I could do was worry the unknown to death
with a teenage why why why
a lifetime later I pass 33 Union Square West
a number so loaded with inventors
artists creators hoping for bolts from the blue
it's practically branded into my skin . . .
Yitgadal v'yitkadash
going past number 33 I walk faster
looking up
expecting no blessing

Herringbone Overcoat

Jacob Gusewelle

I always wanted a herringbone overcoat. I had one once, I never wore it, I carried it around from aimless homeless place to place. Then someone said this thing takes up space, you never wear it, it's impractical, get rid of it, and I did. I gave it to the Salvation Army, which maybe needed it more than I but maybe not, it all depends upon how you value things. Once I took it to a tailor—it didn't fit, you see—and he said this thing is impractical, it would cost more to alter than it's worth, it's just an old herringbone overcoat, very old, out of style, material's good though, but really not worth anything, he said, this very old herringbone overcoat. It belonged to my father and was always too big for me, just as he was too big for me because he died in that Polish place and I didn't but should have and that's my fault somehow—it's always seemed that way. I don't even know how I came by the herringbone overcoat—very old herringbone overcoat—made way back then when the world was still sane. They said my father wrapped me in it the night they slipped me through the wire. It wasn't impractical then. They said I remained wrapped in it across Poland and Russia and south to the Judean hills. They told the Russian soldiers who stopped them it was just a bundle of rags and the Russian soldiers didn't look inside. It was worth something then. They said I remained wrapped in it across a sea and an ocean and a sea and all through that cold winter of '42. It didn't take up space then. When I thought about the old herringbone overcoat I went to the Salvation Army to try and buy it back. They said they couldn't find it in the bundles of rags and couldn't be bothered to look, and anyway, they said, it isn't worth anything.

Insects Won the Battle

Herman Taube

God is the mystery of life, enkindling inert matter with
inner drive and purpose.

— Rabbi Mordecai Kaplan

Our tormentors called us vermin,
identified us as disposable matter,
germs, insects to be exterminated.
We coped with wind and winter,
the darkness of the Holocaust.
We survived the inferno like snow-flies,
like ladybug beetles beneath the snow.
We outlasted our enemies, resembling
tiger-beetles in larva tunnels deep
underground, wrapped in rags like
moth pupas wrapped in leaf cocoons,
weathering the storm hanging on trees.
Our bodies were skinny like the praying mantis
persevering inside the hardening egg cases
on stalks . . . We outlived the human beasts
as goldenrod gallflies survive
in a larva inside hollow ball-galls
in goldenrod plants. Our lives
were hanging on thin, silken hair,

like cabbage-butterfly pupas, attached
to weed stalks by silken slings.
We persisted. The insects won the battle:
Our tormentors perished, We Are Here! . . .

My Mother's Prayer Book

Shel Krakofsky

is her childhood siddur
smuggled out of Poland
saved from the book
burnings and fire that
consumed her favorite
friends and relatives

every morning she gives back names
to the lives erased with numbers
using pages soiled with old
and current tears
smudged with decades
and layers of lipstick

she whispers benedictions
in her kitchen throne room
this monarch prays
with a kerchief crown
then guards her domain
from milk touching meat

like the siddur, her spine
is still straight at 80
she goes to the doctor yearly
to see how he is
and with head uncovered I thank God
for somehow forgetting about her

as she turns a page
there is a flutter
of her ministering angels
and the distance between us quivers
over the soil where she
planted the gnarled roots

that always allowed this son
to fly

In a Bicycle Repair Shop

Shel Krakofsky

bent and missing
spokes
among rusted and
inadequate frames
battered brakes
emaciated tires
piled up
and tangled
like the bodies
in mass graves
impossible to be
put together again
like the survivors
who line
their therapists'
bicycle shops
with the same chance
of being reassembled
and repaired

The Survivor

A. Alvarez

The skull in my hands is my life's. It stares at me.
My child peers out through its eyes. My wife's lips move
Across the polished bone where its lips should be.
Her hair is soft on the crown and burns for love.

We are held in a single death: child, husband, wife,
Mixed blood, mixed feelings, fingers mixed and minds
Burn in a single flame across our lives.
And I am left with a delicate skull in my hands.

Strange that a bone should flame as though dipped in pitch,
Strangely intense in death, strange tenderness
In blood that once leapt to a cheek now cold to my touch.
Death clasps them bone to bone against his chest.

Only the skull is left, the last hard fact
That turns in my hands, in my blood, under my skin
Pacing my life like a traveler who taps
The earth and cries, "Dear mother, let me in."

1960

An Old Story

B. Z. Niditch

The day I lost
out to the shameful sky
I was handed a star
and told that invitations
to my death had been arranged
by various parties
from a chorus of nations
all clamoring that I join in
their program;
autos-da-fé were included
crusades, inquisitions,
pogroms, expulsions,
banishments during intermission,
with chambers of the latest gases
invented especially for me;
I was only a child
five thousand years old.

Sonnets

Richard Newman

25

"It was, of all the ways we ever touched,
the most intimate. I cradled his head.
His belly, shot open, poured guts and blood,
a steaming puddle on the street. I pushed
his insides back inside—they saw, they watched—
and carried him to the doctors, and prayed.
They followed like bloodhounds, and when he died
they dumped him in a mass grave. That night, I retched
through seven corpses till I recognized
his wounds and lifted him one last time,
properly, into the earth. He was cold,
hard. After I laid him out, I held
his hands to my breasts, and called his name.
He didn't warm. I kissed him. His eyes stayed closed."

29

"Women, he once said, should run things here.
Then, more men could join the labor force.
Three of you can do the work of one horse,
so harness yourselves to haul those goods. Spare
no one. Older children can do their share,
and, with a kindergarten, the absurd farce
of Jewish family life will end as the source
of one more parasitic drain on the care
you get here. Useless people should be dead.

We altered census counts and gave false work
permits. We pulled on every chain they had
us by and saved lives with each inch of slack.

We were the hands and eyes that helped them do
what they could not have done without us. It's true."

30
"After each transport was gassed, we'd remove
the gold teeth and fillings and peel off the skin,
especially if it was young and had been
tattooed. What was left we took to the grave
that never seemed to fill. I didn't grieve
till flesh that had been my wife, my daughter and son
passed before me as I worked. I broke down
and asked the nearest SS to shoot me. His laugh
is with me still, *And who gave you the right*
to say when you will die? Or are you god?
I could've thrown myself into the pit,
or let myself collapse. I would have been dead.
The Nazi looked at me and turned away.
I'd chosen life. Or had it chosen me?"

33
"The debate went on for hours. Did Jewish art
require Jewish subjects? And were we bound
as Ghetto artists to be more disciplined
in content so our work could take the part
of history?
            That week, a woman's skirt
was found at the Ghetto gate to be lined
with smuggled food. She was sure they'd send

her first to the Gestapo, then to the fort,
and so rehearsed the life she'd claim as hers—
single with no living relatives—
to try and save her family. The officers
stripped her, spread her legs and probed with knives
before they let her go. She brought her shame
to me, and I wrote it down, including her name."

In Memory of Smoke

Michael Waters

I found her again this morning,
my mother, sleeping
with her head in the oven,
on a pillow of human hair.

On her knees, exhausted,
wanting the oven forever clean,
she might have been praying
in memory of smoke.

I don't know her reasons.
I guess something simple
as cleaning the oven
becomes a compulsion for those

who have been lost in snow,
in childhood, wandering
from town to burning town
in search of a family.

I guess you might recognize
the family as smoke
billowing over black trees.
So I let my mother sleep.

I know she would never shut
her eyes, place her cheek
on the burning pillow each night,
without a prayer for her family,

giving thanks
for the work she manages daily,
in memory of smoke,
in fear of the coming snow.

Pinochle Day

Frieda Arkin

Max the music-hater rubs
the outdoors from his hands, gloves
pocketed. Unwinds the muffler
which since March has lain
dusted with crystals of naphthalene.
Luke's palsied hands chime the whiskey glasses.
Dave with age's lizard's face
sets the cards and chips in place
circling the bottle's golden heart.
Pulling chairs, the old men home
in on the table. They own
the new November dusk, and meld, and grunt,
toss chips, drink Scotch, crack jokes
seasoned like old oak until the dark
swells in between the cracks.
Luke gives the stereo a twist
and in the arc of Paganini-Liszt
smiles like an impresario. "How Richter plays
is enough to make your shoes fall off."
Dave waits, considers, nods.
Only Max. His cards slide flat.
This music is the silver tilt of time
that sweeps him back to Hildesheim,
his daughter's sounds. Sweet prodigy,
sweet child of fire. Her face
through his face: to this day

he has to turn his eye away from mirrors,
his ear from sounds like these.
Old man—who hears Beethoven's *Ode to Joy*
and sees gas chamber queues.
No waiting till the record stops.
Stands. Walks. Takes coat and muffler,
opens door and leaves. Old man—
smelling of mothballs and schnapps.

Outcast

Bina Goldfield

Memory puts me
in discord with nature,

is longer than the time
saplings took to replace
the electrified fence;

is stronger than winds of four decades
that robbed the air
of the stench of burning flesh;

is harder than packed earth
that denies it was
blood drenched.

When I die,
will my memories pass on
to the worms?

Remembering

Enid Shomer

For my husband

Your mother hoards flour and sugar
whenever the news is grim.
No matter weevils get most of it.
It is stored in her heart and head,
fuel for a memory she stokes and fans.

I, too, keep expecting war
but each morning smells of diesel,
bread and donkeys.
All day at the zoo peacocks scream
but they are only laying eggs.

We take the train for Jerusalem.
The woman across the aisle
has those numbers on her arm,
but breathes deeply,
reads a paper.
Later at a roundhouse, you watch
an engine turn and pass out cold,
remembering men gaffed and drowned
near a platform in Minsk.
The doctor says it is memories
that make you sick,
suggests next time you look away.

At Yad Vashem, memorial
to the six million, you close your eyes
as we grope our way along the damp walls,
past the silent brass roll call.
Later you tell me the engraved
names of the dead bloomed
like flowers in your hands.

Forging Links

> European Jewish civilization — language, culture, institutions —
> was wiped out utterly.
>
> — Cynthia Ozick

In the early morning silence, reading *The Drowned*
and the Saved, a vision of Primo Levi
comes to me: his eyes clouded behind spectacles squint

as he trudges each cobbled street searching for traces
of Turin's Jews. In and out my dreams I see their house
usurped by neighbors, the mezuzahs on the doors

torn away, desecrated, though the shadows of the dead
still visit the doorposts like kisses children feel
on their foreheads long after they grow old. Late March

and it is snowing, though I know nothing will remain,
that these fat flakes are no more than memories
disappearing into trees, like my children leaving their wooden

swingset to me and the squirrels. Each time they come back
home, I tell them another of my parents' Holocaust truths.
The Church orders not sheltering Jews. Hanka

Haranin brings us bread, empties our bucket.
In the town of burnt corpses Hanka heats the ground
to dig their graves.

It was as if all our corpses
streamed to heaven in the full moon with its red ring.
The only way to link us to that other world we'll never know.

What keeps haunting me? Making me remember
that museum in Florence, Michelangelo's disembodied
torsos. *When I hammer I release imprisoned shapes.*

Arbeit Macht Frei*

Reva Sharon

For a survivor—the night before Bitburg

You work hard
and never complain
and never explain why
you work late into hours
when shadows across your desk
darken into that black alphabet
arched above the entrance
where you sounded out
the words phonically
trying to read

the signs
Old men naked
Sagging women naked
Cowering children naked
blue numbered
stripped of the yellow stars
torn by the barbed wire
rusting your years
Silently they file through
the drawn slats of your blinds

....

*German: Work makes you free.

Herded into showers
they cried out
Shema*
but the steel
door clanged shut
On the cold concrete floor
that scraped the skin on your back
your mama cradled you
laid over you
whispering
Then she fell . . .

Smoke curls
from the ashes
and embers grow cold
in your hearth
You switch on the light
and work hard
and long past
memory and dream
but never enough
to be free

*Hebrew: Hear.

Lettuce for Anne Frank

Janice Townley Moore

Whenever I see lettuce
shining in a wet garden,
cool in the crisper
I think of how in the dark
of the secret annex
they had to boil it.
It was only fit for boiling,
carried on an ugly truck,
bruised under canvas.
Later, someone swept it
from the corners of a remote market,
smuggled it in a paper sack
with vermin.
Even the lettuce forgot
what it had been:
rooted in the moist earth,
growing green in the sun.

Berlin: Savoy Hotel

Herman Taube

The bathroom at the Savoy Hotel
is immaculately brushed, spotless.
The toilet seats are furnished with
a rotary motor that cover the seats
with fresh towels after every flush.

Mr. Ganz, a native Berliner, who
lives in Haifa, Israel, came back to
his place of birth, after an absence of
49 years, invited by Berlin's City Senate,
is hesitant to sit down and use the toilet.

Leaving the lavatory, he shares
with me some thoughts and memories:
On Kristallnacht, November 9, 1938
I was arrested and taken to Buchenwald
with my father and a younger brother.

The latrine barrack was awash with feces,
we stood in line deep in human excrement,
my brother, weakened by dysentery, fell off
the plank into the deep ditch, I tried to
help him. The guard hit me with his whip.

I returned to my barrack soaked with blood,
my father washed my face and kept asking:
Where is my son? I lied: "They took him away."
My father died crawling on his hands and knees
in the torture chambers of Buchenwald . . .

Mr. Ganz, I asked, why did you come to Berlin?
My spouse insisted we visit the cemetery here,
my mother is also buried here, fortunately, she
died before Kristallnacht. Doesn't sound silly?
I can't use the hotel toilet. Too deep the scars . . .

El Tango Fabuloso

Asher Torren

Among the 90,000 bodies unearthed and burned in Ponary,
Ely the Black recognized his wife and daughter.

You always passed out
When I held you so close,
When every tango was
Our first and last.

Limed, putrid figure
I dug you out,
Smothered Ponary quarry,
Cut marble of my eyes.

Let us glide again, then turn,
Before I torch your body
Good-bye, and go on
Wedded to our tango,
Shackled to the pit
You left behind.

Lithuania

Myra Sklarew

Excerpts from the book-length poem Lithuania

I

At three-thirty in the morning in America
I have filled an enamel soup pot with cold water
from the sink and I am watering
the apple tree I planted a summer ago.
I am watering the false camellia tree I planted
in March, the crown-of-thorns cactus,
the plant with tiny blue flowers, I am trying
to remember something.

I am trying to remember something I couldn't
possibly know. I am trying,
as I was two days ago in Lithuania,
to move by feel, to know when I was close
to where they had been. At first
I just walked in the Jew's town
without anyone helping me, without anyone
telling me. I walked until I remembered.

But how could I? I had not been here
before. Christ could not show me
the way. Neither Petras nor Regina—neither stones
nor saints nor royalty. Perhaps a man
who bit the throat of a Lithuanian

before they cut him into pieces. Perhaps
a tiny red poppy I picked from the trench
of the massacre of Keidan—they say the weeds grew
here twice as tall as anywhere else. How
beautiful it is in Lithuania.

3

But is this the way their story will end?
Not this way. Not yet.
For here is the place where the young brother
was killed, his wife, the infant nearly ready
to enter this world. In the fire that burned
the mother alive, the baby exploded from her
belly like the sacred letters of the scroll
Akiba was wrapped in when the Romans

set him afire. Wedged between the life
before life and the life to come, for a single
moment the child looked upon this world
before it too entered the flames. An old woman—
her face so close I hear her labored
breathing, I smell her skin—who thinks we are
survivors come back, pierces the silence with a voice
so calamitous, tells us about her neighbor

who escaped from the pit in Krakiai
where all others were murdered. He went
to the people to whom he had entrusted his
property, but they betrayed him, sending
him back to his death. Is she one of the righteous

or one who is haunted by the past? Or one
who fears the survivor who will turn up
one day at her door and ask for his house

back, ask for a place to breathe again, ask
what has become of his small son?
They cut off the head of the rabbi
of this town and set it in the window. Was he
to be a talisman, keeping watch over
them like a ship's figurehead sighting
the dangers before them? Or an object
of ridicule? Or by fixing his head

like a beacon light in their window, they could hold
imprisoned the heart of his people? What hatred, what
fear carries human action to this place?

6

Be wary of old forts—they have a history
of killing; their walls are used to the screams
of prisoners, the silence of death. Their walls
are impervious to the last messages
scrawled in blood. There is no poetry in any
of this. These forts have witnessed
the deaths of over 100,000 Jews. Be wary
of names. Those who took the long

road from ordinary life to the ghetto and
from the ghetto to the Ninth Fort called that way
Via Dolorosa—Christ's walk
to Golgotha. The road that led uphill from

Kovno to the Ninth Fort. The Germans called it
the Way to Heaven—Der Weg
zum Himmel-Fahrt. And in secret they named it
Place of Extermination No. 2, Vernichtungstelle nr.2.

Not existing place, *vernichtungstelle.* No,
that's not quite it. A transitive word, more active—
place to make nothing, to nullify, cancel, annul.
You must say these names yourself. Taste
the strange mixtures of annihilation, the Jew
using Christian iconography, going in columns
of a hundred along the sorrowful way.
In the Ninth Fort the power went off. We

stood in the cold dark, in the cold, in the
dark. We could smell the air they had breathed.
I wanted, above all, to escape. But I kept
my feet on the ground. We lighted candles
and we walked through the steel blackness.
The woman with me had worked there twelve years.
Her face had no expression as she talked about what
happened there, the voice drilling into my head.

A Letter to Hans Puvogel

Paul Cummins

In 1936 Hans Puvogel, a twenty-five-year-old doctoral student in Saxony, successfully explained to his examiners that an individual's worth to the community "is measured by his or her racial personality. Only a racially valuable person has a right to exist in the community. A racially inferior or harmful individual must be eliminated."

How has time treated you, Hans?
Did you at all costs survive?
Have you been able to measure
Love in tests of blood?
Did you find a pure woman
To mount in pure sweat and sire
Pure children—credits to their race?
And do you explain to your children
How the Aryan language
Has purified their blood?
Do you tell them how the world's value
Has been increased because their food
Has been fertilized by
Ashes of Jewish children?
Do you on cold winter nights
Feel warmth and comfort
Recalling the aroma of Auschwitz
Smoke as the impurities burned off
Rising from the chimney stacks
To melt into your pure blond air?

Inspection

Deborah DeNicola

Believe, if you will, that he isn't guilty.
But brighten the bare bulb a little at each denial.
The red tile will glare at him, his story drifting

like the lies he spits out to keep us off him.
When he's drunk on the sheer volume of our voices,
and the quiet is such you can hear the moths

shitting in the dust—when the yellow wall waves
like some crazy oasis, remember we'll lose our features
and, faceless, we'll remove ourselves

from this blight of "unchristian acts" as you say;
we're only instruments of the Party following orders.
In just a few hours after dinner and brandy with our wives,

this cell will be silent as angels, a space
we never entered. And later tonight,
when you cup your mistress's buttocks in your fingers,

you'll forget that glassy stare in his rheumy eyes.
But for now, consider his filth, the animal quality
of his moans. His muscles are slack, his hair's

falling out, his jaw can't hold the phlegm in his mouth.
One toe beneath your boot will crush like a bulb of garlic
the chef at the club rubs into the roast.

The same thing goes for a testicle.
The bones that protrude through his arms are especially fragile.
The crack when they're wrenched to the back will be nothing

you didn't expect. Besides, tonight, going home
we can stop on the road for a couple of ales.
The thick froth will soothe our throats from the shape

of these difficult questions. Other men will be worse,
there will always be those who whisper of rats and experiments;
those who spread rumors of transports to pits;

those who tell jokes. Always the jokes.
After a month on the job you'll look back at your qualms
and laugh at yourself. Remember, you're young

and torture gets old like everything else.

Cinema III

Christopher Fahy

If—as some of you still contend—
it had actually happened—
If smoke from burning human flesh
had dimmed the summer sun—
could blond-headed boys and girls
have happily played in the meadows
beside the walls?

Could meticulous, hygienic bourgeoisie like us
have willingly wallowed day after day
in excrement, maggots, rats, contagious disease?
—Or rosy-cheeked fräuleins in uniform
have laughed, sipped coffee,
digested linzertorte at linen-lined tables
beside the foul stench of real graves?

The buildings? All models,
including the ovens.
We Germans excel at toys.
The bodies? Just dummies, just dolls,
by today's standards rather crude.
Often they lack detail;
the heads and limbs are poorly attached,
flop about too much; the facial expressions
are far too coarse and startled,
no one believes them.

Those tottering, sticklike survivors
are simply a matter of makeup and lighting,
the right camera angle, their nudity
a trick of the costume department.
The figures frozen in desperate flight,
charred in barbed-wire fences
—mere papier-mâché
rubbed with lampblack.

Some complain that the plot is repetitious:
the trains arrive,
the occupants are sorted out,
shot, gassed, or put to work.
The dead are burned. The trains arrive. . . .
Well, subtleties tend to suffer in wartime,
we were rushed, the budget was tight.
The effects got star billing, all right,
and still impress:
the piles of horsehair,
pebbles painted to look like gold teeth,
the vats of chicken fat. . . .
Some viewers, even now,
grow pale, gag, choke and faint,
though their minds scream:
It's only a movie!

Which it is, of course.
All that's real is the backdrop,
the mountains and lake.
How gullible people are!

We liked our Jews, still do,
though most of them
—it must be something in their blood—
have left for a warmer climate.

The point of it all?
We had to do something
to take our minds off the chocolate shortage,
and everyone loves a good horror tale.
Remember *Nosferatu?* Our classic vampire show?
We felt we could top it.
I think you'll agree we did.

Art and Politics

Barry Ivker

They played Beethoven in Theresienstadt—
For a while—gaunt and bony-fingered—
The sounds arose—the musicians lingered—
Pampered just a bit—a month or so—then shot,
Or gassed, and burned—it really mattered not
Once they were selected out. Tones even
That might ope the rusted doors of heaven
Could not derail for long a führer's plot.
Beauty may set military feet tapping.
It may caress the palate like aged wine—
While connoisseurs re-create a state—*judenrein*—
listen to fists on shower doors—rapping—
And hand the violins on down the line,
Trusting the next concert will be just fine.

Criminal Sonnet XXXVIII

Phyllis Koestenbaum

He actually said he only did his
job, the infamous Barbie, Butcher of
Lyon. He dispatched to Auschwitz's ovens
an entire Jewish orphanage, his
job. Other crimes he thinks we should forget:
executing 4000, torturing
thousands more, deporting like the orphans
to gas chambers or atrocities worse
than gas, 75 hundred *Juden.*
The worst retribution he could get
for deeds he's forgotten is life, death kaput
in France. I can't make this poem better.
The first draft was as good or as bad as
this; I'm as far from the light as I was.

Ronald Reagan in Germany

Joanne Seltzer

1. Response from Bergen-Belsen

All of us buried
in this mass grave
say that the president
of the USA
doesn't belong
at Bitburg
and furthermore
we don't want him here.

Forgiveness
has its limits.

2. Response from Bitburg

Hearing the band play
"I Had a Comrade,"
watching the president
of the USA
lay flowers
upon my grave,
I repeat
what I said before:

I was only
following orders.

Our Holocaust Dead

Hilary Tham (Goldberg)

Just last month, someone denied
them, said it never happened.
The celluloid horrors of *Friday
the 13th, Nightmare
on Elm Street, Pet Sematary* are
acceptable but lampshades of human skin,
six million reels of unfinished lives
thrown into the fire, char the mind.
Yet teenage boys in Central Park
bouncing a lead pipe on a woman's skull "for fun"
is fact. They died, these ordinary
people like you and me, who wanted to live
ordinary lives, they died for lack of blue
eyes, they died because boys acted out
horror fantasies without need
for fake blood or plastic corpses.
Let us not kill them again.

May 5, 1989

Waiting to Go Home

$Bill\ Siegel$

The liberation of Auschwitz camp, 1945

For years, I thought the faded picture
showed wounded soldiers lying on the ground,
waiting to be taken home.
I imagined smiling faces through the bandages,
the woolen coats, the fog
that had blurred the old photo.
Tired, but on their way home.

"Too terrible to be seen," my mother said.
"Out of sight somewhere," she said.
When I asked, my father took it out;
that same old blue cardboard box
I had looked through a hundred times
growing up. "There," he said,
pulling out one small photo.
"These are some of the bodies we found."
I looked closer,
without my child's eyes this time,
and saw the lips pulled impossibly back
from the teeth, the eyes sunken
within the skulls, the child
face down between rag-wrapped corpses,

the blackened skin, and the bones it barely covered.
"Some people say this never happened,"
he said in a quiet, even voice.
"But they forgot to tell the people at this camp."

I look up from the photo,
and see my father's face behind the camera:
tired, waiting to go home.

How Can They Say It Never Happened?

Joan Fondell

My father wouldn't lie to me.
He showed me pictures of his parents.
They're gone.
His father died of pneumonia in Theresienstadt.
His mother gassed at Auschwitz.
His number tattooed on his arm.
How can they say it never happened?

He told me how harsh the camps were.
Soup, mostly water.
Starving, cold, only wooden shoes.
He couldn't brush his teeth, no toilet paper.
Lice. Jaundice.
How can they say it never happened?

The Nazis took pictures of their treasures.
Gold fillings, eyeglasses, suitcases, coats, jewelry.
Ovens, mass graves, hangings, medical experiments.
How can they say it never happened?

He dreams at night. Frightening nightmares. Cold sweats.
Chills. He remembers.
How can they say it never happened?

Psalm 1*

David Curzon

Blessed is the man not born
in Lódz in the wrong decade
who walks not in tree-lined shade
like my father's father in this photo, *nor*
stands in the way of sinners waiting for
his yellow star,
nor sits, if he could sit, in their cattle car,

but his delight is being born
as I was, in Australia, far away,
and on God's law he meditates night and day.

He is like a tree that's granted
the land where it is planted,
that yields its fruit by reason
of sun and rain in season.

The wicked are not so, they
burn their uniforms and walk away.

Therefore the wicked are like Cain
who offered fruit which God chose to disdain.

*From *Midrashim* (1991).

and *the way of the righteous* is Abel's, whose
slaughtered lambs God chose to choose
and who was murdered anyway.

Blessed is the man who walks not in the councel of the wicked, nor
stands in the way of sinners, nor sits in the seat of scoffers; but his
delight is in the law of the LORD, and on his law he meditates day and
night. He is like a tree planted by streams of water, that yields its fruit
in its season, and its leaf does not wither. In all that he does, he pros-
pers. The wicked are not so, but are like chaff which the wind drives
away. Therefore the wicked will not stand in the judgement, nor sin-
ners in the congregation of the righteous; for the LORD knows the
way of the righteous, but the way of the wicked will perish.

Translation: Revised Standard Version

Adam*

Yevgeny Vinokurov

On the first day, gazing idly around,
He trampled the grass down and stretched himself
In the shade of the fig tree.

    And placing
His hands behind his head,
        dozed.

Sweetly he slept, untroubled was his sleep
In Eden's quiet, beneath the pale blue sky.
And in his dreams he saw the ovens of Auschwitz
And he saw ditches filled with corpses.

He saw his own children!
    In the bliss
Of paradise, his face lit up.
He slept, understanding nothing,
Not knowing good and evil yet.

Translated from the Russian by Daniel Weissbort

---

*The poet portrays innocence in relation to the death camps by means of a midrash on Adam. The narrator relates what Adam dreamed on his first night in the Garden of Eden, before Eve was created or fruit was eaten from the Tree of Knowledge of Good and Evil.

Songs of Songs*

Iakovos Kambanelis

Have you seen the one I love?

— Song of Songs 3:3

How lovely is my love
in her everyday dress
with a little comb in her hair.
No one knew how lovely she was.
Girls of Auschwitz
girls of Dachau
have you seen the one I love?

We saw her on the long journey.
She wasn't wearing her everyday dress
or the little comb in her hair.

How lovely is my love
caressed by her mother,
kissed by her brother.

---

*Iakovos Kambanelis, an important Greek literary figure (primarily a play-wright) and a survivor of Mauthausen, uses a question from Song of Songs 3:3 as the epigraph for his poem. The refrain of the poem is addressed to prisoners in the death camps. This poem is well known in Greece, where it was set to music by Mikis Theodorakis as part of a cycle of laments on Mauthausen. On May 6, 1994, Carnegie Hall in New York was filled for a concert of music by Theodorakis. When the Mauthausen cycle was played, the largely Greek audience joined Maria Farandouri in singing the laments.

No one knew how lovely she was.
Girls of Belsen
girls of Mauthausen
have you seen the one I love?

We saw her in the frozen square
with a number on her white arm
and a yellow star over her heart.

Translated from the Greek by Gail Holst-Warhaft

BEYOND LAMENT

Testimony*

Dan Pagis

No No: they definitely were
human beings: uniforms, boots.
How to explain? They were created
in the image.

I was a shade.
A different creator made me.

And he in his mercy left nothing of me that would die.
And I fled to him, floated up weightless, blue,
forgiving—I would even say: apologizing—
Smoke to omnipotent smoke
that has no face or image.

Translated by Stephen Mitchell

---

*Dan Pagis, a survivor who emigrated to Israel as a teenager after the war, wrote many poems in Hebrew dealing either directly or indirectly with the Holocaust. Here, Pagis uses Genesis 1:27, "And God created man in His image," as the implicit prooftext for a poem of witness addressed to humanity at large.

Draft of a Reparations Agreement*

Dan Pagis

All right,
gentlemen who cry blue murder as always,
nagging miracle-makers,
quiet!
Everything will be returned to its place,
paragraph after paragraph.
The scream back into the throat.
The gold teeth back to the gums.
The terror.
The smoke back to the tin chimney and further on and inside
back to the hollow of the bones,
and already you will be covered with skin and sinews and you will
live,
look, you will have your lives back,
sit in the living room, read the evening paper.
Here you are. Nothing is too late.
As to the yellow star:
It will be torn from your chest

---

*In Ezekiel 37, God shows the prophet a valley with dry bones; He proceeds to
bring the bones together and cover them with flesh and skin, then causes breath
to enter into them. After they have stood up, God tells Ezekiel that these bones
are "the whole House of Israel," who were cut off in exile to Babylon. In this
midrashic poem, Pagis has God speak and promise to do for those killed in the
Holocaust the equivalent of the miracle of the dry bones.

immediately
and will emigrate
to the sky.

Translated by Stephen Mitchell

Written in Pencil in the Sealed Railway Car*

Dan Pagis

here in this carload
i am eve
with abel my son
if you see my other son
cain son of man
tell him that i

Translated by Stephen Mitchell

*As in his poem "Testimony," Pagis draws on a text of universal application and affirms that, as the Bible says, no one, not even a mass murderer, is to be regarded as a demon but as "my other son," the "son of man."

Deathfugue*

Paul Celan

Black milk of daybreak we drink it at evening
we drink it at midday and morning we drink it at night
we drink and we drink
we shovel a grave in the air there you won't lie too cramped
A man lives in the house he plays with his vipers he writes
he writes when it grows dark to Deutschland your golden hair Margareta
he writes it and steps out of doors and the stars are all sparkling he
    whistles his hounds to come close
he whistles his Jews into rows has them shovel a grave in the ground
he orders us play up for the dance

Black milk of daybreak we drink you at night
we drink you at morning and midday we drink you at evening
we drink and we drink
A man lives in the house he plays with his vipers he writes
he writes when it grows dark to Deutschland your golden hair Margareta

*This poem takes as its prooftext a passage from the Song of Songs, which reads, in
the Jewish Publication Society's 1917 translation:

> Return, return, O Shulamite;
> Return, return, that we may look upon thee.

> What will ye see in the Shulamite?
> As it were a dance of two companies.

Celan interprets this last line as the dance of death between German masters and
Jews under their control. In Jewish Bibles the last phrase is chapter 7, verse 1; in
Christian Bibles, where the book is called Song of Solomon, it is chapter 6, verse 13.

your ashen hair Shulamith we shovel a grave in the air there you
    won't lie too cramped
He shouts jab this earth deeper you lot there you others sing up
    and play
he grabs for the rod in his belt he swings it his eyes they are blue
jab your spades deeper you lot there you others play on for the
    dancing

Black milk of daybreak we drink you at night
we drink you at midday and morning we drink you at evening
we drink and we drink
a man lives in the house your goldenes Haar Margarete
your aschenes Haar Shulamith he plays with his vipers
He shouts play death more sweetly this Death is a master from
    Deutschland
he shouts scrape your strings darker then rise up as smoke to the sky
you'll have a grave then in the clouds there you won't lie too cramped

Black milk of daybreak we drink you at night
we drink you at midday Death is a master aus Deutschland
we drink you at evening and morning we drink and we drink
this Death is ein Meister aus Deutschland his eye it is blue
he shoots you with shot made of lead shoots you level and true
a man lives in the house your goldenes Haar Margarete
he looses his hounds on us grants us a grave in the air
he plays with his vipers and daydreams
    der Tod ist ein Meister aus Deutschland

dein goldenes Haar Margarete
dein aschenes Haar Shulamith

1944–45

Translated by John Felstiner

O the chimneys

Nelly Sachs

And though after my skin worms destroy this body,
yet in my flesh shall I see God.

— Job 19:26*

O the chimneys
On the ingeniously devised habitations of death
When Israel's body drifted as smoke
Through the air—
Was welcomed by a star, a chimney sweep,
A star that turned black
Or was it a ray of sun?

O the chimneys!
Freedomway for Jeremiah and Job's dust—
Who devised you and laid stone upon stone
The road for refugees of smoke?

O the habitations of death,
Invitingly appointed
For the host who used to be a guest—

---

*The epigraph from Job 19:26 has been taken from the King James translation. In the German original, however, Nelly Sachs used the 1917 Jewish Publication Society edition: "And when after my skin this is destroyed, then without my flesh shall I see God." As in Celan's "Deathfugue," the biblical text has been illustrated with shocking irony but no actual denial: yes, my people have, without their flesh, seen God, just as Job believed, and this is the way it happened.

O you fingers
Laying the threshold
Like a knife between life and death—

O you chimneys,
O you fingers
And Israel's body as smoke through the air!

Translated by Michael Roloff

A Shade from Auschwitz

Cornel Adam

How shall I praise you, Lord, at this late hour?
How can I magnify your name?

They washed me in lye and purged me with Zyklon-B;
They removed my circumcised part
and pulled out my teeth.

They converted my marrow into soap
to send in a matchbox to my begetters.
They ground up my bones for fertilizer,
to improve the earth, they said.

How shall I praise you, O Merciful Lord?
How can I magnify your name?

THE LORD: Avoid pollution and ingratitude.
Bury old bones and ashes.
Fly through the chimney as dust if you must.

Sing hosannas, if you can.
I am what I am!
(Spare me your lamentations!)

Ezekiel in the Valley

Cornel Adam

Shall these dry bones that crumble in the darkness,
A barren heap, so marred and charred and broken,
Old shards of faith that hold no living waters,
Reclothe themselves in flesh when I have spoken?
And feel a fresh wind blowing through the breastbone,
The heart like wild wings beating in its hollows?

Then rise, pale bones, and wrap yourselves in sinew:
The spell that bound you to the pit is broken.
Find living eyes and heart and hope within you:
Roll out into the sun—the grave is open.
Now celebrate the breath that stirs within you,
O twice-burned bones twice-born—the word is spoken!

Where Were You

Lily Brett

Where in Warsaw
were you
when the ghetto was burning

that small city
of streets
crowded with corpses

and skinny remains
of uncles aunts
cousins and brothers
mothers and fathers

that they set alight
to burn
for days and nights

were you
watching in the middle
of that heated cheering crowd
on the Aryan side

while Fela
holding her baby
leapt from the top
of a blazing building

like a sparkler
spinning
through the sky

or did you cry
in excitement
as Moniek and his mother
exploded into the night

maybe you
were dazzled
by the display

when Pola
and then Adek
blasted
into the dark

and Shimon who was two
left
like a Catherine wheel
somersaulting off the earth

were you
part of that flushed crowd
that clapped

here goes
another one
with her son

where in Warsaw
were you
when the ghetto was burning.

On the Propensity of the Human Species to Repeat Error

Christina Pacosz

And if they kill others for being who they are
or where they are
Is this a law of history
or simply, what must change?
— Adrienne Rich, *Your Native Land, Your Life*

The world is round.
This should tell us
something, this should
have been our first clue.

> *what goes around*
> *comes around*

Scientists are studying
a rent in the roof of sky
over the South Pole
right now, but poets
need not adhere
to the caution
of the scientific method.

The message is simple:

what goes around
comes around

The battery acid of
Plato's Republic
has finally reached
the ozone layer,
a membrane, protective
like skin or an amniotic sac,

permeable and destructible.

what we take
for granted
will get us
in the end

The Sioux woman's breast
severed from her body,
dried into a pouch
for tobacco,
what book was that?

Or a chosen people's skin
stretched across the heavens,
shade for us to more easily
read the harsh lesson
of history.

It Is Raining on the House of Anne Frank

Linda Pastan

It is raining on the house
of Anne Frank
and on the tourists
herded together under the shadow
of their umbrellas,
on the perfectly silent
tourists who would rather be
somewhere else
but who wait here on stairs
so steep they must rise
to some occasion
high in the empty loft,
in the quaint toilet,
in the skeleton
of a kitchen
or on the map—
each of its arrows
a barb of wire—
with all the dates, the expulsions,
the forbidding shapes
of continents.
And across Amsterdam it is raining
on the Van Gogh Museum

where we will hurry next
to see how someone else
could find the pure
center of light
within the dark circle
of his demons.

Response

Linda Pastan

a ban on the following subject matter: the Holocaust, grandparents,
Friday night candle lighting . . . Jerusalem at dusk.

— from the poetry editor of *Response*

It is not dusk
in Jerusalem
it is simply morning

and the grandparents have disappeared
into the Holocaust
taking their sabbath candles with them.

Light your poems, hurry.
Already the sun is leaning
toward the west

though the grandparents and candles
have long since burned down
to stubs.

God Teaches Us How to Forgive, But We Forget

Louis Phillips

The Night & Fog Decree:
Under cover of darkness,
Persons I love are spirited away.
On this highway, no immunity.
Thru the February fog,
One can see
Valentines of barbed wire,
One is enchanted by
Waterfalls of blue gas,
Geysers of quicklime.
Soil takes on the smell of fat
& even the rain does not help.
What is the good of men
Who dispatch their own kind?
Think of an answer.
I cannot.
God invented forgiveness
To shame His enemies,
But I am grieving planet
Blown off course.
Look, you murdering bastards,
I shall not forget what you did,

What your fathers did,
& their fathers before them.
Nacht-und-nebel erlass.*
What was once human
Is hurt forever.

---

*The Night and Fog Decree (an order in the dead of night).

Perhaps You Wish to Learn
Another Language

Louis Phillips

Sometime in the late twentieth century,
While you watch blue flowers tattoo a field,
An acquaintance will mention, offhand,
Trying to make it seem casual,
Auschwitz or Belsen and so many dead Jews.
Of course, the conversation must change.
The four-dimensioned world rattles.
"Yes, yes, it was all on television,
The cyanide that blossomed into bones."
So you sigh and drink the final cup of coffee,
Lukewarm, sugared, black,
like breathing that refuses to be stilled.
Perhaps you wish to learn another language?
A yellow star rises into our sky,
But there is no shining from it.

The Unseen

Robert Pinsky

In Kraków it rained, the stone arcades and cobbles
And the smoky air all soaked one penetrating color
While in an Art Nouveau café, on harp-shaped chairs,

We sat making up our minds to tour the death camp.
As we drove there the next morning past farms
And steaming wooden villages, the rain had stopped.

Though the sky was still gray. A young guide explained
Everything we saw in her tender, hectoring English:
The low brick barracks; the heaped-up meticulous

Mountains of shoes, toothbrushes, hair; one cell
Where the Pope had prayed and placed flowers; logbooks,
Photographs, latrines—the whole unswallowable

Menu of immensities. It began drizzling again,
And the way we paused to open or close the umbrellas,
Hers and ours, as we went from one building to the next,

Had a formal, dwindled feeling. We felt bored
And at the same time like screaming biblical phrases:
I am poured out like water; Thine is the day and

Thine is also the night; I cannot look to see
My own right hand . . . I remembered a sleep-time game,
A willed dream I had never thought of by day before:

I am there; and granted the single power of invisibility,
Roaming the camp at will. At first I savor my mastery
Slowly by creating small phantom diversions,

Then kill kill kill kill, a detailed and strangely
Passionless inward movie: I push the man holding
The crystals down from the gas chamber roof, bludgeon

The pet collie of the commandant's children
And in the end flush everything with a vague flood
Of fire and blood as I drift on toward sleep.

In a blurred finale, like our tour's—eddying
In a downpour past the preserved gallows where
The Allies hung the commandant, in 1947.

I don't feel changed, or even informed—in that,
It's like any other historical monument; although
It is true that I don't ever sleep at night anymore

Prowl rows of red buildings unseen, doing
Justice like an angry god to escape insomnia. And so,
O discredited Lord of Hosts, your servant gapes

Obediently to swallow various doings of us, the most
Capable of all your former creatures—we have
No shape, we are poured out like water, but still

We try to take in what won't be turned from in despair:
As if, just as we turned toward the fumbled drama
Of the religious art shop window to accuse you

Yet again, you were to slit open your red heart
To show us at last the secret of your day and also,
Because it also is yours, of your night.

Gypsy Soup

Morrie Warshawski

Tonight I eat
Gypsy Soup
with my wife and

daughter. We break bread
together and try to
remember the words to

a prayer. We three
gypsies spoon up
songs to one another

on imaginary violins.
Sad songs. Songs that
take us from pain to

joy and back again.
If I tell a joke this
all might disappear.

But, tonight, nothing
is funny. The mad
men downtown are hard

at work before dawn
sprucing up our city
with lies. The

joke is so funny it
hurts. I know
gypsies died too

in the ovens.
Their big feet and
garish shoes passed

down, like my weak
right arm, from
generation to generation.

Daughter, tonight my
soup has onions and
garlic all mixed with

love for you and
for a life that will
someday sit

in a sports car laughing
slicing through a stiff
wind straight ahead.

THE AFTERMATH

Yellow Stars

Michael Waters

*Starting on April 29, 1942, the Dutch Jews were forced to wear a
yellow Star of David.*

Crossing the Prinsengracht canal
   from the greengrocers' shops
      to the bookstalls and cafés,

grasping my mother's hand,
   the water below sweeping
      winter's debris to the sea,

I spotted three yellow stars
   bicycling toward me, fallen,
      I guess, from the sky.

I gazed through layers of air—
   daylight, but I could tell
      the stars were no longer there.

Later I saw yellow stars
   everywhere: on trams, swaying
      to Wagner in the park,

yellow stars trying to feel
   at home, hovering over
      little stars, their children.

But soon the stars floated
    away, puffs of smoke
        over the opening fields,

the icy blossoms of jasmine.
    Then winter again, our flowers
        gone, the stars vanished.

Where did the yellow stars go?
    Do you, like me, long to know,
        staring into the night

sky to search among the white,
    thermal stars, the flaring
        orange, for those few

yellow stars that returned
    home, that call down now
        to this strange planet:

behold us in the milky
    light of creation
        waiting to be born.

Vigil in the Darkness

Dean Smith

I

The instruments of torture
preside above the village
in the castle dark

from the time of Luther
reserved for heretics,
peasant rebels and witches,

each painful deviation
given a strong prescription.

The Hacker's Chair, a throne of spikes
called Maiden's Womb,
tightened to the witches' dimensions

enough to leave an impression
on any aspiring demoness.

The *Schädleknacker* or "headcrusher"
a primitive device to shrink
heads of heretical conviction,

and the *Säge*, a jagged-tooth saw
with henchmen on either side
of the ingrate, hung upside down

straddling the blade, designed
to keep him alive until
the teeth reached the sternum.

II
And even these lowly devices
cannot begin to compare
with the industrialization of hatred

at Auschwitz, Bergen-Belsen, and Dachau
genius turning inward upon
life itself, and these names

supposedly deterrents against
the recurrence of history
as I try to sleep

amidst news of another attack
on a party of immigrants
with a Molotov cocktail, a faint

reminder of the poisonous gas,
an indelible scar, bandaged by time
and threatening to open fresh wounds.

III
Drunk with sadness in the Kleige Möhr*
a German man wept about the murders
("Do you know our history?")

---

*Name of a bar in Heidelberg.

before he crashed to the floor
unable to make a difference,
escaping from the outside world

where anything can happen
if we forget the idea of Holocaust,
and give up the vigil in the darkness.

There Are Times You Must Wonder

J. R. Solonche

There are times you must wonder what
you would have done had you been there.
You would have run at the first foot on
the step, the first knock, or fought right
there, at the door, right then, or given in,
meekly, and gone with them the way the others
went, like sleepwalkers. And later, at
the rail station, you would have grabbed
under a guard's arm for his gun, shot
as many of them, him at least, before you
yourself were shot by another one. And later,
in one of the cattle cars, with no light,
with no air, certainly with no more hallucinations
of hope, you would have taken your glasses off,
dropped them to the floor, stepped on them,
and with a shard of the lens, cut a vein.
And later you would have refused to eat,
given away the food, or let it be stolen.
You never wonder if you would have lived.
You never would have lived. That was a sin.

Pinball Wizards

Mike Frenkel

in the pinball wizardry
of human history
a metal ball is fired
and rolls through streets
and villages.
lights flash,
sirens sound,
points are tabulated.

Hitler's mustache dances.
his eyes are frozen black
as he humps the machine;
white knuckles enforce
his rhythm.
FDR flicks an ash.
Stalin peers over
the swastika shoulder;
he is drooling as he
again awaits his turn.

Feeding Stray Cats

Yala Korwin

To his wife, Sammy;
to son and daughter, Daddy.
The neighbors say he's g.ntle,
a grandpa feeding stray cats.

Twice a day he walks
almost twenty minutes
to the temple Beth-Sholom,
so they can have a minyan.

The congregation is grateful
for the velvet ark curtain
donated in honor
of his mother and father,

sisters Rachel, Sarah,
brothers Avram and Joel,
wife Dinah and baby
murdered by the Nazis.

To former camp inmates
he was a Bloody Szymek,
a handsome six-footer
who raged sputtering insults.

To the sickly laggard
unable to walk fast enough,
a punishing fist crushing
a skull like a walnut.

To the starving thief
who made a hasty meal
of a stolen rabbit,
he was a well-fed hangman.

To the score of wretches
in the hospital hut,
the angel of death
denying a handful of coal.

To the rabbi's daughter
in the women's enclosure,
a son of Lilith,
demon of frenzy and lust.

To his wife, Sammy;
to son and daughter, Daddy.
The neighbors say he's gentle,
a grandpa feeding stray cats.

The Distance between Two Towns

Enid Shomer

Halfway between the Black Sea
and the Baltic, in the bulge
east of Lublin which often
changed flags (now Polish,
now Russian), were two Jewish
hamlets less than forty miles
apart: Shepatovka and Kremenets.

For twenty years I thought
finding you was ordinary luck,
meeting as we did in mid-Atlantic
on a Greek ship bound for Tel Aviv.
But now I know the map threw
its fine blue net around us.
Though my grandfather left

Shepatovka for America in 1905,
though the Nazis killed every child
in Kremenets but you,
our marriage looks the product
of a matchmaker's scheme:
the granddaughter of the carpenter
wed to the neighboring coachman's son.

The only accident, it seems,
was spotting the design in my atlas.
I was searching for my roots
on the pale green of the Soviet Union
when my finger, touching my town,
touched yours. The names are side
by side, only us between them now.

Daily Stones

Shel Krakofsky

every day
the smooth, unmortared
wall of stones beckons
to this distant suburb
every day
the cobblestones under
my grandparents' feet
remain under my own
every day
the harsh rocks that
encircled their ghettos
are erected elsewhere
every day
Ishmael throws stones
at his half-brother
and they strike me
every day
I desire neither David's
slingstone nor Goliath's
spear and armor
every day
I wish David had smitten
the Philistine with his
harp and song

A Night Out

Dannie Abse

Friends recommended the new Polish film
at the Academy in Oxford Street.
So we joined the ever melancholy queue
of cinemas. A wind blew faint suggestions
of rain toward us, and an accordion.
Later, uneasy, in the velvet dark
we peered through the cutout oblong window
at the spotlit drama of our nightmares:
images of Auschwitz almost authentic,
the human obscenity in close-up.
Certainly we could imagine the stench.

Resenting it, we forgot the barbed wire
was but a prop and could not scratch an eye;
those striped victims merely actors like us.
We saw the camp orchestra assembled,
we heard the solemn gaiety of Bach,
scored by the loud arrival of an engine,
its impotent cry, and its guttural trucks.
We watched, as we munched milk chocolate,
trustful children, no older than our own,
strolling into the chambers without fuss,
while smoke, black and curly, oozed from chimneys.

Afterward, at a loss, we sipped coffee
in a bored espresso bar nearby
saying very little. You took off one glove.
Then to the comfortable suburb swiftly
where, arriving home, we garaged the car.
We asked the au pair girl from Germany
if anyone had phoned at all, or called,
and, of course, if the children had woken.
Reassured, together we climbed the stairs
undressed together, and naked together,
in the dark, in the marital bed, made love.

Between the Lines

Michael Hamburger

Yesterday, just before being transported back to prison, I committed a terrible gaffe. Two people came out of the interrogation room. One of them, tall, elegant, speaking a very cultivated French, looked so tormented, as though about to break down. I asked him with concern: "Vous ont-ils malmené?" "Qui ça?" "Mais eux." He looked at me, shrugged his shoulders, and walked on. Then the German sentry said: "But that's a Gestapo man."
— Prison diary of E. A. Rheinhardt
Nice, 22 January 1944

Later, back in my cell, back in the thick stench
From the bucket shared with three men whose dreams are of flesh
Not for beating or fondling but eating, I laugh, laugh
As never before in that place, even when gorged with a treat
Of gift food from a parcel. For then I would drift
Away from our common attrition by hunger and filth
To my garden, those hardly believable flowers
That may open again though I am not there to tend them,
To my bed and, almost, the mingling of bodies in lust,
And would hate the voice that clattered into my refuge
With a curse or a joke. Now they are close to me,
My fellow victims, decent men at the most,
Blundering into death as I do, devoid of a fury to hurl
Against our tormentors, the furious burners of books
Numb with the icy need to know nothing, be strong.
I laugh, laugh at their strength, at our feebleness
And laughing feel how one I could not believe in

Allows me to blaze like his martyrs, consumes me
With love, with compassion; and how the soul
Anatomists cannot locate even now will rise up
when my turn comes to blunder again, when I cry
To the killer who cracks my joints: "Je te comprends, mon ami . . ."

In a Cold Season

Michael Hamburger

Part 1 of a five-part poem concerning Adolf Eichmann

I

Words cannot reach him in his prison of words
Whose words killed men because those men were words
Women and children who to him were numbers
And still are numbers though reiterated
Launched into air to circle out of hearing
And drop unseen, their metal shells not broken.
Words cannot reach him though I spend more words
On words reporting words reiterated
When in his cage of words he answered words
That told how with his words he murdered men
Women and children who were words and numbers
And he remembered or could not remember
The words and numbers they reiterated
To trap in words the man who killed with words.
Words cannot reach the children, women, men
Who were not words or numbers till they died
Because ice-packed in terror shrunk minds clung
To numbers words that did not sob or whimper
As children do when packed in trucks to die
That did not die two deaths as mothers do
Who see their children packed in trucks to die.

Hidden

Anne Kind

They have forgiven us
It is official
Acclaimed by the Senatskanzlei.

We were never proved guilty
Although Jesus of Nazareth
Remains a problem between us.

Thoughts unwind
Like a bandage across the eyes;
The wound is weeping.

Who was waving flags
Daubing stars, throwing stones
On Kristallnacht?

No one claims that notoriety.
Für einen Augenblick*
Sight is restored and then
The bandage is rewound.

---

*For a split second, in the blink of the eye.

Trying to Hide Treblinka

Jon Silkin

For Jon and Elaine Glover

Blessed is the lupine sown to thwart
what our soldiers' hands raised to the light:
a camp with no architectural style,
with a name like this, Treblinka,
and the unnameable, blessed be He, God. *Schlaf*,
as You must, in sleep's grace
of abandoned bliss. And you, God's sweet.
Blessed be He.

Maculate flower.
Blessed the lupine, thick snapable haulm
with innocuous hairs; blessed its noxious seed,
petals, a bird-shaped milky blue.
Blessed the lupine, with no mind to choose a soil
but what sustains it, and what flowers
its unending ignorance. The animal God,
this salmon-spawner, blesses.

The camp, a hole in the eye; its zone, the flowers' assart.
A hill swells with breath and flowers: some blue,
some faded blood ones, that sink their roots
in shreds of carbon made visible
with hours of damp archaeology. Unappeasable
the claws, as they travail
that earth their hands troweled.

Friends

Lotte Kramer

To call you faithful would not be enough.
You came at night because the laws were wild
With hate. It could have meant a broken, rough
Diminished life for you and for your child;

It could have been your end. But when they burnt
The temples, when they rent the doors apart
That held our coffined world, when they interned
And chained the silent men and many hearts

Translated fear to death, you found the way
To us. Even before the cattle trucks
Ordained a new stage of the cross, that day,
Your comfort marked a constancy. It brushed

all bitterness away I might have clutched
As a distorting mask. With love you judged.

Neither Nor

Georg Kreisler

Do you consider it easy?
Do you consider it difficult?
It's neither easy nor difficult, believe me.
Do you consider it foul?
Do you consider it fair?
It's neither foul nor fair, believe me.
Just forget about having a home
for the rest of your life!
And don't ever say: "I'm going home,"
because you're not!

Do you consider it a matter of intelligence?
Do you consider it a matter of stupidity?
It's neither intelligent nor stupid, believe me.
You think screaming will help?
You think being silent will?
Neither screaming nor silence, believe me.
You'll just have to work more and get less than
the others,
without constantly feeling sorry for yourself.
And it's immaterial whether you're intelligent or
stupid.

Because they'll say:
"He's just a stupid Jew,"
or they'll say: "That Jew's too smart for his own
good."

Do you consider that rotten?
Or do you consider it all right?
It's neither rotten nor all right, believe me.
Does it make you afraid?
Or, on the contrary, courageous?
Neither afraid nor courageous, believe me.
You'll just have to keep wandering on the edge
of the world.
But don't be angry about that.
It's sufficient that you know
that you are like everybody else,
and that everybody else knows
that you are different.

English version by the author

Walls

Willy Verkauf-Verlon

If the walls between us
were made of glass,
we'd have shattered them
long ago
and we'd have walked
over the pieces
to each other.

But the walls between us
are invisible.
They are hard to penetrate
since they run through
our hearts and spirits.

Love of Austria

Herbert Kuhner

No one
loved Austria
like its Jews

That love
apparently
couldn't be
destroyed
by humiliation

it couldn't be
expunged
by the theft
and destruction
of property

Nor could it be
beaten out
whipped out
bitten out by dogs

It had to be
gassed out

All the Generations Before Me

Yehuda Amichai

All the generations that preceded me contributed me
in small amounts, so that I would be erected here in Jerusalem
all at once, like a house of prayer or a charity institution.
That commits one. My name is the name of my contributors.
That commits one.

I am getting to be the age my father was when he died.
My last will shows many superscriptions.
I must change my life and my death
daily, to fulfill all the predictions
concerning me. So they won't be lies.
That commits one.

I have passed my fortieth year.
There are posts they will not let me fill
because of that. Were I in Auschwitz,
they wouldn't put me to work.
They'd burn me right away.
That commits one.

Translated by Robert Friend

Dachau

Joan McGinnis

Dachau,
an extra day in Munich and Dachau so close.
Could I do it, could I go?
So much easier to go somewhere else, somewhere pleasant.
But that would be cowardly, not facing the fear.
Would it make me physically sick?
Could I not go and live with myself later?
I had spent so many years in an intellectual search
for the answer to the question, "How could the German
people not know the Holocaust was taking place?"

Six million Jews. The sheer vastness of that number
made such an impression on a nine-year-old mind.
So many human lives lost.
Did no one care enough to do anything?
Now, here I was so close to Dachau, I must go.

A raw, gray, rainy day.
The train was on time,
a short trip through the Munich suburbs.
A bus to the camp.
Dachau, a Bavarian suburb,
till the bus turned the corner and stopped.
All the passengers got off, not really sure where to go.
Directly across the street high hedges and I. M. Farben.
This was a work camp as well as a death camp!

Of course they knew! How could the residents
of that town, the other workers of that factory
be in contact day after day and not know?

One of the passengers headed back away from the bus,
without speaking we all followed not sure where to go.
The pavement led into the camp.
A modern list on the wire fence of things visitors
were prohibited from doing
seemed to establish a restrictive mood.
No guides, only a diagram on the wall of the
first building. Ahead the barracks.
People had broken into groups of 2 or 3,
most walked silently alone
through the lightly falling rain.

The barracks, why did they seem so familiar,
like every movie I had seen of them. STARK.
The photos graphic. And all so neat, so symmetrical.
Count the foundations, how many had passed through here?
Back toward the religious memorials, one each.
All so stark so barren. The only human touch
was in the Protestant building
where it was possible to sign your name.

The ovens. Off to the left, across a
small stream. White inside, neat. Why
the strong feeling of revulsion that drove
me quickly outside? The increasing
sense of the size of the camp, the desolation.
Outside, a small memorial and flowers.

Out of place or fitting?
I went to the next building.
Down the long driveway. The solitary confinement building.
What did solitary confinement mean in a place like this?
What kind of extra punishment was that?
There was no sense of humanness here, but solitude, alone.

Exiting the building, the rain had increased,
I put up my umbrella and stepped over
to offer cover for a woman exiting at the same time.
"Thank you," she said, in an American accent.
"You're welcome," I replied.
"Oh, you're an American!"
There was an instant bond in her tone.
We had both been shaken in that building, and a human
connection was welcome. We both needed to express to
each other our need to have come here.
To have it make sense.

She was a Jewess from Chicago, in her late thirties.
Her parents did not understand her need
to come here, to Germany.
Her unspoken message asked me to understand.
Her words queried my motive,
I was not a Jew, what drove me to come?
We talked as we walked through the rain to the
final building with the displays,
parted as we entered. We had established contact,
human warmth and an understanding at one of the most
moving moments of my life. A connection.

We had entered the building at the exit.
I went through the exhibits in that direction,
effect to cause. The aerial photographs at the time of the
Allied Liberation confirming the size and position
there adjacent to the highway, the factory,
the surrounding homes. The numbers who entered
each year from 1932 to 1945. The symbols
each group was forced to wear. The gold Star of David,
the pink triangle, the others. All the groups
who died. The lists of books, of authors whose
works were banned, were burned.
Conformity that led to death.
I had studied it all for so long, had sat
in graduate classes for hours viewing the
propaganda films the Nazis had produced.
It was all so familiar.
Why? How could it happen?
It did. And they knew. They had to know.
That fact was clear in my mind.

Slowly something else became clear.
My quest had been a metaphor
for my own situation. How could my family
not have noticed what had happened
to that 6-year-old girl? Raped by an uncle,
but never told.
Is denial so strong in the human psyche,
that the most horrendous acts can be committed
by one human upon another, that bystanders
can't bear to remember? Deny it really happened?
Denial and its consequences are forever.

Hate Shall Not Impale Me

Marguerite M. Striar

I collect poems on the Holocaust
Words woven out of pain remembered
threads of empathy.

There must be happier themes
to engage my daytime thoughts,
my nighttime dreams,
more robust and healthier companions
than these skeletons of Jews,
their unrepentant murderers.

Now, the poems chosen,
pages numbered,
awaiting only the publisher's decision
and the reader's,
you'd think I could sleep at last
but, eyes closed, I tremble
as SS troops surround me,
their bayonets impale me,
hunger gnaws, torture, terror . . .
naked, I crawl on all fours on frozen ground
to the ovens,
the path well marked in scarlet calligraphy.
Flames consume me.
I end in smoke
that finally floats free.

I wake and, shaking, ask
What now my task?
As a Jew?
A member of the human race?
Shall I let hate impale me?
And so perpetuate
the downward plunge?

God, let me remember with rage
how Nazis dared evil our world
into a rotting abattoir.
Let me be aware and wary
of other tyrants, incomplete and unevolved,
even now committing,
scheming to commit,
such crimes again.

Do I then, sentient, sink backward
into the same muddy morass
of hate and revenge?

Or is there another way?

Biographical Notes

A

DANNIE ABSE is a respected British physician as well as a renowned poet. He was born and grew up in Wales and is now a Londoner. Many of his story poems are based on his medical experiences or on Jewish tradition. The two poems in this anthology, "A Night Out" and "No More Mozart," are from *White Coat, Purple Coat: Collected Poems 1948–1988*, first published in England by Century Hutchinson, Ltd., in 1989 and in the United States by Persea Books in 1991. *Remembrance of Crimes Past* was published by Persea Books in 1993.

CORNEL ADAM. *See* CORNEL LENGYEL

A. ALVAREZ is a poet, novelist, literary critic, and author of many nonfiction books on topics ranging from suicide to divorce, poker, and mountaineering. His most recent book, *Night: Life, Night Language, Sleep and Dreams,* published by W. W. Norton in 1995, is based on the author's research and personal experience. His books of fiction include *Hers* (Random House, 1981), *Hunt* (Bantam Books, 1981), and *Day of Atonement* (Random House, 1992). His books of literary criticism include *The Shaping Spirit, The School of Donne, Beyond All This Fiddle: Essays 1955–1967,* and *Samuel Beckett* (Viking Press, 1973). Collections of his poetry are *Lost, Penguin Modern Poets No. 18, Apparition* (with paintings by Charles Blackman), and *Autumn to Autumn and Collected Poems 1953–1976.* Alvarez lives in London and is a frequent contributor to the *New Yorker.*

YEHUDA AMICHAI, Israel's most famous poet, was born in Würzburg, Germany in 1924. In 1936, his idyllic childhood was interrupted when he and his family fled to Palestine to escape the Nazis. Educated in Jerusalem, he became a teacher and a soldier, fighting first with the British Army's Jewish Brigade in World War II, then with the Palmakh in 1948 in Israel's War of Independence, and with the Israeli Army in 1956 and 1967. A writer of novels and plays as well as poetry, his writing reflects his own history and that of Israel. The Holocaust is ever in his consciousness. When he writes of the commonplace and of our common humanity, it is with poignancy and humor. His poetry collections include *Songs of Jerusalem and Myself* (1973); *Amen* (Harper and Row, 1977); *Time: Poems* (Harper and Row, 1979); *Love Poems: A Bilingual Edition* (Harper and Row, 1981); *The Selected Poetry of Yehuda Amichai* (Harper and Row, 1986); and *Even a Fist Was Once a Palm with Fingers* (Harper Perennial, 1991). His poetry has been translated into many languages, and his novel *Not of This Time, Not of This Place* has been translated into English (Harper and Row, 1968).

ROBERT ANBIAN's first collection, *Bohemian Airs & Other Kefs* (Night Horn Books), appeared in 1982; his second collection, *Antinostalgia* (Ruddy Duck Press), appeared in 1992. Anbian is an editor and journalist in San Francisco who writes on politics, books, film, and video. His poems have appeared in *City Lights Review, Oxygen,* and the electronic journal *R if/t.* His mother, a native Frenchwoman, was a teenager in occupied Paris who lost two brothers in the French Resistance.

FRIEDA ARKIN has published a novel and eleven short stories, one of which appeared in *American Short Fiction* published by University of Texas Tech Press in 1991. She is a retired teacher of anthropology (Hunter College, New York City). Several members of her family (on her mother's side) were murdered by the Nazis.

LINDA ASHEAR's work has been published in many literary magazines. In 1989, her first book of poems, *Toward the Light,* was published by The Croton Review Press. Presently, she runs writing workshops for children and adults in Westchester County, New York.

B

CRYSTAL V. BACON is assistant professor of communications at Gloucester County College in New Jersey. She has published poems in *Ontario Review* and *Massachusetts Review*. Referring to her poem "Kristallnacht, 1991," Bacon says, "My mother grew up in Nazi Germany and says very little about the Holocaust. Whatever the truth is, it is elusive. Only the pain of one's history is real. This poem reflects my continual vigilance against the treason of forgetting."

ANNA BART's poetry has appeared in many literary journals, including *Lip Service, Borderlands, Embers, Rhino,* and *La Bella Figura. The Dream Book: An Anthology of Writings by Italian-American Women* (Schocken Books, 1985) includes four of her poems. Her book on the creative art of the mentally retarded has been published by Charles C. Thomas. She lives in Connecticut, where she is working on a collection of short stories.

JILL BART's poem "The Shower" won first prize for poetry in the *West Wind Review* in 1991. Her poetry collection *First Light* was published by Paumanok in 1988; *The Naked & The Nude* was published by Birnham Wood in 1993. Her poems have appeared in *Ms., Poetry East,* and *Xanadu.* She is a recipient of a Taproot/NEA grant.

WALTER BAUER was born in Merseburg, Germany, in 1904. In 1952 he emigrated to Canada. After years of hardship he became a professor of German literature at the University of Toronto. He died in Toronto in 1976. He is the author of some forty volumes of poetry and prose.

BRUCE BENNETT is the author of three volumes of poetry: *Straw into Gold* (Cleveland State, 1984), *I Never Danced With Mary Beth* (FootHills), and *Taking Off* (Orchises, 1992). He is professor of English and director of creative writing at Wells College in Aurora, New York.

JUDITH BERKE's first book, *White Morning,* was published by Wesleyan University Press in 1989. Her chapbook *Acting Problems* was published by Silverfish Review in 1993.

LISA BERNSTEIN's poetry books include *Anorexia* (Five Fingers, 1985) and *The Transparent Body* (Wesleyan University Press, 1989). Her poems have been published widely in periodicals and anthologies. She received a fellowship from the National Endowment for the Arts in 1992. She is also a singer, songwriter, spoken-word artist, and rapper whose EP, *Be the Word* (Piece of Pie Records), can be heard nationwide on college and noncommercial radio.

HAROLD BLACK was born in Goniatz, Poland in 1920. His family escaped the Russian-Polish War by migrating to Mexico and entered the United States in 1929. Now retired from his career in urban planning and housing, he devotes himself to writing full time. He began writing poetry while a student at Wayne State University and has been widely published in literary magazines. His work has appeared in several anthologies, including *Ears Chamber* and George Washington University's *Evidence of Community.*

ARIEL BLOCH is emeritus professor of Semitic linguistics at the University of California at Berkeley. Most of his books and articles deal with Arabic and Hebrew syntax and semantics. He has translated *The Window: Selected Poems of Dahlia Ravikovitch* and *The Song of Songs* in collaboration with Chana Bloch. Among his awards are a National Endowment of the Humanities Senior Fellowship, the President of the University of California's Research Fellowship in the Humanities, and a National Science Foundation grant.

CHANA BLOCH is professor of English literature and director of the creative writing program at Mills College. She has published two books of poems, *The Secrets of the Tribe* (Tilbury House, 1980) and *The Past Keeps Changing* (Sheep Meadow Press, 1992), and a critical study of George Herbert, *Spelling the Word* (University of California Press, 1985). Her translations include *The Selected Poetry of Yehuda Amichai* (with Stephen Mitchell), *A Dress of Fire* and *The Window* by Dahlia Ravikovitch, and *The Song of Songs* (the last two with Ariel Bloch). Among her awards are the Discovery Award, the Poets & Writers Exchange Award, and the Columbia University Translation Center Award.

JOHN BRADLEY teaches creative writing and composition at

Northern Illinois University and is the editor of *Atomic Ghost: Poets Respond to the Nuclear Age,* an international poetry anthology published by Coffee House Press in 1995. He won the 1989 Washington Prize for his book *Love in Idleness: The Poetry of Roberto Zingarello* (Wordworks, 1989).

REEVE ROBERT BRENNER, besides being a writer, is a rabbi, scholar, and social activist. He has written on a wide variety of Jewish subjects including the Holocaust. His book *American Jewry and the Rise of Nazism* received the 1967 YIVO Jewish Scholarship Prize. For nine years he conducted research among survivors in Israel on the way Holocaust victims themselves came to understand the meaning of the Holocaust in the light of Jewish belief and practice. The result was the book *The Faith and Doubt of Holocaust Survivors,* first published by the Free Press in 1980 and reprinted by Jason Aaronson Publishers in 1997. In a lighter vein he wrote *A Yiddle's Riddles: The Jewish Riddle Collection* (Shapolsky Publishing, 1991). His current book project is *Eternal Jerusalem Poetry.* During his stay in Israel he invented a new sport, bankshot basketball, which allows athletes in wheelchairs or with other handicaps to compete equally with everyone else.

LILY BRETT was born in Germany after the war and emigrated to Australia with her parents in 1948. She has published six collections of poetry and three volumes of fiction. Her novel *What God Wants* (University of Queensland Press, 1991) won Australia's National Steele Rudd Award in 1992. She is the only writer to have won Australia's highest award for fiction as well as poetry. *The Auschwitz Poems* (Scribe, 1986) won the 1987 Victorian Premier's Award for Poetry. Her second book, *Poland and Other Poems* (Scribe, 1987), won the Mattara Poetry Prize, and her third, *After the War* (Melbourne University Press, 1990), was short-listed for the 1990 Victorian Premier's Award for Poetry. *Things Could Be Worse* (Melbourne University Press, 1990), her first collection of fiction, also received prestigious honors. In 1994, her novel *Just Like That* (Pan Macmillan) was published simultaneously with her fifth volume of poetry, *In Her Strapless Dresses* (Picador/Pan Macmillan). In 1997, she published *Mud in My Tears* (Picador/Pan Macmillan), a book of poems, and *In Full View* (Macmillan), a volume of essays. She lives in

New York with her husband, the Australian painter David Rankin, and their three children.

C

P. M. CALLEN's poems, short stories, and essays have appeared in *Outerbridge, WOMANEWS, Horses All, Cats! Magazine,* and *The Animals' Voice.* She is a frequent contributor to *Between the Species: A Journal of Ethics,* published by the Albert Schweitzer Foundation at the University of California, Berkeley. Her poetry has been included in various anthologies. Her poem "Meditation" was included in an encyclical presented to Pope John Paul II at the conclusion of the international March for Animals to Rome. In 1994, she was awarded the first prize for fiction by Negative Capability Press.

JOAN CAMPION is the author of *In the Lion's Mouth: Gisi Fleischmann and the Jewish Fight for Survival* (University Press of America, 1989) and co-author, with Randall Forte, of a one-act play about Mrs. Fleischmann, *A Woman of Bratislava.* Her articles on a wide variety of subjects have appeared in dozens of magazines and newspapers. A non-Jew, Campion's work has been funded in part by the Memorial Foundation for Jewish Culture and by Simon Wiesenthal's Dokumentationszentrum, Vienna.

MARK CANNADAY was born in the South in 1948. He is an Episcopal priest serving as canon to the Bishop of West Texas. He performed as Otto Frank in *The Diary of Anne Frank.* "As I came to know Otto," he says, "my awareness of the Holocaust and the people who endured it grew more vivid and sacred. I grew up in a new way through that experience and I am changed forever. I offer you this poem as my gift of witness, lament, love and Hope. I survive the Holocaust because of those who suffered, died, survived and continue in Hope. For that, from them, I am eternally grateful."

GRACE CAVALIERI was the producer and host of the radio program *The Poet and the Poem* on WPFW in Washington, D.C., from 1957 to 1997. She is the author of six books of poetry and eighteen produced plays. She is the editor of the *WPFW Poetry Anthology* (1992) and in 1991 produced a dramatic poem performance piece, "Migrations," based on her own life story. Her awards include the PEN/Syndicated Fiction Award and the Corporation for Public Broadcasting's medal for poetry programming. She is currently affiliated with St. Mary's College in Maryland and its poetry workshop.

PAUL CELAN said that his poems were "messages in a bottle," which might or might not be picked up. His poetry was based on the anguish of his experience. Although he survived physically, the Holocaust and its mass killings became a lifelong obsession. Accepting the impossibility of describing Auschwitz literally, he nevertheless felt impelled to find parallel images that would express his psychological asphyxiation.

Born Paul Antschel (then Ancel, then Celan) at Czernowitz in Bukovina, Romania, on November 23, 1920, he became a medical student in France in 1938. He returned to his hometown in 1939, where he continued his studies until 1941, when the German and Romanian forces herded Jews into a ghetto. There he studied Russian. In 1942 his parents were taken to an extermination camp, where his father died of typhus and his mother was murdered by a shot in the neck. Celan was sent to a forced labor camp where he worked on road building. In 1944 the Soviets reoccupied Bukovina. Celan then worked for a while as a field surgeon in the psychiatric unit and continued his studies. In April 1945 he moved to Bucharest, where he obtained work as a publisher's reader and translator of Russian texts into Romanian. Leaving Romania illegally in 1947, he stayed briefly in Vienna, then settled in Paris and began the study of German literature. After receiving his degree in 1950, he became a lecturer in German literature. He married Gisele Lestrange, a graphic artist, in 1952, and had two sons. Celan lived in Paris until he committed suicide by drowning in 1970 at the age of forty-nine. Six volumes of his poetry were published between 1952 and his death, and three more collections posthumously. With the translation of his works into English and other languages, he has achieved worldwide renown.

JUDITH CHALMER's poems have appeared in several literary journals, including *Seneca Review, Spoon River Poetry Review,* and *Prairie Schooner.* She was first-prize winner in the New England

Writers Association annual poetry competition, and also received an honorable mention for both the Pushcart Poetry Prize and the Wildwood Poetry Prize. Her first collection of poems, *Out of History's Junk Jar*, was published by Time Being Books in 1995. She teaches literature and creative writing at Norwich University in Vermont and also to frail elders in a day-care center. Chalmer has dedicated the past several years to researching the life of a woman, now living in Switzerland, who saved many Jews, including Judith's family, as part of the Dutch Resistance during World War II.

LENA L. CHARNEY was born in Poland. She lived in Russia and Germany, then came to the United States by way of Paris and Montreal. A former educator and administrator, she turned to poetry when she retired. Her poems have appeared in *Black Buzzard Review, Wind, Blue Light Review, Gypsy, Elf, Hydra, The Plastic Tower,* and *Breakthrough.*

ELAYNE GOLDMAN CLIFT is a writer and health communication specialist in Potomac, Maryland. Her award-winning fiction, poetry, essays, and articles have appeared in over two dozen magazines and periodicals in North America and abroad. Her books of collected essays include *Telling It Like It Is: Reflections of a Not So Radical Feminist* (Knowledge, Ideas, and Trends, 1991) and *The Road to Radicalism: Further Reflections of a Frustrated Feminist* (OGN Publications, 1994). *Demons Dancing in My Head: Collected Poems 1985–1995* was published by OGN Publications in 1996, as was a short story collection entitled *Croning Tales.* In addition to working in print journalism, she serves as Washington, D.C., reporter for *WINGS Radio,* a globally syndicated news program by and for women.

JEAN COLONOMOS's poems have been published in *Inkling, Iris, 13th Moon, Roh Wedder,* and *West Wind Review,* among other publications. Her plays have been produced in New York City and Los Angeles. Her play *Palm Fever* won the Los Angeles Playwriting Award. She dedicates her poems in this anthology to Lola.

ESTHER CRYSTAL currently teaches creative writing and Holocaust literature at Touro College in New York. She is managing editor of

Emunah Magazine and has had poems published in a variety of anthologies, including an anthology of Jewish women's verse called *From Adam to Tzipporah.* She is a daughter of Holocaust survivors, and a great deal of her work focuses on Holocaust and second-generation issues.

PAUL CUMMINS, a writer and an educator, is the author of *Dachau Song: The Twentieth-Century Odyssey of Herbert Zipper,* which tells the story of Zipper, born in 1904 in Vienna, who was a composer, a conductor, an educator, and a concentration camp survivor. The book was translated into Chinese in Beijing, China, in 1991 and published in 1992 by Peter Lang Publishing, New York. Paul Cummins is the founder of the Crossroads School and is currently its headmaster. His publications include a booklet on Richard Wilbur, several articles on education, and numerous poems. He and his family live in Santa Monica, California.

BRUCE V. J. CURLEY has been published in *Texts-Sounds-Texts, Home Planet News, American Man, Mad Poets Review,* and *The Federal Poet.* Bruce grew up in a diverse Jewish neighborhood where some of his neighbors were Holocaust survivors. While writing a paper on Joseph Goebbels for a class on fascism at the American College in Paris, he had the opportunity to view original Nazi war documents such as newspapers, magazines, posters, and movies. His impressions were made more vivid when he viewed a PBS special on the Holocaust. He committed his feelings to paper in "This Broken Silence."

DAVID CURZON was born in Melbourne, Australia, and has lived in New York City for the past twenty years. He holds a bachelor's degree in physics and a doctorate in economics, and worked for the Australian government, NASA in Washington, and as a professor of economics before joining the United Nations, where he is currently chief of the Central Evaluation Unit. A collection of his poems, *Midrashim* (Cross-Cultural Communications), was published in 1991; *Modern Poems on the Bible: An Anthology* (Jewish Publication Society) was published in 1994; and *The Gospels in Our Image* (Harcourt Brace) was published in 1995. His work also appears in two Oxford anthologies and *The Norton Anthology of World Poetry.* His poetry has been collected in *Dovchik* (Penguin Books Australia,

1996) and *The View from Jacob's Ladder* (Jewish Publication Society, 1996).

Rivka Rass, in a profile of David Curzon for the newspaper *Forward,* writes: "Mr. Curzon . . . is a master synthesizer, bringing together worlds as far apart as Australia and the U.S.A., bureaucracy and poetry, matter and spirit, and most important, the secular and the religious." After writing many poems synthesizing his own secular attitude with traditional biblical texts, he realized that his own family history mirrors much of Jewish history. His father was born in Łódź, Poland, graduated from the Sorbonne in medicine, and emigrated to Australia in 1939, where he married and his son David was born. However, his own parents and younger sister were sent to their deaths in Auschwitz. His only living relative was a sister who survived the war by living in Bulgaria. When David was seventeen, his father killed himself and later his aunt in Bulgaria killed herself, too. In an effort to piece together the fragments of his family, Mr. Curzon has circled the globe between Australia, Israel, Bulgaria, and Poland.

RUTH DAIGON is editor of *Poets On* and author of *A Portable Past* (Realities Library, Contemporary Poets Series, 1987). She won The Eve of St. Agnes Award (Negative Capability) in 1993 and was runner-up in 1994. Her latest poetry collection, *Between One Future and the Next,* was published by Papier-Mâché Press in 1995. She has been a performing poet for the Connecticut Commission on the Arts as well as a professional singer and soprano soloist with New York Pro Musica and Columbia Recordings.

PATRICIA D'ALESSANDRO is a freelance writer, poet, and photographer recently retired from the International Women's Health Coalition in New York City, where she was administrative assistant to the president. She introduced Poetry on the Buses in San Francisco and was the first-place winner of the California Writers Poetry Award of Mills College in 1975. Her work has appeared in many anthologies, among them *Death and Transformation: An Anthology of Poetry from the Sacramento Women Artists and Writers Exhibition, "Un Dia De Muerte," 1994.*

PETER DANIEL was born in Vienna in 1963. His articles have appeared in Jewish journals in Austria and elsewhere, including *Aufbau* in New York. His publications include *Lab-Art: A Manifesto* (David Press, Vienna); *Homage to G'd: Experimental Concrete Text Symbols* (Das Froehliche Wohnzimmer Edition, Vienna); *En-Sof, Eternally, Concerning the Eternal Power of Hebrew Letters* (Edition Splitter, Vienna). Daniel also is the creator of graphics, sculpture, and objects composed of Hebrew letters.

ANNIE DAWID has had short fiction published in *Response: A Contemporary Jewish Review* and in the Spring 1992 issue of the *Jewish Review*, a special issue devoted to the Holocaust. Her poetry has been published in *Eleventh Muse, Voices of America*, an anthology of Western poets, and *Painted Hills Review*. Her first novel, *York Ferry*, published in 1993, is in its second printing from Cane Hill Press.

MARGARET DelGUERCIO is associate professor of English at Monmouth College in West Long Branch, New Jersey, where she teaches Shakespeare and serves as president of the faculty union. Her poetry has been published in little magazines across the country. Recent work has appeared in the *Chattahoochee Review, Journal of N.J. Poets, Sulphur River Literary Review*, and *Treasure House*.

DEBORAH DeNICOLA's book *Where Divinity Begins* was published by Alice James Press in 1994. Her work has appeared in *Antioch Review, Fiction International, The Journal, North American Review*, and other journals. She is currently editing an anthology of contemporary poems on Greek myth entitled *Orpheus & Company*. She teaches creative writing at Massachusetts College of Art and lives in Brookline, Massachusetts.

PETER DESY has had work published in the *New England Review, Literary Review, Quarterly West*, and *Southern Poetry Review*. He is a retired English professor (Ohio University). He has published two chapbooks, one of poetry and one of fiction; his poetry collection *Driving from Columbus* was published by Edwin Mellen Press in 1992.

E

DINA ELENBOGEN has had her poetry published in *Without a Single Answer* (Judah Magnes Press, Berkeley, Calif.), a volume of poems about contemporary Israel; in *Sarah's Daughters Sing* (Ktav, 1990), a sampler of poems by Jewish women; and in *Prairie Schooner.* She has spent a lot of time in Israel and has written extensively on the new Ethiopian immigrants. She received an M.F.A. from the University of Iowa Writer's Workshop and now teaches English and literature of the Holocaust at the University of Illinois at Chicago.

SUE SANIEL ELKIND was born in Pittsburgh in 1913 and died there in 1994. She began writing at age sixty-five with no formal training, and had over six hundred poems published in magazines such as *Negative Capability, Kansas Quarterly, Centennial Review,* and *Crosscurrents.* Her published books were: *No Longer Afraid* (Lintel, 1985); *Waiting for Order* (Naked Man Press, 1987); *Dinosaurs and Grandparents* (MAF Press, 1988); *Another Language* (Papier-Mâché Press, 1986); and *Bare as the Trees* (Papier-Mâché Press, 1992). Elkind's work has appeared in several anthologies. She was awarded the 1977 Esther Scheffler Prize for a poem that appeared in *Centennial Review.*

MARY ENGEL has had poetry appear in *Poet Lore, Cream City Review, Western Medical Journal, the new renaissance,* and *Tar Heel,* as well as the anthology *Peace Is Our Profession* (East River Anthology, 1983). She was awarded first place in a poetry contest sponsored by the Kentucky State Poetry Society and won an award from the Poetry Forum of Pennsylvania.

SAMUEL EXLER was a soldier in the 104th Infantry (Timberwolf) Division, which saw combat during World War II in Belgium, Holland, and Germany; the 104th liberated Nordhausen. Exler's book *Ambition, Fertility, Loneliness* (Lintel Publishing, 1982) was praised by Robert Bly with these words: "I am often moved . . . by the grieving weight of these poems." Exler has published in *Poetry East, Plainsong, International Poetry Review, Literary Review, Newport Review, New York Quarterly,* and other literary magazines.

F

CHRISTOPHER FAHY is the author of the novels *Nightflyer* (Jove, 1982), *Dreamhouse* (Zebra, 1987), *Eternal Bliss* (Zebra, 1988), *The Lyssa Syndrome* (Zebra, 1989), and *The Fly Must Die* (Wash. Inst. Creative Activity, 1993); a volume of short stories, *One Day in the Short Happy Life of Anna Banana* (Coatwise Press, 1988); and a book of poetry, *The End Beginning* (Red Earth Press, 1978). He has published widely in anthologies, and was the winner of the 1987 Maine Arts Commission Fiction Competition.

JOHN FELSTINER is a writer and translator who teaches English and Jewish studies at Stanford University. He is the author of *The Lies of Art: Max Beerbohm's Parody and Caricature* (Knopf, 1972); *Translating Neruda: The Way to Macchu Picchu* (Stanford University Press, 1980); and most recently, *Paul Celan: Poet, Survivor, Jew* (Yale University Press, 1995).

CHARLES FISHMAN is director of the visiting writers program at SUNY Farmingdale and Distinguished Service Professor of English and Humanities in the State University of New York. His most recent book-length titles include *Catlives*, a co-translation of Sarah Kirsch's *Katzenleben*, and *Blood to Remember: American Poets on the Holocaust*, both released in 1991 by Texas Tech University Press. Fishman's *As the Sun Goes Down in Fire* won the 1992 Anabiosis Press chapbook competition, and his volume of poems on the Holocaust, *The Death Mazurka* (Texas Tech University Press, 1989), was nominated for the Pulitzer Prize in Poetry in 1990. His most recent chapbook of poetry, *Nineteenth-Century Rain*, was released by Whistle Press in 1995. Fishman is currently at work on *Flames Ascending: World Poets on the Holocaust*.

JOAN FONDELL received a B.A. in English from UCLA in 1982 and J.D. from Loyola Law School in Los Angeles in 1985. She is a partner in Russo & Fondell, a legal search consulting firm in Galisteo, New Mexico. She is working on a memoir and a law firm mystery.

Fondell is the daughter of a Holocaust survivor—Kurt Fischl

(known as Curt Fondell in the United States), born July 31, 1921, in Brno, Czechoslovakia. He survived Theresienstadt and was transported to Auschwitz in 1942, where he survived the death march and escaped into the woods on the last day of the war. His father, Alexander Fischl, died of pneumonia at Theresienstadt in 1942. His mother, Bertha Jellinek Fischl, was gassed on arrival at Auschwitz in 1942. Curt Fondell died in Los Angeles in 1987.

ROBERT FRAUENGLAS is a freelance writer who has been published in numerous countries. He has been a Jewish activist since 1967, as well as an environmental activist, Soviet Jewry activist, and a veteran of the antiwar movement. He has done human rights work throughout pre-glasnost Eastern Europe and the USSR. In 1978, he completed a 1,200-mile solo hike through Western Europe on behalf of Soviet Jewry.

MIKE FRENKEL was born in Paris in 1950. His parents survived the Holocaust in Romania, but his grandparents and uncle did not. He taught English in the New York City public high schools for many years and is currently an administrator at New York City Technical College of the City University of New York. His poetry has appeared in *Blood to Remember: American Poets on the Holocaust* (Texas Tech University Press, 1991), the *New Press Literary Quarterly*, and *Perspectives* (1991–92).

D. DINA FRIEDMAN has been published in *Amelia, Calyx, The Sun, Hurricane Alice, Earth Daughters, Sh'ma,* and *Home Planet News.* She runs creative writing workshops in Northampton, Massachusetts.

KENNY FRIES has had poetry published in *Five Fingers Review, The American Voice,* and *Mudfish.* He received the Gregory Kolovakos Award for AIDS Writing in 1991 and a Lambda Literary Award nomination for his book of poems *The Healing Notebooks* (Open Books, 1990). He is the author of *Body Remember: A Memoir* (Dutton) and *Anesthesia: Poems* (Adiscado Press), and editor of *Staring Back: The Disability Experience from the Inside Out* (Dutton Plume).

4

DAVID GERSHATOR'S poetry and translations have appeared in *Confrontation, Jewish Currents, Anthaeus,* and *The Caribbean Writer. Play Mas' (Downtown Poets),* a collection of Caribbean poetry, was published in 1981. He edited and translated Federico García Lorca's *Selected Letters* (New Directions, 1983). A poetry chapbook, *Elijah's Child,* was published by Cross Cultural Communications in 1992. His poem "Jars" won an award from the Judah Magnes Museum in Berkeley, and he received a New York State Creative Arts Public Service Award for poetry.

JACOB GLATSTEIN is one of the most important figures in modern Yiddish literature. Glatstein's prodigious literary output included sixteen volumes of poetry, seven volumes of essays and criticism, and four novels. Critic Irving Howe has called him "a major writer in any language." For fifty-eight years Glatstein lived and wrote in New York City (he came to the United States from Poland at age seventeen), establishing himself as a noted publicist, editor of many Yiddish-language periodicals, and coeditor of several important anthologies, including one of the first anthologies of Holocaust literature in English. Glatstein, whose work has been translated into Spanish, French, German, Polish, Hebrew, and English was the recipient of a number of prestigious literary prizes for both poetry and prose. Before his death in 1971 he recorded his work for the Harvard Vocarium Series. In November 1972 the first Jacob Glatstein Memorial Prize was awarded by *Poetry* magazine.

BARBARA GOLDBERG'S grandparents died in Auschwitz and her uncle was a Holocaust survivor. Her most recent books are *After the First Rain: Israeli Poems on War and Peace* (Syracuse University Press in association with Dryad Press, 1998) and *The First Yes: Poems about Communicating* (American Speech-Language-Hearing Foundation in association with Dryad Press, 1997). She is the coeditor of *The Stones Remember* (The Word Works, 1991), an anthology of contemporary

Israeli poetry, which received the Witter Bynner Foundation Award and was selected as an Outstanding Book in 1993 by *Choice* magazine. She has twice won the PEN/Syndicated Fiction Project Award (1983, 1985), has held two fellowships from the National Endowment for the Arts (1991, 1996), and received three Maryland State Arts Council Grants (1987, 1992, 1997). Goldberg is the executive editor of *Poet Lore* and director of editorial services for the American Speech-Language-Hearing Association. She lives in Chevy Chase, Maryland.

DARCY GOTTLIEB's poems have been published in many small magazines and anthologies. She is the winner of the Dylan Thomas and Christopher Morley Awards given by the Poetry Society of America. Her first book of poems, *No Witness but Ourselves,* was published by University of Missouri Press in 1973. In 1980, *Matters of Contention,* a chapbook of revisionist poems about women in history and legend, appeared. Until 1997 she taught composition at the University of Miami.

ROBERTA GOULD's books include *Dream Yourself Flying* (Four Zoas Press, 1979), *Writing Air, Written Water* (Waterside Press, 1980), *Only Rock and Other Poems* (Folder Editions, 1986), *Esta Naranja* (Lince Editores, 1988), and *Not by Blood Alone* (Waterside Press, 1990).

MIMI GROSSBERG was born in 1905 in Vienna. Before emigrating to the United States, she was librarian for the Volkshochschule Ottakring. She has published volumes of her own poetry and has gained distinction as the editor of anthologies of poetry by Austrian émigrés in America.

JACOB GUSEWELLE writes poetry and short stories. He has a Ph.D. in European history from the University of California and has been a college professor. He has a special interest in the Holocaust because "I survived it and 6,000,000 didn't."

LEO HABER is adjunct professor of Hebrew language and literature at Hebrew Union College in New York. He is also consulting editor at the Jewish monthly *Midstream*. He has taught Hebrew and English at the City College of New York, and Hebrew, English, and Latin at Lawrence High School in Cedarhurst, New York. His poetry, fiction, and essays on music, literature, and current affairs have appeared in a variety of publications, including the *New York Times, Saturday Review, Commentary, Midstream, Louisville Review,* and *Literary Review.* He received a first prize in poetry from the Poetry Society of Dallas and from Embers in Connecticut, as well as a first prize in fiction from Negative Capability. He and his wife, Sylvia, live in Brooklyn and are the parents of two sons.

ISRAEL HALPERN is the editor of *Long Island Poetry Collective Newsletter* and *Sampler,* the annual poetry publication of the Fresh Meadows Poets in Fresh Meadows, Queens. He has led poetry workshops at Beyond Baroque Literary Center and the Social Public Art Resource Center in Venice, California. His poetry has appeared in *California Poetry Quarterly, Rhyme Scheme, Katmandu Review, Copenhagen Christian Boxcar,* and *Alchemy.* Recently, the opportunity to travel to Russia and meet with other writers also allowed him to see where his parents spent their youth.

MICHAEL HAMBURGER was born in Berlin in 1924, escaping with his family to England early in the Hitler period. He has been writing and publishing books for fifty years. His first book, published in 1943, was a translation from the German of *Poems of Hölderlin* (Nicholson and Watson). His reputation as a translator grew significantly with his groundbreaking anthology *East German Poetry* (Carcanet, 1972) and *German Poetry 1910–1975* (Humanities Press, 1981). Recent translations include the work of Günter Eich, Paul Celan, Rilke, Brecht, Hans Magnus Enzensberger, and Günter Grass. In 1986 he received the German Federal Republic's Goethe Medal for his services to German literature. In 1990 he was awarded the first European Community Translation Prize for his *Poems of Paul Celan* (Anvil Press and Persea, 1988) and in 1992 the Petrarca Prize Modena, Italy and the O.B.E. Equally renowned as a poet and a critic, Hamburger's books of poetry include *Flowering Cactus, Weather and Season, Travelling,* and a new edition of his *Collected Poems 1941–1994* (Anvil Press, 1994). *The Truth of Poetry* (Penguin, 1972), a book of criticism, analyzes modern poetry in Europe and America. *String of Beginnings,* a book of memoirs of Hamburger's early years, was published by Skoob Books in 1991.

In a tribute to Michael Hamburger at seventy, Rodney Pybus, editor of *Stand Magazine,* called him "a cutting from the great continental German-Jewish plant, rooted well in English soil and still flowering strongly."

ANTHONY HECHT was born in 1923. His first book of poems, *A Summoning of Stones,* was published by Macmillan in 1954. It was followed by *The Hard Hours* (Atheneum, 1967), which won the Pulitzer Prize for Poetry in 1968, *Millions of Strange Shadows* (Atheneum, 1977), and *The Venetian Vespers* (Atheneum, 1980). He is the translator (with Helen Bacon) of *Aeschylus' Seven Against Thebes* (Oxford University Press, 1973), and coeditor (with John Hollander) of a volume of light verse, *Jiggery-Pokery* (Atheneum, 1967). Several poems about the Holocaust have been published in *Collected Earlier Poems* (Oxford University Press, 1991). His most recent book is *Flight among the Tombs: Poems* (Knopf, 1998). Professor Hecht has taught at several colleges and universities. At present he is University Professor in the Graduate School of Georgetown University.

Professor Hecht was awarded the Prix de Rome in 1951. Since then, among other awards and prizes, he has received the Brandeis University Creative Arts Award, 1965; the Miles Poetry Prize, 1968; the Russell Loines Award, National Institute of Arts and Letters, 1968; the Bollingen Prize, 1983; the Librex-Guggenheim Eugenio Montale Award for Poetry, 1984; and the Ruth Lilly Prize, 1988. He is a chancellor of the American Academy of Poets and is a trustee of the American Academy in Rome.

ANDRÉ HELLER was born in 1947 in Vienna. He is active as a poet, chansonnier, and entrepreneur. He has produced numerous theatrical spectacles but has not neglected his literary output.

CHAIA L. HELLER was born in Stamford, Connecticut, and has spent the last ten years living in Iowa and Vermont, where she has taught women's studies at Burlington College and the Institute for

Social Ecology. She has been a psychotherapist, activist, speaker, and poet for years, dealing mainly with issues of women's creativity and liberation. She is a member of the "Speak Out" speakers bureau, sponsored by South End Press, and she tours nationally, speaking on issues of feminism and ecology. Her poetry has appeared in such periodicals as the *Grinnell Review, Sinister Wisdom,* and *Burlington Review.* She currently lives in Western Massachusetts, where she teaches, gives workshops, and writes.

HELENE HOFFMAN is the daughter of Holocaust survivors from Czechoslovakia who emigrated to Cleveland after World War II. Hoffman, now residing in Chicago, is an attorney and a writer. She has been published in anthologies and won several awards for her writing. She is very interested in preserving Yiddish as a language and has had several articles on the subject published in *The Bookpeddler.*

JEAN HOLLANDER left Vienna with her family as a child when Hitler took over the country. Many years after that traumatic flight, she expressed her thoughts in poetry. Her poem "Isolde, Dead in Vichy France" memorializes a cousin who died in a concentration camp. A lecturer at Princeton University, Hollander is also director of the Annual Writers' Conferences at Trenton State College. Her book of poems *Crushed into Honey* was published by Saturday Press in 1986 and won the Eileen W. Barnes Award. She received a first prize in the Billie Murray Denny Poetry Contest and has twice been a winner (1980 and 1981) in the Poetry Society of America Bulletin Contest.

GAIL HOLST-WARHAFT was born in Australia and lived for six years in Greece, where she worked as a musician and journalist. She has written a number of books about Greek music and literature, including *Road to Rembetika* and *Dangerous Voices* (Routledge, 1992). Holst-Warhaft has translated some of the major poets and prose writers of modern Greek into English, including Kambanellis, whose *Mauthausen* was released in English in 1995. She teaches Greek literature at Cornell University.

I

COLETTE INEZ was born in Brussels of French parentage. She was reared in a Catholic home for children in Brussels. Inez is on the faculty of Columbia University's Writing Program and has taught at a number of colleges and universities. She has read her poetry nationwide and has conducted poetry workshops at New York's Cooper Union, the West Side YMCA, and at a number of writers conferences. She has received fellowships from the Guggenheim Foundation, the Rockefeller Foundation, and the National Endowment for the Arts. Other honors include a Pushcart Prize and awards from the Poetry Society of America and the New York State CAPS program.

Books by Colette Inez include *Getting Underway: New and Selected Poetry, Family Life, Eight Minutes from the Sun, Alive and Taking Names* (Ohio University Press, 1977), and *The Woman Who Loved Worms* (Doubleday, 1972), which received the 1972 Great Lakes Colleges Association National First Book Award and was reissued last year by Carnegie Mellon University Press Classic Contemporaries Editions. Her most recent collection, *Naming the Moons*, was released in late 1994. She resides in New York City with her husband, freelance writer Saul Stadtmauer.

ROSELINE INTRATER, currently a Gestalt-oriented psychotherapist in Toledo, was for many years adjunct professor of modern literature at the Cleveland College of Jewish Studies. She has also taught at Indiana University and at Case Western Reserve University. She is the author of *An Eye for an "I": Attrition of the Self in the Existential Novel* (Peter Lang Publishing, 1988), and articles on Yehuda Amichai, Martin Buber, Heinrich Heine, and others.

BARRY IVKER currently teaches English at Xavier University and is a practicing clinical social worker. He is the unofficial Ba'al Kriya at Tikvat Shalom Conservative Synagogue in New Orleans and tutors some congregants for bar and bat mitzvahs; he also leads the New Orleans International Folk Dance Group. He has been involved with collage for over twenty years and has had several exhibitions. He plays piano and harpsichord in the Jupiter Chamber Ensemble, has had several of his one-act plays produced, and is a writer of children's stories and poetry.

J

EMILY CAROLYN JOYCE is a learning facilitator in the White Plains (New York) Public Schools. She lived and traveled in Europe, and has been published in magazines and journals both in the United States and in Canada. Her favorite living writer is Elie Wiesel.

IAKOVOS KAMBANELIS was born in Athens and is one of the leading playwrights of modern Greece. He was involved in the resistance to the German occupation of his country and spent two years in the Mauthausen concentration camp. In 1965 he published a memoir of his experiences in the camp during and after the liberation. When the book *Mauthausen* was about to be released in Greek, he wrote a set of poems which he sent to the composer Mikis Theodorakis, who immediately set them to music. One of them, the "Song of Songs," is as popular in Israel as it is in Greece.

TSIPI KELLER was born in Czechoslovakia, raised in Israel, and has lived in New York City since 1974. She studied French literature at Tel Aviv University and at the Sorbonne, and holds an M.A. in English from New York University. Her poems and short fiction have appeared in various publications; her novel, *The Reverse Turn of the Heart*, was published in 1995 by Sifriat Hapoalim, Israel. She is a recipient of CAPS and NYFA awards in fiction as well as an award from the Translation Center at Columbia University for her translation of poems by Dan Pagis in the *Quarterly Review of Literature* (1992).

MIRIAM KESSLER's poems have appeared in *The Alchemist, Poet Lore, River Styx, Kalliope, Peregrine,* and other literary magazines. Several of her poems have been published in anthologies.

RITA KIEFER lives in Greeley, Colorado, where she teaches English and women's studies at the University of Northern Colorado. Before her marriage to her husband, Jerry, she was a Catholic nun for eighteen years. Two collections of her poetry are *Unveiling* (Chicory Blue Press, 1993) and *Trying on Faces* (Monkshood Press, 1995).

ANNE KIND was born in Berlin and came to Britain in 1934, where she continued her interrupted education. Trained as a nurse and administrator, and married to a doctor, she worked for many years for the Family Planning Association. Her poetry has been published in *Stand, Other Poetry*, and *Wayfarer. Come and See This Folks* was published in 1994 by Volcano Press.

MARTA KNOBLOCH has written three books of poetry: *The Song of What Was Lost* (Artscape, 1988), which won the Baltimore Literary Arts Award; *Sky Pond* (1993); and *The Room of Months* (Book Editore, Bologna, 1995) in both English and Italian.

PHYLLIS KOESTENBAUM was born in Brooklyn in 1930. Her books are: *oh I can't she says* (Christopher's Books, 1980); *Hunger Food* (Jungle Garden Press, 1980; a chapbook); *Crazy Face* (Mudborn Press, 1980; a chapbook); *That Nakedness*, (Jungle Garden Press, 1982); and *14 Criminal Sonnets* (Jungle Garden Press, 1984; limited fine press edition). *oh I can't she says* won an honorable mention in the first annual book award of the Poetry Center at San Francisco State University and was named one of the Best Titles of 1981 in the *Library Journal*'s "Small Press Roundup." Her work has been published in *The Best American Poetry* anthologies for 1992 and 1993, in *A Formal Feeling Comes: Poems in Form by Contemporary Women* (Story Line Press, 1994), *Each in Her Own Way: Women Writing on the Menopause and Other Aspects of Aging* (Queen of Swords Press), and *Her Face in the Mirror: Jewish Women on Mothers and Daughters* (Beacon Press, 1994). She is an affiliated scholar at Stanford University's Institute for Research on Women and Gender.

YALA KORWIN, poet, artist, and Holocaust survivor, is the author and illustrator of *To Tell the Story: Poems of the Holocaust* (formerly Holocaust Library, 1987; now published by U.S. Holocaust Memorial Museum). Her poems on the Holocaust have been anthologized in: *Anthology of Magazine Verse, Yearbook of American Poetry 1986–1988*, ed. A. F. Pater (Monitor Book Co., 1988); *Sarah's Daughters Sing*, ed. Henny Wenkart (KTAV, 1990); and *Blood to Remember: American Poets on the Holocaust*, ed. Charles Fishman (Texas Tech University Press, 1991). Other poems and illustrations were published in magazines such as *Midstream, Bitterroot, Amelia,*

BIOGRAPHICAL NOTES

and *Blue Unicorn.* She exhibits her paintings in group and solo shows in the New York area.

SHEL KRAKOFSKY received the 1993 Toronto Jewish Book Award for Creative Writing. He practices medicine in London, Ontario, and was previously a journalist with the *Globe and Mail* and a former English teacher. The recipient of several literary awards and a Canada Council Reader, some of his recent work has been anthologized in such diverse books as *The Great Big Book of Canadian Humour* (Macmillan, 1992); *Sing, Shout and Celebrate—Canada Is 125!* (British Columbia Ministry of Education, 1992); and *The Naked Physician* (Quarry Press, 1990). A collection of poetry, *The Reversible Coat,* was published by Moonstone Press in 1991. His newest book, *Listening for Somersaults* (Moonstone Press, 1993), has been acclaimed for creating memorable characters that define the cultural quality of being Jewish and Canadian. He is the editor of *Parchment,* Canada's national journal of Jewish writing.

LOTTE KRAMER was born in Germany and came to England as a child refugee in 1919. She worked in a laundry, dress shop, and as a ladies' companion while studying art and the history of art in evening classes. She began to write poetry during the 1970s and has been widely published in England, the United States, Canada, Ireland, and Germany. Her collections of poetry are: *Ice Break, The Shoemaker's Wife* (Hippopotamus Press, 1987), *A Lifelong House* (Hippopotamus Press, 1983), *Family Arrivals* (Poet & Printer, 1992), *The Desecration of Trees* (Hippopotamus Press, 1994), and *Earthquake and Other Poems* (Rockingham Press, 1994).

GEORG KREISLER was born in Vienna in 1922. He went to Hollywood in 1938 and in 1942 joined the United States Army. He returned to Vienna in 1956 and later moved to Berlin. Besides being a poet and a translator, Kreisler is a leading composer, librettist, and singer of satirical songs working in cabaret, musicals, and TV. In the late 1950s he was pianist and chansonnier at the Monkey Bar in New York City. Herbert Kuhner, his future editor, lived across the street at 55 East 54th Street, but unfortunately their paths did not cross.

HERBERT KUHNER was born in Vienna in 1935. In 1939 his family was forced to leave Austria. Kuhner grew up in the United States and was educated at the Lawrenceville School and Columbia University. He has been a resident of Austria since 1963. He is the editor and translator of the bilingual anthology of Holocaust poetry *If the Walls Between Us Were Made of Glass* (Verlag Der Apfel, 1992). He has also completed individual bilingual volumes of the following poets who deal with the Holocaust and its aftermath: Willy Verkauf-Verlon, Else Keren, Tamar Radzyner, and Stella Rotenberg. His own recent bilingual volume of poetry, prose, and drama, *Love of Austria,* deals not only with the Holocaust but with remigration and Austrian affairs. Together with Michael Lay, he is working on a book of interviews of concentration camp survivors and converts to Judaism. Among his publications are *Nixe* (Funk and Wagnalls, 1968), *Broadsides and Pratfalls* (Menard Press, 1976), and *Austrian Poetry Today* (Schocken Books, 1985). His nonfiction novel *Der Ausschluss (Memoirs of a 39er)* was published in 1988 by Edition 39/Verlag Der Apfel. Kuhner is also the author of *The Assembly-Line Prince,* which is both in novel and drama form. His works and papers are collected by Boston University Library.

L

ALVIN M. LASTER is a retired dentist who is now a freelance writer with a regular column in a local newspaper in Southbury, Connecticut. A book of poetry, *Arabesques, Trumpets and Grace Notes,* was published by Northwoods Press in 1989. Dr. Laster is president of the Southbury Connecticut Poetry Society and has judged poetry competitions for the State Society.

KENDALL LeCOMPTE published his first poem in 1968. He has published poems in several literary journals, including *Commonweal, Manhattan Poetry Review, Chester H. Jones Anthology, Gryphon, Alura, Apalachee Quarterly,* and *Gold Dust.*

BARBARA LEFCOWITZ has published five books of poetry, including *Shadows and Goatbones* (SCOP Publications, 1992) and *Minarets of Vienna* (Chestnut Hill Press, 1996), as well as a novel, *Red Lies and*

White Lies (East Coast Books, 1993). She has published short stories, essays, and poems in over one hundred journals. Lefcowitz has received fellowships from the National Endowment for the Arts and the Rockefeller Foundation.

MERRILL LEFFLER is an environmental and science writer at the Maryland Sea Grant College of the University of Maryland. He is the author of *Partly Pandemonium; Partly Love* (Dryad Press, 1982), a collection of poetry, and editor of *The Changing Orders: Poetry from Israel* (Poet Lore, 1996). His most recent collection of poetry, *Take Hold*, was published in 1997 by Dryad Press. He is the cofounder and editor of Dryad Press.

CORNEL LENGYEL, who fled the city in his early thirties for eighty acres in the woods of El Dorado National Forest near Georgetown, California, has been writing and publishing poetry since he was a teenager and is still at it at 82. He said once, "The most improbable, impractical thing I can think of is being a poet. Yet I am still writing poetry. It's like an adolescent vice. It persists through life." He is credited with having invented a new kind of verse: the blank verse sonnet. His books of poetry include *The Lookout's Letters* (Dragon's Teeth Press, 1971), *Fire Watch, Latter Day Psalms*, and *Four Dozen Songs* (Dragon's Teeth Press, 1970). Lengyel is a historian, playwright, and essayist as well as a poet, author of *Four Days in July: The Story Behind the Declaration of Independence* (Doubleday, 1958), and *I, Benedict Arnold: The Anatomy of Treason* (Doubleday, 1960). His play *The Atom Clock* won the Maxwell Anderson Award for poetic drama. Other plays are *Will of Stratford, Doctor Franklin*, and *Shadow Trap*.

LEATRICE LIFSHITZ has had poetry published in many poetry journals and anthologies. She was a prize winner in the 1989 World Haiku Contest and has twice received an honorable mention for the Anna Davidson Rosenberg Poetry Award (1987, 1989). In 1986 she received first prize in the Hans S. Bodenheimer Poetry Award. She is the editor of *Her Soul Beneath the Bone: Women's Poetry on Breast Cancer* (University of Illinois Press, 1988) and of *Only Morning in Her Shoes: Poetry about Old Women* (Utah State University Press, 1990). Lifshitz is the founder of Rockland Poets and the Rockland County Haiku Society.

TOBY LORBER is a graduate of the High School of Performing Arts in New York City and attended Brooklyn College. Her poems have appeared in *Metropolis, Nocturne, The Writer, Taking Shape,* and *Genesis.* She lives on Long Island, attends Nassau Community College, and is currently working on a collection of poems.

μ

ARLENE MAASS's poems have appeared in *Jewish Currents, Rhino,* the *Rockford Review,* and *Cornerstone* magazine, as well as the anthology *Concert at Chopin's House: An Anthology of Polish-American Writers* (New Rivers Press, 1988). In 1994 she won the first prize of the National Federation of State Poetry Societies NFSPS Award for "Uncle Max Always Said I'd Amountanuthin'." Maass presently is managing editor of *Kesher* (Connection), the quarterly of the American Messianic Fellowship International, and manages and writes for *Sechel,* the biannual forum for the fellowship of Messianic congregations. She resides in Buffalo Grove, Illinois, with her husband, Eliezer, a messianic pastor, and their son, Aaron.

JOAN McGINNIS was born in Philadelphia and has taught in the public schools in New England for a number of years. She currently resides in Hamden, Connecticut, where she is employed as a medical librarian. She wrote the poem "Dachau" one year after returning from a trip to Czechoslovakia, Austria, and Germany, shortly after the fall of the Berlin Wall in 1989. McGinnis is a member of the International Women's Writing Guild (IWWG).

SEYMOUR MAYNE, raised and educated in Montreal, has been teaching at the University of Ottawa since the early 1970s. He has also taught at the University of British Columbia, Concordia University in Montreal, and the Hebrew University of Jerusalem, where he also served as writer-in-residence. Founder of a number of little magazines and literary presses, he has edited anthologies and critical texts in Canadian literature, including *40 Women Poets of Canada* (1971), *Irving Layton: The Poet and His Critics* (1978), *Essential Words: An Anthology of Jewish Canadian Poetry* (Oberon

Press, 1985), and *Jerusalem: An Anthology of Jewish Canadian Poetry* (Zehicule Press, 1997). He has translated poetry from several languages. His translations from Yiddish and Hebrew include: *Burnt Pearls: Ghetto Poems of Abraham Sutzkever* (Mosaic Press, 1981); *Generation: Selected Poems of Rachel Korn* (1982); *Crossing the River: Selected Poems by Moshe Dor* (1989); *Jerusalem as She Is: New and Selected Poems of Shlomo Vinner* (Bookmark/UMKC, 1991); and *Night Prayer and Other Poems* by Melech Ravitch (Mosaic Press, 1993). He received an ALTA (American Literary Translators Association) Poetry Translation Award in 1990 for his translations from the Yiddish. His own poetry has been collected in some thirty-five books, chapbooks, and broadsides. His collection *Name* (Press Porcepic, 1975), won the J. I. Segal prize in English-French literature and the York Poetry Workshop Award. Recent volumes of poetry include *The Impossible Promised Land: Poems New and Selected* (Mosaic Press, 1981), and two collections comprising poetry and prose, *Children of Abel* (Mosaic Press, 1987) and *Killing Time* (Mosaic Press, 1992), as well as a selection of biblical poems, *Going Up.*

RICH MICHELSON's *Tap Dancing for the Relatives* was published in 1985 by University Press of Florida. *Did You Say Ghosts?* was published in 1993 by Macmillan Children's Books (illustrations by Leonard Baskin). Recent work has appeared in the following anthologies: *Unsettling America: An Anthology of Contemporary Multicultural Poetry* (Penguin Books, 1994), *Men of Our Time* (University of Georgia Press, 1992), *Blood to Remember: American Poets on the Holocaust* (Texas Tech University Press, 1991), and *Ghosts of the Holocaust: An Anthology of Poetry by the Second Generation* (Wayne State University Press, 1989). In 1990 he was the recipient of the Felix Pollak Prize in Poetry.

BERNARD MIKOFSKY, now retired, taught Russian and other Slavic languages, Romance languages, and German at Kent State University, Indiana University, Bethlehem Steel Corporation, and elsewhere. From 1943 to 1946 he was an officer in U.S. Signal Corps Intelligence, a cryptanalyst-translator working mainly with Japanese.

E. ETHELBERT MILLER has long been a literary presence in Washington, D.C., both as literary activist and as founder of the

Ascension Series of readings. He is the author of several collections of poems. *First Light: New and Selected Poems* was published in 1994 by Black Classic Press. *In Search of Color Everywhere* is an anthology of African-American poetry edited by Miller and published in 1994 by Stewart, Tabori and Chang. Miller is a board member of the Institute for Policy Studies as well as a member of the board of the PEN/Faulkner Foundation.

JIM IGNATIUS MILLS, whose poem in this anthology is about Raoul Wallenburg, says, "As much as any individual of this century, Raoul Wallenberg demonstrates the potential for humankind to find light in the depths of total darkness." His poetry and prose has appeared internationally, including a centennial anthology of Idaho poets published by the University of Idaho Press.

CZESŁAW MIŁOSZ was born in 1911 into a Lithuanian family of Polish descent. He is a distinguished poet, essayist, translator, and novelist who teaches in the Department of Slavic Languages and Literatures at the University of California at Berkeley. He was a leader in the avant-garde poetry movement in Poland in the 1930s. During World War II, he was a member of the Resistance and active in underground literary publications. He lived in Warsaw during the German occupation and served as a diplomat for the Communists after the war. Defecting in 1951, he lived in Paris until 1960, then came to the United States. Miłosz was awarded the Neustadt International Prize for Literature in 1978 and the Nobel Prize for Literature in 1980. Many of his poems on the Holocaust are included in *Selected Poems* (Ecco Press, 1996). *The Witness of Poetry* (Harvard University Press, 1983) contains critical essays on the impact of the events of the twentieth century on literature. His most recent book is *Striving Towards Being: The Letters of Thomas Merton and Czeslaw Milosz* (Farrar, Straus and Giroux, 1997).

VICTOR MINGOVITS, born in New York City, now lives in Missoula, Montana, where he manages the production department at a weekly newspaper. "Mystery My History" originally appeared in his collection of poetry *A Satan Worshiper's Guide to the American Northeast,* published in 1991 by Watershed Press. His work also appears in *A Living Testimony: Remembering Loved Ones Lost to*

AIDS, edited by Lesléa Newman and published by The Crossing Press. He is currently working on a novel.

STEPHEN MITCHELL has translated many books, including *The Selected Poetry of Rainer Marie Rilke* (Random House, 1992), *The Book of Job* (HarperCollins, 1992), *The Gospel According to Jesus* (HarperCollins, 1991), and a volume of poems by Pablo Neruda, *Full Woman, Fleshly Apple, Hot Moon* (HarperCollins, 1997). He has edited the poetry anthologies *The Enlightened Mind* (HarperCollins, 1992) and *The Enlightened Heart* (HarperCollins, 1993).

JANICE TOWNLEY MOORE teaches English at Young Harris College in Georgia. Her poetry has appeared in numerous publications, such as *Southern Poetry Review, Confrontation, New Virginia Review, Kansas Quarterly, Florida Review, Negative Capability, Anthology of Magazine Verse,* and *The Bedford Introduction to Literature.*

N

ROCHELLE NATT, a professional psychic in New York, has published short fiction and poetry in many literary magazines, such as *Negative Capability, The Mac Guffin Story Review,* and *Pearl.* Her work has been included in several anthologies. In 1985 she won the Brannan Memorial Award for an essay in *Negative Capability.* She was a finalist in the Eve of St. Agnes poetry competition and in the 1991 *Colorado Review* contest. In 1993, she was a finalist for the Judah Magnes Award for a poem on the Jewish experience.

JO NELSON is an antiquarian bookseller in Seattle. Her poetry has been published in dozens of national magazines, among which are *The Archer, Chariton Review, The Eagle, Poetry Seattle, San Fernando Poetry Journal, West Wind Review,* and *The Wise Woman.*

STANLEY NELSON's book of stories, *The Unknowable Light of the Aliens* (The Smith), was named a Small Press Book of the Year by *Library Journal.* Nelson's poems have appeared in such publications as *TriQuarterly, Beloit Poetry Journal, Kansas Quarterly, Confron-*

tation, Turnstile, and several anthologies. His most recent book, *Immigrant,* an epic poem in four volumes, was published by Birch Book Press, volume 1 in 1990 and volume 4 in 1998. Other poetry collections are *The Passion of Tammuz* (Bellosguardo Press), *Idlewild* (The Smith), *The Brooklyn Book of the Dead* (The Smith), *Nightriffer* (Birch Brook Press), *101 Fragments of a Prayer* (Midnight Sun), and *Driftin' on a Nightriff* (Sub Rosa Press).

RICHARD NEWMAN teaches English and English as a Second Language at Nassau Community College on Long Island. For many years, since he was in high school and yeshiva, he has been writing a long poem dealing with the Holocaust. At least fifty parts of this poem are fully formed sonnets. As he writes, he has plagued himself "with questions about the legitimacy of fitting not only the Holocaust, but also sexual abuse and illegal abortion, into a poetic form historically reserved for love, for meditative contemplation. . . . I worried that giving coherent form to horrors popularly thought to be transcendent of the limits of understanding would trivialize what I was trying to say about them."

B. Z. NIDITCH has contributed to *Midstream, Response, Jewish Spectator,* and *Rashi.*

O

ALICIA OSTRIKER, a poet and critic, has authored seven volumes of poetry. Her most recent works are *The Imaginary Lover* (University of Pittsburgh Press, 1986), which won the 1986 William Carlos Williams Award from the Poetry Society of America, and *Green Age* (University of Pittsburgh Press, 1989). As a critic, she is the author of *Vision and Verse in William Blake* (University of Wisconsin Press, 1965) and editor of Blake's *Complete Poems* (Penguin), and has written two books on American women's poetry, *Writing Like a Woman* (University of Michigan Press, 1983) and *Stealing the Language: The Emergence of Women's Poetry in America* (Beacon Press, 1986). *The Nakedness of the Fathers: Biblical Visions and Revisions* was published by Rutgers University Press in 1994.

BIOGRAPHICAL NOTES

She has received awards from the New Jersey Arts Council, the National Endowment for the Arts, the Rockefeller Foundation, and the Guggenheim Foundation. She lives in Princeton, New Jersey, and teaches English and creative writing at Rutgers University.

P

CHRISTINA PACOSZ has published four books of poetry, including *Notes from the Red Zone* (Seal Press, 1983); *Some Winded, Wild Beast* (Black and Red, 1985); and *This Is Not a Place to Sing* (West End, 1987). She has been an artist-in-the-schools for the Washington State and South Carolina Arts Commissions, a North Carolina Visiting Artist, and is on the roster for the Alaska State Council on the Arts and Nevada State Council on the Arts artist-in-the-schools programs. She currently lives with her husband in Delta Junction, Alaska, where she teaches children with learning disabilities.

DAN PAGIS (1930–86) was born in Bukovina, originally in Austria. His father emigrated to Palestine just before the war but was unable to bring out his family as he had planned. Pagis, a boy of eleven, and his mother were taken to a concentration camp in the Ukraine, from which he was able to escape after three years, in 1944. He emigrated to Israel in 1946 and taught on a kibbutz, then, in 1956, moved to Jerusalem, where he earned a doctorate and became a professor of Hebrew literature at the Hebrew University. He also taught at Harvard University, the University of California at Berkeley, and the Jewish Theological Seminary. He wrote many poems in Hebrew, dealing directly or indirectly with the Holocaust and his camp experience.

LINDA PASTAN, poet laureate of Maryland, is the author of nine books of poetry, the most recent of which is *Carnival Evening: New and Selected Poems 1968–1998* (Norton, 1998). Other books are *An Early After Life* (Norton, 1995), *Heroes in Disguise* (Norton, 1991), *The Imperfect Paradise* (Norton, 1988), *A Fraction of Darkness* (Norton, 1985), *PM/AM: New and Selected Poems* (Norton, 1982), *Waiting for My Life* (Norton, 1981), *The Five Stages of Grief* (Norton, 1978), *Aspects of Eve* (Liveright, 1975), and *A Perfect Circle of Sun* (Swallow Press, 1971). A recipient of fellowships from the National Endowment for the Arts and from the Maryland Arts Council, Linda Pastan has won the Dylan Thomas Award, the Di Castagnola Award, the Bess Hokin Prize of *Poetry Magazine,* and the Maurice English Award. Pastan is on the staff of the Bread Loaf Writers' Conference in Vermont. She lives in Potomac, Maryland, with her husband and three children.

MARK PAWLAK has been an editor of Hanging Loose Press since 1981. He grew up in Buffalo and has lived in the Boston area for more than twenty-five years. He presently teaches mathematics at the University of Massachusetts at Boston. He is a founding member of the October Poetry Theatre, along with poet Dick Lourie and theater director Steve Seidel. He recently appeared in *News from Crazy Horse,* a fully staged theater production that uses poems as its text. His poems and translations from the German of Bertolt Brecht and others have appeared widely in magazines and anthologies. He is the author of three poetry collections, *The Buffalo Sequence* from Copper Canyon Press (1997), *All the News* from Hanging Loose Press, and *Special Handling: Newspaper Poems New and Selected* (Hanging Loose Press, 1993). He is coeditor, with Dick Lourie, of *Smart Like Me: High School–Age Writing from the Sixties to Now,* and *Bullseye,* a sequel.

T. W. PERKINS writes, "I am neither a Holocaust survivor, nor Jewish, but started studying the Holocaust at a young age, and in particular the literature of survivors. As a poet, I write in the voices of all who touch my heart or soul."

LOUIS PHILLIPS is a poet and short story writer. He lives in New York City with his wife, Patricia Ranard, their twins, Ian and Matthew, and an assortment of elusive rodents and reptiles. His collection of short stories, *A Dream of Countries Where No One Dare Live,* was published by Southern Methodist University Press in 1993. Aran Press has published his play *The Ballroom in St. Patrick's Cathedral.* Phillips teaches creative writing at the School of Visual Arts in New York City.

ROBERT PINSKY served as the 1997–98 Poet Laureate of the United States. His first book of poems, *Sadness and Happiness*

(Princeton University Press, 1975), was followed by *The Situation of Poetry: Contemporary Poetry and Its Traditions* (Princeton University Press, 1976), a landmark work of criticism. Since then, Pinsky has published two prize-winning books of poetry, *An Explanation of America* (Princeton University Press, 1979) and *History of My Heart* (reissued by Farrar, Straus and Giroux, 1997). *Poetry and The World* was published by Ecco Press in 1988; *The Inferno of Dante,* a new verse translation, was published by Farrar, Straus and Giroux in 1994. His most recent book is *The Figured Wheel: New and Collected Poems, 1966–1996* (Farrar, Straus and Giroux, 1997).

KARL PLANK is an associate professor of religion at Davidson College, Davidson, North Carolina, where he teaches modern Jewish literature and thought. He has recently published a critical study, *Mother of the Wire Fence: Inside and Outside the Holocaust* (Westminster John Knox Press, 1994).

RODNEY PYBUS was born in Newcastle upon Tyne, England, in 1938. Educated at Cambridge University, he has worked in both the mass media and education, including at Macquarie University in Sydney, Australia. He is also an editor of *Stand Magazine.* The most recent of six collections of his poems are *Cicadas in Their Summers: New and Selected Poems* (Carcanet, 1988) and *Flying Blues* (Carcanet, 1994).

R

TAMAR RADZYNER died while the anthology *If the Walls Between Us Were Made of Glass* (Verlag Der Apfel, 1992), in which she is represented, was in progress. Shortly before her death, she wrote: "I was born in Poland too late to enjoy the Golden Twenties. After I was successful in the art of surviving I have attempted to combine my excessive idealism with political activity. I live in Vienna as a housewife and mother, and instead of consulting a psychiatrist I express my fears in my poetry."

DAHLIA RAVIKOVITCH was born in 1936 in Ramat Gan, a suburb

of Tel Aviv. She studied at the Hebrew University in Jerusalem, and later worked as a journalist and teacher. She has published five volumes of poetry, *The Love of an Orange, A Hard Winter, The Third Book, Deep Calleth Unto Deep*, and *Real Love*, a book of selected poems; *All Thy Breakers and Waves*, a book of short stories; *A Death in the Family*; and two books of poetry for children, *Family Party* and *Mixed-Up Mommy*. She is the recipient of many of Israel's literary awards, including the Shlonsky, Brenner, Ussishkin and Bialik Prizes, as well as the Award of the Municipality of Ramat Gan. Her most recent collection in English, *The Window: New and Selected Poems*, translated and edited by Chana Bloch and Ariel Bloch, was published by the Sheep Meadow Press in 1989.

ELIZABETH REES grew up in Minneapolis. She received her M.F.A. from Boston University in 1986 and has taught creative writing, literature, and composition at Boston University, Macalester College, Harvard University, the U.S. Naval Academy, and Howard University. She has also served as a consultant at the U.S. Holocaust Memorial Museum. Her poems have been published in *Partisan Review, Kenyon Review*, and *Poet Lore*. She was a recipient of a D.C. Commission for the Arts grant in poetry in 1990 and is working on a poetry collection.

DONNA REIS's poetry has appeared in numerous anthologies and literary journals including *Art Times, Hanging Loose, New York Quarterly, Piedmont Literary Review*, and *Riverrun*. The story told in her poem "Photo, Kraków 1939" is of her great-great-grandmother. Donna lives in Warwick, New York, with her husband, Jim Delahanty.

BETTY RENSHAW taught English for a number of years at various colleges and now writes full time. Her two published collections of poems are *To Audre and Alice* (Springhouse Press, 1985) and *Roses in Young Cabbage-Heads* (Print 3, 1991).

LISA RESS's first collection, *Flight Patterns*, the 1983 Associated Writing Programs' Award Series in Poetry winner, was published by the University Press of Virginia in 1985. In 1984 she received a National Endowment for the Arts grant, in 1991 an Illinois Arts Council grant, and in 1987 her poem "Setting the Table, Eating What

Is Served" won the Word Works' Washington Prize. Her poems have appeared in a variety of literary periodicals, most recently in *Spoon River Quarterly* and *Sycamore Review*. She has taught at Cornell University, the University of California at Irvine, and Hollins College; she currently teaches at Knox College, Galesburg, Illinois.

ELLIOT RICHMAN won a National Endowment for the Arts grant in poetry in 1993. His full-length collections are *Walk On, Trooper* (Viet Nam Generation Press, 1994), *Honorable Manhood: Poems of Eros and Dust* (Asylum Arts, 1994), and *The World Dancer* (Asylum Arts, 1993).

ELISAVIETTA RITCHIE is a writer, poet, editor, translator, photographer, occasional creative-writing instructor, and poet-in-the-schools. Her *Flying Time: Stories and Half-Stories* (Signal Books, 1992 and 1996) includes four pieces that won the PEN/Syndicated Fiction Award. *A Wound-Up Cat and Other Bedtime Stories* was published by Palmerston Press in Toronto in 1993. *Elegy for the Other Woman: New and Selected Terribly Female Poems* was published by Signal Books in 1995, *The Arc of the Storm* in 1998. Individual poems have appeared in *Poetry, American Scholar,* the *New York Times, Christian Science Monitor, Amelia,* and *New Republic.* She is also the editor of *The Dolphin's Arc: Poems on Endangered Creatures of the Sea,* published by the Center for Marine Conservation in 1990. The United States Information Agency has sponsored her readings in Brazil, the Balkans, and throughout the Far East. She lives in Washington, D.C., with her husband, the writer Clyde Farnsworth.

CURTIS ROBBINS was born in 1943 in New York City. He became deaf at the age of one after a near-fatal case of tonsillitis and a possible adverse reaction to a mycin drug used for treatment. He received a B.A. from Gallaudet University in 1967, an M.A. from New York University in 1972, and an M.A. and Ph.D. from the University of Maryland in 1985. He has worked as a vocational evaluator, vocational rehabilitation counselor, career counselor, sign-language teacher, Jewish history teacher, computer programmer, and assistant professor of educational technology. Robbins began writing poetry at the age of fourteen. His poem "Nod" appears in *The Second Jewish Catalog* (Jewish Publication Society, 1976).

STELLA ROTENBERG was born in 1916 in Vienna, where she studied medicine. In 1939 she emigrated to Britain, where she has remained. She has continued to write in German and has published several volumes of poetry.

DIANA K. RUBIN's poetry books include *Panorama* (Gusto); *Visions of Enchantment* (JVC Books); *Spirits in Exile* (Guyasuta Publishers, 1990), which was nominated for the Pulitzer Prize in Poetry; and the award-winning collection *Poet's Lullaby* (The Cognitive Overload Press). She has also published a book of short stories, *Love Like a Distant Bell*. Her poetry and fiction have been published both nationally and internationally, and have appeared in *Poetry*, *The Quest* (India), New York University's *Minetta Review*, University of Wisconsin's *Fox Cry*, and *Antigonish Review* (Nova Scotia).

LARRY RUBIN teaches English at Georgia Tech in Atlanta and has published three volumes of poems, most recently *All My Mirrors Lie* (Godine, 1975). He has had poems published in the *New Yorker*, *Harper's Magazine*, *Saturday Review*, *Sewanee Review*, *American Scholar*, and other literary journals, as well as in about fifty anthologies, including the *Norton Introduction to Literature* (1991). He received annual awards from the Poetry Society of America in 1961 and 1973.

CYNTHIA PINKUS RUSSELL is a psychosynthesis psychotherapist in private practice and on the clinical faculty of the Yale Department of Psychiatry. She grew up during the Depression and Second World War, raised her children during the Vietnam War era, and has been a volunteer to the Holocaust Film project and the Peace Movement. Russell became Jewish in 1960. Her work has been published in many periodicals, including the *New York Times* and the *Jerusalem Post*. She is the author of three books and has created the video "Patient as Teacher" (Hartley Films).

∫

NELLY SACHS was born in Berlin in 1891. In 1940, she escaped with her mother to Sweden, partly through the good offices of the Swedish writer Selma Lagerlof (1858–1940). Her early work, rooted in the German romantic tradition, underwent a transformation as the Nazis rose to power. In 1943, she began to write book after book in German dealing with the murder of her people. To help her to come to terms with this momentous theme, she sought recourse in her Jewish tradition taking as her model the Cabala, especially the Zohar, a commentary on the Pentateuch. Translations of her work appear in *O the Chimneys!* (Farrar, Straus and Giroux, 1967), which includes the text of *Eli,* a mystery play in verse of the sufferings of Israel, and in *The Seeker and Other Poems* (Farrar, Straus and Giroux, 1970). In 1966, she was the co-winner, with Samuel Agnon of Israel, of the Nobel Prize for Literature. Sachs died in 1970.

JANE SCHAPIRO is a freelance writer whose first collection of poetry is *Tapping This Stone* (Washington Writers Publishing House, 1995). The Holocaust is part of her family's history. She has lived in Arad, Israel, as part of the work/study program (UUJS) and worked on a kibbutz. Schapiro lives in Annandale, Virginia, with her husband and three daughters.

PAULINE K. SCHMOOKLER has been a teacher of literature, a poet, playwright, and novelist. When her children were very young and she could not continue working in the theater, she turned to playwriting, converting her prize-winning short story into a one-act play, which was produced at several universities and little theaters. She turned to poetry after the premature death of her husband. Since the early 1970s, her poems have been published extensively in *Identity, Jewish Spectator, Unknowns, Monacacy Valley Review,* and in the *National Poetry Anthology.* Four of her poems have been included in a collection dealing with grieving and healing edited by Mike Bernhardt: *Voices of the Grieving Heart* (Cypress Point Press, 1994). She has written a novel, *Anuska,* based on her mother's life story.

WILLA SCHNEBERG was a winner of the 1990 Anna Davidson Rosenberg Award sponsored by the Judah Magnes Museum in Berkeley, California. In 1992 she received second prize in the Allen Ginsberg Poetry Awards sponsored by the Poetry Center of Passaic County Community College. Among the publications in which her poetry has appeared are *Tikkun, Jewish Calendar, Sifrut, Cincinnati Judaica Review,* and *Israel Horizons.* She was awarded an Oregon Literary Arts Fellowship in Poetry for 1994. She currently resides in Portland.

NEIL C. SCOTT was born in Munich. He came to the United States when he was thirteen. In 1974 he received a B.A. in German literature from the University of Virginia. At present he is employed by Boley Centers for Behavioral Health Care in St. Petersburg, Florida. About the Holocaust he says, "I am not Jewish but feel strongly about the subject."

GARY SEA has been translating from German and modern Greek since 1980. Some of his translations appear in *Blue Unicorn, Collages and Bricolages, Gryphon, International Poetry Review, New Renaissance,* and *Webster Review.* He has lived and worked in both Germany and Greece for extended periods, and returns to San Francisco periodically, "when in need of cash," to work as a legal word processor in a law office. In 1980–81, while working in Berlin as a technical translator, he discovered in the library a two-volume set of "memorials" to Germans who fought in the Resistance and were subsequently captured and killed. Sea says, "I concentrated exclusively on women in the Resistance—their roles often being downplayed or ignored by after-the-fact male historians—and wrote a series of poems in which I attempted to project myself into their personas . . . I've tried to keep them as simple and direct as possible. . . . The intention is to celebrate the courage of each of these great women."

JOANNE SELTZER has published over four hundred poems in literary journals, newspapers, and anthologies, including *Minnesota Review,* the *Village Voice,* and *When I Am An Old Woman I Shall Wear Purple,* ed. Sandra Martz (Papier-Mâché Press, 1991). Her essays, book reviews, and short fiction have appeared in magazines such as *Small Press Review* and *Studia Mystica.* Her most recent poetry chapbook, *Inside Invisible Walls,* was published by Bard Press in 1989.

GREGG SHAPIRO's first short story collection, *Indiscretions,* was published on computer disc by Spectrum Press in 1994. Both his poetry and fiction have been published or are forthcoming in a wide variety of magazines and anthologies, including *Modern Words, Christopher Street, The Evergreen Chronicles, Amethyst, Hammers, Private, The Quarterly, Blood to Remember* (Texas Tech University Press, 1991), *Mondo Barbie* (St. Martin's Press, 1993), *Unsettling America* (Viking/Penguin, 1994), *Mondo Marilyn* (St. Martin's Press, 1995), *Reclaiming the Heartland,* and *Full Circle.* He lives in Chicago's Andersonville neighborhood with his life-partner, playwright Rick Karlin, their dog, Sasha, and cat, Goober.

REVA SHARON's poems have appeared in many journals and anthologies in the United States and Israel. Her book *Pool of the Morning Wind* was published in Jerusalem in 1989. An exhibition of her photography was held at the gallery of the American Cultural Center in Jerusalem in 1993, and her photo essays have been published in the *Jerusalem Post Magazine.* She is the Coordinator of Literary Readings for the Association of Americans and Canadians in Israel. She has lived in Jerusalem since 1987.

ENID SHOMER's prize-winning poems and stories have appeared in the *New Yorker, Atlantic, Poetry, Paris Review, Tikkun,* and other publications. Her third book of poetry, *Black Drum,* was published by the University of Arkansas Press in 1997. She is also the author of *Imaginary Men* (University of Iowa Press, 1993), which won both the Iowa Short Fiction Award and the Southern Review/LSU Short Fiction Award. She served as writer-in-residence at Thurber House in Columbus, Ohio, in 1994 and at Florida State University in 1997.

JOAN SELIGER SIDNEY has been a special research associate/ writer-in-residence at the University of Connecticut Center for Judaic Studies and Contemporary Jewish Life. In 1995 she taught the first creative-writing workshop offered by the English department at the Université de Grenoble, France. Her poems have appeared in *Midstream, Massachusetts Review,* and *New York Quarterly.*

BILL SIEGEL has had poetry translations published in the *International Poetry Review,* and original poetry and drawings in the *Worcester Review.* He was a finalist for the Massachusetts Artists Fellowship in Poetry. His poem "Waiting to Go Home" is based on a story his father told him abut photographs he took when, as a twenty-one-year-old infantryman, he was among those "cleaning out" concentration camps after they were liberated by American and Soviet troops.

JOAN I. SIEGEL's poetry has appeared in *Commonweal, Yankee, Literary Review, Cumberland Poetry Review, Poet and Critic, Amicus Journal, Journal of the American Medical Association, The Bridge, Tennessee Quarterly,* and others. She is the coeditor of *Wordsmith,* a poetry and art journal.

LAYLE SILBERT's poetry has been published in magazines and anthologies and as a book, *Making a Baby in Union Park Chicago* (Downtown Poets, 1983). She has published three books of fiction: *Imaginary People and Other Strangers* (Exile Press, 1985); *Burkah and Other Stories* (Host Publications, 1992); and *New York, New York* (St. Andrews Press, 1995). Silbert also works as a freelance photographer specializing in the photography of literary personalities.

JON SILKIN founded the literary magazine *Stand* forty-three years ago in London and remains senior editor of this popular periodical. As a poet, Silkin has published ten books of poetry, the most recent being *The Lens-Breakers* (Sinclair-Stevenson and David Godine, 1992). Known as a modernist "with grit," Silkin's concerns are with violence in man and his continued self-destructive separation from nature. Silkin writes in a Hebraic tradition with a strong sense of history and moral justice. He says, "All my writing adult life I have been trying to write about this [the Holocaust], and I have written about it, both directly and obliquely."

MYRA SKLAREW, former president of Yaddo, professor of literature and codirector of the M.F.A. program in creative writing at the American University, is the author of *From the Backyard of the Diaspora* (Jewish Book Council Award in Poetry 1977 and cowinner with Erica Jong of the Poetry Society of America's Di Castagnola Award 1972), *The Science of Goodbyes, Altamira,* and *Like a Field Riddled by Ants* (Lost Roads, 1987). *Eating the White Earth* was published in Hebrew in 1994. A portion of her book-length poem *Lithuania* received the Anna Davidson Rosenberg Award from the

Judah Magnes Museum in 1993. The second edition of *Lithuania: New and Selected Poems* was brought out by Azul Editions in 1997.

DEAN SMITH, a 1989 graduate of the M.F.A. program in creative writing at Columbia University, has had poems published in *Poetry East, The Pearl, Cultural Studies Times,* and *Charlotte Review.* He lives and writes in New York City.

J. R. SOLONCHE lives and teaches in New York State. His poems have appeared in the *American Scholar, New Criterion, Poetry Northwest, Literary Review, Yankee Magazine, Tennessee Quarterly,* and the anthology *Mixed Voices: Contemporary Poems about Music.*

LESTER SPEISER, a retired New York City high school principal, has been active on the "poetry circuit" as a member of the Fresh Meadows Poets, reciting in libraries, schools, and on various campuses. Other activities include a dramatic production, based on his Adirondack poetry, in an upstate theater, and several Holocaust Memorial programs. While not a survivor, Speiser has written about the impact of the Holocaust on his life now. He is a veteran of World War II and a first-generation American. His parents were born in Eastern Europe, having emigrated to the United States before World War I. His father, Morris A. Speiser, served in the Jewish Legion, which liberated Jerusalem from the Turks.

ELAINE STARKMAN is both a prose writer and a poet. Her prose includes *Learning to Sit in the Silence: A Journal of Caretaking* (Papier-Mâché Press). "In the Kibbutz Laundry" has become part of the Yom Hashoah service in the Northern California community where she lives and is recited every year. She is the coeditor, with Leah Schweitzer, of *Without a Single Answer: Poems on Contemporary Israel,* published by the Judah Magnes Museum Press in 1990. She is the coeditor, with Marsha Lee Berkman, of *A World of New Jewish Stories: An International Anthology of Short Fiction* (Jewish Publication Society, 1998). *The Best Time,* a collection of her poems about maturity and the aging process, was published by Sheer Press in 1992.

JULIA STEIN has published two books of poetry, *Under the Ladder to Heaven* (West End Press, 1984), and *Desert Soldiers* (California Classics, 1992).

BRADLEY R. STRAHAN is the director of VIAS (Visions International Arts) and editor of *Visions, The Black Buzzard Review,* and the Black Buzzard Poetry Chapbook series. He has developed an international reputation for his work, which includes three books of poetry and over four hundred poems published in such places as *Crosscurrents, Seattle Review, Poet Lore, Midstream, Jewish Spectator,* and *Israel Today.* His poetry has been translated into several languages, including French, Spanish, and Korean, and anthologized in a number of volumes. He has led the Washington Poets Workshop since 1977. He has also recently translated a book of poems by Bulgaria's leading poet, Nikolai Kantchev.

CHARLES STRECKFUS has been a scientist at the National Institutes of Health. He is currently a professor of diagnostic sciences at the University of Mississippi, where his research focuses on breast cancer. He has published numerous poems and has coauthored a book of poetry entitled *Hungry Ghosts.*

MARGUERITE M. STRIAR, born in Boston, is a writer, poet, editor, artist, and teacher. She has taught art in the public schools and at the University of Maryland. Her poetry has been published in magazines and anthologies, and two collections of her poetry are being prepared for publication. A short story, "The Vulture," published in *Virginia Country Magazine,* was nominated for the O. Henry Best Short Story award in 1991. Striar has been an editor and regular columnist for the original *Washingtonian* magazine and for *Washington Illustrated.* Her feature stories have appeared in the *Washington Post* and *Essence* magazine. She has written radio scripts for the Voice of America and for WCCM. Although her writing focuses on issues of war, peace, racism, and politics, she has also written about art and artists and on science. Striar lives in Washington, D.C., with her husband, Robert. They have three children.

ABRAHAM SUTZKEVER was born in Byelorussia in 1913, studied literature and criticism at Vilna University, and at age twenty received the acclaim of the Yunge Vilne writers for his poems in Yiddish. During the German occupation, Sutzkever wrote poetry in hiding, then in the Vilna Ghetto, and later in the forest as a partisan. He is one of the earliest and most articulate poets of the Holocaust. His poems dating from 1941–45, written not in retrospect or at a distance from the events they describe but during the daily misery of ghetto life and under constant threat of death, were his way of preserving his sanity and of protecting himself against despair. He believed that each day he survived was a gift and deserving of his highest artistic effort. His later work, beginning with *Di festung* (The fortress) in 1945, is informed by his wartime experiences. Sutzkever settled in Palestine in 1947. He has been the editor of the premier Yiddish journal, *Di Goldene Keyt*, since 1948.

T

HERMAN TAUBE, through his poetry, stories, and essays in English and Yiddish, interprets the Jewish soul with sensitivity and passion, with pathos, humor, and hope. Born in Łódź, Poland, he was orphaned as a small child and brought up by his grandfather, who was the first Jew killed in Łódź by the Nazis. A Holocaust survivor, he arrived in the United States in 1947, obtained an American college education and citizenship, and has become a prolific writer and lecturer, not only on the Shoah but on the whole span of Jewish life and experience. He writes not only of the 400,000 martyrs of the Polish ghetto, but of the happier aspects of life and of the beauty of nature. Among Taube's eighteen published books are *Between the Shadows* (Dryad Press, 1986); *Autumn Travels: Devious Paths, Land of Blue Skies* (Refugee Village, 1992); and his latest novel, *My Baltimore Landsman* (Dryad Press, 1995). His latest poetry collection is *Golden Leaves: New and Selected Poems* (Board of Jewish Education of Greater Washington and Dryad Press, 1998). A resident of Rockville, Maryland, Taube is referred to as a Washington-area treasure.

HILARY THAM (GOLDBERG) was born in 1946 in Kelang, Malaysia. She is a graduate of the University of Malaya and a Jenny Moore Fellow. She has been tutor to Malaysian princesses, a health insurance claims reviewer, and chairman of the coalition to resettle Vietnamese refugees in Northern Virginia. She lives in Arlington, Virginia, with her husband and three daughters, and teaches creative writing in high schools. Her poems have been published in Malaysia, Singapore, England, Israel, and the United States. Her work is included in *The Second Tongue* (Heinemann, 1976), a definitive anthology of Malaysian poetry. Her books are *Tigerbone Wine* (1992), *No Gods Today* (1969), *Paper Boats* (1987), and *Men and Other Strange Myths* (1994), all published by Three Continents Press. *Bad Names for Women* (Wordworks, 1989) won second prize in the 1988 Virginia Poetry Prize contest. Her most recent book is *Lane with No Name: Memoirs and Poems of a Malaysian/Chinese Girlhood* (Lynne Reiner Publishers, 1997).

ASHER TORREN was born in 1936 in Haifa. From 1953 to 1956 he served in the Israeli Air Force, and since 1968 he has taught biology at the Borough of Manhattan Community College. His poetry has appeared in many magazines in the United States, Germany, England and Israel. *Seven Portholes in Hell,* a book of Holocaust poems, was published by Holocaust Publications in 1991.

V

LOIS VAN HOUTEN, a professional poet of many years standing, has received numerous grants over the years and is the author of six published books of poetry, the most recent of which is *Coming to Terms with Geese,* published in 1987. She is vice-president of Bergen Poets, and has read extensively at colleges, poetry centers, and cafés in Manhattan and in Bergen and Passaic Counties in New Jersey, as well as on radio and television. Over three hundred of Van Houten's poems have appeared in magazines and anthologies, and many of her poems have won awards.

WILLY VERKAUF-VERLON was born in 1917 in Zurich and died in 1990 in Vienna. He came to Vienna in 1921. In 1934 he emigrated to Palestine but also spent time in London. He returned to Austria in

1945. In addition to being a poet, he was a noted artist and expert on Dada. He worked as a publisher, bookseller, and gallery owner.

SANDRA COLLIER VERNY is a psychotherapist in Toronto. Her most recent publication, "My Father's Gold Tooth," appeared in *Gifts of Our Fathers* (Crossing Press, 1994).

THOMAS R. VERNEY is a doctor and psychiatrist. He is the founder of the Pre- and Perinatal Psychology Association of North America. His nonfiction books include *Inside Groups* (McGraw-Hill, 1974), *The Secret Life of the Unborn Child*, with John Kelly (Summit Books, 1981), *Parenting Your Unborn Child* (Doubleday, 1988), and *Nurturing the Unborn Child*, with Pamela Weintraub (Delacorte Press, 1991; Dell, 1992). He is also the author of numerous papers in professional journals and articles in the lay press. In 1982 he wrote a weekly column, "Lifelines," for the *Toronto Star*. His many years of involvement in issues of conception, pregnancy, and birth have led to an exploration of the process of creation and creativity in myths, fairy tales, and his own psyche. This in turn resulted in an expansion of his writing to include short fiction and poetry.

DORIS VIDAVER is a prize-winning poet, playwright, translator, and fiction writer. Born in Detroit, she was educated at the Universities of Michigan and Minnesota, and at Harvard University. Her poetry, fiction, and essays have been published in many journals and anthologies, including the *Literary Review, Poetry, Prairie Schooner, Midstream, Panorama, Scandinavian Review, Another Chicago Magazine, Today's Poets, Chelsea,* and *American Scholar*. Her book of poems *Arch of a Circle* was published by Swallow Press/Ohio University Press in 1980. Her awards include the First Chelsea Prize in Fiction (1990); the Public Radio Drama Award (1985); and the National Endowment for the Humanities Project Award.

YEVGENY VINOKUROV, a Russian who fought in World War II, has written poems that record the shock to his innocence given by the grisly wounds and deaths he saw in combat.

W

DAVI WALDERS, a resident of Chevy Chase, Maryland, is a poet, education consultant, and former teacher and school administrator. Her work has been published in *Ariel IX, CrossCurrents, Journal of Rehabilitation, Painted Hills Review,* and *Virginia Education Journal.* She has held poetry residencies at the Virginia Center for the Creative Arts, Château de la Napoule, and Château de Lesvault in France.

MITCHELL WALDMAN writes and revises legal articles for a law book publisher. His poems and stories have been published in a number of magazines, including *Poetry Motel, Innisfree, Unknowns, Poetalk, Poetry Forum,* and *Poetry Peddler.* He lives in Rochester, New York, but was raised in Skokie, Illinois, site of the infamous attempt of American Nazis to march in a community heavily populated with Jewish Holocaust survivors and their families.

MORRIE WARSHAWSKI is a writer and consultant whose poems, stories, and articles have appeared in a number of publications, including the *Los Angeles Times Syndicate, Toronto Globe and Mail,* and *Videography.* Warshawski's parents survived the Holocaust in Poland.

MICHAEL WATERS teaches at Salisbury State University on the eastern shore of Maryland. His six volumes of poetry include *Bountiful* (1992), *The Burden Lifters* (1989), and *Anniversary of the Air* (1985), all published by Carnegie Mellon University Press; the most recent is *Green Ash, Red Maple, Black Gum* (BOA, 1997). He has been the recipient of a fellowship in creative writing from the National Endowment for the Arts.

TOM WAYMAN is the Squire of "Appledore," an estate in the Selkirk Mountains of Southwest British Columbia. Recent books include *In a Small House on the Outskirts of Heaven* (poems, 1989), *Paperwork* (an anthology of contemporary U.S. and Canadian poems about daily work, 1991), *A Country Not Considered: Canada, Culture, Work* (essays, 1993), *Did I Miss Anything? Selected Poems 1973–1993,* and *The Astonishing Weight of the Dead* (poems, 1994).

VERA WEISLITZ, a poet, sculptor, and teacher, in her first volume of poems and stories draws on her own experience at Theresienstadt, where she spent two years, as well as on the universal lesson of the Holocaust. Born in Ostrava, Moravia, Weislitz escaped to Prague with her family when the war broke out. She and her sister were among the hundred children out of fifteen thousand who survived Theresienstadt. Her mother died during the war, her father died in Dachau. Weislitz's art is riddled with anxiety about the destiny of mankind, about the special role of Jews during the war era, and about the existential questions of the sickness of the world that led to the genocide. Some of her poems were part of the exhibition "Precious Legacy," which traveled around the United States in 1986. After the war, in a Jewish orphanage, she met the novelist Arnošt Lustig, who became her husband. They emigrated to the United States with their two children in 1970.

"Writing is the only way in which I can talk about the past, about the unspeakable," she says. "My children urge me to do so. For myself, it is a way to talk to my mother, father, grandmother, to ask them questions I had no chance to ask while they were alive."

DANIEL WEISSBORT was born in London in 1935 of Polish Jewish émigré parents. In 1975 he came to the United States, where he is director of the translation workshop at the University of Iowa. He has published several collections of his own poetry, including *Lake: New and Selected Poems* (Sheep Meadow Press, 1993), and translated much poetry, mostly from the Russian. He has also assembled various anthologies, including *The Poetry of Survival: Post-War Poets of Eastern and Central Europe* (Penguin Books, 1992). Since 1965 he has been the editor of *Modern Poetry in Translation.*

JOHN FOSTER WEST, an emeritus professor of English at Appalachian State University in Boone, North Carolina, is a novelist, poet, and folklorist. One of his three novels, *Time Was,* was published by Random House in 1965. The son of a tenant farmer in the foothills of western North Carolina, the first schools he attended had only one room. Today he lives in a chalet, Cloud 10, on the crest of the Blue Ridge Mountains. "I wept when I visited the house where Anne Frank was concealed in Amsterdam," he writes, "and I wept more profusely when I exited the Memorial for Children in Jerusalem. I am delighted that I can have my say, however brief, concerning the Holocaust."

JOANNA M. WESTON was born in England and has lived in Canada since 1958. She has an M.A. from the University of British Columbia and has been published in the United Kingdom, Canada, and the United States. Three of her chapbooks have been published: *One of These Little Ones* (1987), *Cuernavaca Diary* (1990), and *Seasons* (1993).

EVELYN WEXLER is a former English teacher and guidance counselor. Except for two years spent in Budapest as a young child—an experience she draws on repeatedly in her work—she has lived all her life in the Bronx. She is married and the mother of two sons. Her work has been published in *Negative Capability, Nimrod, Pittsburgh Quarterly Review, Poets On, South Coast Poetry Journal, Classical Outlook,* and many other publications. She is the 1990 recipient of the Bronx Council on the Arts Grant for excellence in poetry and the William C. Woolfson Memorial Award for the Literary Arts. Her chapbook *The Geisha House* was published in 1992 by Mayapple Press. In 1994 Mayapple Press published her first collection of poems, *Occupied Territory.*

LESLIE WHAT's mother survived the Riga Ghetto, a work camp in Libau, Lithuania, and imprisonment in Hamburg. What is a writer currently working on the memoirs of a survivor of the Warsaw Ghetto.

MICHELE WOLF's poems have appeared in *Poetry, Hudson Review, Antioch Review, Boulevard,* and in the anthologies *When I Am an Old Woman I Shall Wear Purple* and *I Am Becoming the Woman I've Wanted,* both from Papier-Mâché Press. Her collection *The Keeper of the Light* was the 1995 winner of the Painted Bride Quarterly Poetry Chapbook Series. She won the 1997 Anhinga Prize for Poetry and a 1997 Anna Davidson Rosenberg Award for poems on the Jewish experience. *Conversations during Sleep,* her most recent book of poetry, was published by Anhinga Press in 1998. She lives in New York, where she works as a magazine writer and editor.

Z

HARRY ZOHN, born in Vienna in 1923, is professor of German at Brandeis University. His translations from German and Yiddish into English include the works of Theodore Herzl, Walter Benjamin, Gershom Scholem, Martin Buber, Walter Bauer, and Nelly Sachs. He is the author of the articles on Bauer, Sachs, and several others in *Ungar's Encyclopedia of World Literature in the Twentieth Century*. His most recent translation is of *Against All Hope: Resistance in the Nazi Concentration Camps, 1938* by Hermann Langbein (Paragon House, 1994).

Permissions

The following poets, publishers, translators, heirs, and agents are gratefully acknowledged and thanked for their permission to reprint poems in *Beyond Lament*.

Abse, Dannie: "A Night Out" and "No More Mozart," from *White Coat, Purple Coat: Collected Poems 1948–1988*. Copyright © 1977, 1989, 1991 by Dannie Abse. Reprinted by permission of Sheil Land Associates Ltd.

Adam, Cornel: *See* Lengyel, Cornel

Alvarez, A.: "The Survivor," from *Autumn to Autumn and Selected Poems 1953–1976* (London: Macmillan, 1978). Reprinted by permission of A. Alvarez.

Amichai, Yehuda: "All the Generations Before Me." Translated by Robert Friend. Reprinted by permission of Robert Friend.

Anbian, Robert: "Anonymous Recollection," from *Antinostalgia* (Ruddy Duck Press, 1992). Reprinted by permission of Robert Anbian.

Arkin, Frieda: "Pinochle Day" reprinted by permission of Frieda Arkin.

Ashear, Linda: "Auschwitz, August, 1988," reprinted by permission of Linda Ashear.

Bacon, Crystal V.: "Kristallnacht, 1991," reprinted by permission of Crystal V. Bacon.

Bart, Anna: "Collectible," reprinted by permission of Anna Bart.

Bart, Jill: "The Shower," from *West Wind Review* 10 (1991). Reprinted by permission of Jill Bart.

Bauer, Walter: "Two Poems" and "Traveling to the Capitals," translated by Harry Zohn. Reprinted by permission of Professor Henry Beissel, Concordia University, Ontario, Canada.

Bennett, Bruce: "Remembrance," previously published in *The Quarterly* (Spring 1990). Reprinted by permission of Bruce Bennett.

Berke, Judith: "Dachau '44" and "The Tattoo," both first published in *Massachusetts Review* (Fall 1989). Reprinted by permission of Judith Berke.

Bernstein, Lisa: "Inscribed," first published in *Tikkun* (January/February 1992). Reprinted by permission of Lisa Bernstein.

Black, Harold: "Warsaw Ghetto," published in the anthology *The Ear's Chamber* (SCOP Publications, 1981). Reprinted by permission of Harold Black.

Bradley, John: "Letter to Dina," published in *Sun Dog: The Southeast Review* (1992) and in *New Voices: Poetry and Fiction from Colorado State University* (Colorado State University Press, 1994). Reprinted by permission of John Bradley.

Brenner, Reeve Robert: "To Make Sacred," reprinted by permission of Reeve Robert Brenner.

Brett, Lily: "To the Left," "Children II," "Invisible," "Another Selection," "Selection,""The First Job," "Overload," "The Last Day," "The Toilet," "Possessions of the Rich," "Renya's Baby," and "The Sonder Kommando," from *The Auschwitz Poems* by Lily Brett. First published by Scribe Publications Pty Ltd, Australia, 1986. Reprinted by permission of Scribe Publications Pty Ltd and Lily Brett. "The Immigration Man," "Where Were You?" "After the War," "I Have Never Known," "Poland," "The Cake," and "Displaced," from *Poland* by Lily Brett. First published by Scribe Publications Pty Ltd, 1987. Reprinted by permission of Scribe Publications Pty Ltd and Lily Brett.

Callen, P. M.: "See, Nadia," reprinted by permission of Paulette M. Callen.

Campion, Joan: "To Gisi Fleischmann," reprinted by permission of Joan Campion.

Cannaday, Mark: "Learning the Part of Otto Frank," reprinted by permission of Mark Lawson Cannaday.

Cavalieri, Grace: "To Rosa Cavalieri," reprinted by permission of Grace Cavalieri.

Celan, Paul: "Deathfugue," from *Modern Poems on the Bible*, edited by David Curzon (Philadelphia: Jewish Publication Society, 1994). Translated by John Felstiner. Reprinted by permission of John Felstiner.

Chalmer, Judith: "Folk Art" and "Personal to Kaplan," first published in *Cimarron Review* (October 1991). Published in Judith Chalmer's *Out of History's Junk Jar* (Time Being Press, 1996). Copyright © 1993 by Time Being Press, Inc. All rights reserved. Reprinted by permission of Time Being Books.

Charney, Lena L.: "The Synagogue of Florence," reprinted by permission of Lena Charney.

Clift, Elayne Goldman: "Kol Nidre," from Clift's *Demons Dancing in My Head* (Potomac, Md.: OGN Publications, 1995). Reprinted by permission of Elayne Goldman Clift.

Colonomos, Jean: "Female Jewish History: Aunt Anka" and "Female Jewish History: Aunt Tanya," published in 1985 on behalf of the Avron Foundation. Reprinted by permission of Jean Colonomos.

Crystal, Esther: "Grandmother Lost," reprinted by permission of Esther Crystal.

Cummins, Paul: "A Letter to Hans Puvogel," reprinted by permission of Paul Cummins. "Overlooking Jena," published in *Dachau Song* by Paul Cummins (New York: Peter Lang Publishing Co., 1992). Reprinted by permission of Paul Cummins.

Curley, Bruce V. J.: "This Broken Silence," reprinted by permission of Bruce V. J. Curley.

Curzon, David: "The Gardens," first published in *Forward* (1992). Reprinted by permission of David Curzon. "Psalm #1" appeared in Curzon's *Midrashim* (Cross-Cultural Communications, 1991) and in *Modern Poems on the Bible: An Anthology*, edited and with an introduction by David Curzon (Philadelphia: Jewish Publication Society, 1994).

Reprinted by permission of Cross-Cultural Communications, the Jewish Publication Society, and David Curzon.

Daigon, Ruth: *"An Die Musik,"* reprinted by permission of Ruth Daigon.

D'Alessandro, Patricia: "The Sky Was Not a Friendly Place," reprinted by permission of Patricia D'Alessandro.

Daniel, Peter: "The Victims of the Victims," from *If The Walls Between Us Were Made of Glass,* ed. Daniel, Diethart, and Kuhner, trans. Herbert Kuhner (Vienna: Verlag der Apfel, 1992). Reprinted by permission of Herbert Kuhner.

Dawid, Annie: "Taking the Holocaust to Bed," "Goethe's Tree," and "Stateless Person." "Taking the Holocaust to Bed" published in *Out Rage* (Toronto: Women's Press, 1993). Reprinted by permission of Annie Dawid.

DelGuercio, Margaret: "Children's Dreams at Theresienstadt," reprinted by permission of Margaret DelGuercio.

DeNicola, Deborah: "Inspection," reprinted by permission of Deborah DeNicola.

Desy, Peter: "Where We Are," reprinted by permission of Peter Desy.

Elenbogen, Dina: "The History of Night," reprinted by permission of Dina Elenbogen.

Elkind, Sue Saniel: "Kristallnacht," from *Bare as the Trees* (Papier-Mâché Press, 1991). Reprinted by permission of William Elkind.

Engel, Mary: "The Photograph," reprinted by permission of Mary Engel.

Exler, Samuel: "Buchenwald" and "Perhaps a Friend of Anne Frank's," the latter first published in *Home Planet News* 8, no.4 (Fall 1992). Reprinted by permission of Samuel Exler.

Fahy, Christopher: "Cinema III," reprinted by permission of Christopher Fahy.

Fishman, Charles: "The Death Mazurka" and "For Janusz Korczak," first published in *The Death Mazurka* (Timberline Press, 1987; rpt. Lubbock: Texas Tech University Press, 1989). Reprinted by permission of Charles Fishman. "The Children" appears by permission of Charles Fishman.

Fondell, Joan: "How Can They Say It Never Happened," reprinted by permission of Joan Fondell.

Frauenglas, Robert: "Seriatim," reprinted by permission of Robert A. Frauenglas.

Frenkel, Mike: "Pinball Wizards," reprinted by permission of Michael W. Frenkel.

Friedman, D. Dina: "Train to Munich" originally appeared in *Peregrine* 4 (1986), and in *Black Bear Review* 11 (1990). Reprinted by permission of D. Dina Friedman.

Fries, Kenny: "The Burden of Memory" originally appeared in the *San Francisco Sentinel*, 10 April 1987. Reprinted by permission of Kenny Fries.

Gershator, David: "33 Union Square West," reprinted by permission of David Gershator.

Glatstein, Jacob: "Twilight of the World," translated by Doris Vidaver from *Di Fried Fun Yidishen Wort* (London and New York: Der Kval, 1961). Permission to reprint granted by the poet's widow, Mrs. Fanny Glatstein, Elmhurst, New York, and by Doris Vidaver. English translation first appeared in *Prairie Schooner* (Fall 1987). Copyright © 1987 by Doris Vidaver.

Goldberg, Barbara: "Survivor" and "Hearing Him Talk," from Goldberg's *Cautionary Tales* (Tacoma Park, Md.: Dryad Press, 1990). Reprinted by permission of Barbara Goldberg.

Goldfield, Bina: "Outcast" first published in *The Reconstructionist* (Spring 1992). "Sealed" from Goldfield's chapbook (Singular Speech Press, 1992). Reprinted by permission of Bina Goldfield.

Gottlieb, Darcy: "Rehearsal at Terezin," from *No Witness But Ourselves* (Columbia: University of Missouri Press, 1973). Reprinted by permission of Darcy Gottlieb.

Gould, Roberta: "This Week," published in Gould's *Only Rock and Other Poems* (Folder Editions, 1985). Reprinted by permission of Daisy Aldan, Publisher, and Roberta Gould.

Grossberg, Mimi: "Last Rites for Bert Brecht," from *If the Walls Between Us Were Made of Glass*, ed. Daniel, Diethart, and Kuhner, trans. Herbert Kuhner (Vienna: Verlag Der Apfel, 1992). Reprinted by permission of Herbert Kuhner.

Gusewelle, Jacob: "Herringbone Overcoat" and "What Is Required," reprinted by permission of Jacob Gusewelle.

Haber, Leo: "The Book of Lamentations," reprinted by permission of Leo Haber. "The Holocaust Museum in Washington," in the U.S. Holocaust Memorial Museum archives. Reprinted by permission of Leo Haber.

Halpern, Israel: "Being Seemingly Unscathed," reprinted by permission of Israel Irving Halpern.

Hamburger, Michael: "Between the Lines" and extract from "In a Cold Season—Part 1," from Hamburger's *Collected Poems, 1941–1994* (London: Anvil Press Poetry, 1995). Reprinted by permission of Anvil Press.

Hecht, Anthony: "More Light, More Light," from Hecht's *Collected Earlier Poems* (New York: Alfred A. Knopf, 1990). Copyright © 1990 by Anthony Hecht. Reprinted by permission of Alfred A. Knopf, Inc.

Heller, André: "Jankel," from *If The Walls Between Us Were Made of Glass,* ed. Daniel, Diethart, and Kuhner, trans. Herbert Kuhner (Vienna: Verlag Der Apfel, 1992). Reprinted by permission of Herbert Kuhner.

Heller, Chaia L.: "A jew's love for language," reprinted by permission of Chaia L. Heller.

Hoffman, Helene: "Roots," reprinted by permission of Helene Hoffman.

Hollander, Jean: "Isolde, Dead in Vichy France," first published in *Kavitha* (Winter 1983). Reprinted by permission of Jean Hollander. "The Chosen," reprinted by permission of Jean Hollander.

Inez, Colette: "Home Movie of Poland," from Inez's *Alive and Taking Names* (Athens: Ohio University Press, 1977). Reprinted by permission of Colette Inez.

Intrater, Roseline: "Because No One Said No!," reprinted by permission of Roseline Intrater.

Ivker, Barry: "Bone Songs," "Buddha and Me," and "Art and Politics," reprinted by permission of Barry Ivker.

Joyce, Emily Carolyn: "Judische Friedhof: Kaiserslautern," reprinted by permission of Emily Carolyn Joyce.

Kambanelis, Iakovos: "Song of Songs," translated by Gail Holst-Warhaft, from *Modern Poems on the Bible: An Anthology,* edited and with an introduction by David Curzon (Philadelphia: Jewish Publication Society, 1994). Reprinted by permission of Gail Holst-Warhaft.

Keller, Tsipi: "The Shower," first published in *Present Tense* 14, no. 4, (May/June 1987). Reprinted by permission of Tsipi Keller. "My Father's Watches" reprinted by permission of Tsipi Keller.

Kessler, Miriam: "Yahrzeit," published in slightly altered form in *Blood to Remember: American Poets on the Holocaust,* ed. Charles Fishman (Lubbock: Texas Tech University Press, 1991). Reprinted by permission of Miriam Kessler.

Kiefer, Rita: "After Visiting Dachau," reprinted by permission of Rita Kiefer. "Ilse's Poem" previously published in *Antigonish Review* (Summer/Autumn 1986). Reprinted by permission of *Antigonish Review.*

Kind, Anne: "Hidden" and "Role Reversal," first published by *Omens Magazine* (1980). Reprinted by permission of Anne Kind.

Knobloch, Marta: "Kristallnacht '88," first published in *Baltimore Poets Celebrate Peace* (Icarus Press, 1990). Reprinted by permission of Marta Knoblock.

Koestenbaum, Phyllis: "Criminal Sonnet: XXXVIII," from *Fourteen Criminal Sonnets* (Fairfax, Calif.: Jungle Garden Press, 1984). Reprinted by permission of Phyllis Koestenbaum.

Korwin, Yala: "Song Is a Monument," "Feeding Stray Cats," and "Bronze Drama," reprinted by permission of Yala Korwin.

Krakofsky, Shel: "My Mother's Prayer Book," "In a Bicycle Repair Shop," "Daily Stones," "Trapped in Mea Shearim," "Yom Hashoah, Never Again," and "Danger: No Explosives" all from Krakofsky's *The Reversible Coat* (Moonstone Press, 1991). Reprinted by permission of Shel Krakofsky.

Kramer, Lotte: "A New Subject," from *Earthquake and Other Poems* (Rockingham Press, 1994). "The Non-Emigrant," from *The Desecration of Trees* (Somerset, Eng.: Hippopotamus Press, 1994). "Fugue" and "Friends," from *A Lifelong House* (Hippopotamus Press). "On Shutting the Door," from *The Shoemaker's Wife* (Hippopotamus Press, 1987). Reprinted by permission of Lotte Kramer.

Kreisler, Georg: "Neither Nor," from *If The Walls Between Us Were Made of Glass,* ed. Daniel, Diethart, and Kuhner, trans. Herbert Kuhner (Vienna: Verlag Der Apfel, 1992). Reprinted by permission of Herbert Kuhner.

Kuhner, Herbert: "Love of Austria" and "The Class of '38," from *If The Walls Between Us Were Made of Glass,* ed. Daniel, Diethart, and Kuhner, trans. Herbert Kuhner (Vienna: Verlag Der Apfel, 1992). Reprinted by permission of Herbert Kuhner.

Laster, Alvin M.: "Family Tree," from *Arabesques, Trumpets and Grace Notes* (1989). Reprinted by permission of Alvin Laster.

LeCompte, Kendall: "Daughter, a Gift of Red Shoes," published in *Gryphon* 13, no. 1 (1988). Reprinted by permission of Kendall LeCompte.

Lefcowitz, Barbara: "For Mirjam Lenka," published in *Shadows and Goatbones* (College Park, Md.: Scop Publishers, 1992). Reprinted by permission of Barbara F. Lefcowitz.

Leffler, Merrill: "Springtime Near Munich," reprinted by permission of Merrill Leffler.

Lengyel, Cornel Adam: "A Transport of Children," from *Jewish Currents* (April 1973). "A Shade from Auschwitz" published in *Midstream* (June/July 1994). "Ezekiel in the Valley" published in *Midstream* (July 1993). All poems reprinted by permission of Cornel Adam Lengyel.

Lifshitz, Leatrice: "A Jewish Baby in the Warsaw Ghetto," reprinted by permission of Leatrice Lifshitz.

Lorber, Toby: "Rebecca," reprinted by permission of Toby Lorber.

Maass, Arlene: "Traveling to Der Bad," reprinted by permission of Arlene Maass.

McGinnis, Joan: "Dachau" reprinted by permission of Joan McGinnis.

Mayne, Seymour: "Zalman," from *Essential Words: An Anthology of Jewish Canadian Poetry* (Oberon Press, 1985). Reprinted by permission of Seymour Mayne.

Michelson, Rich: "The March of the Orphans," reprinted by permission of Rich Michelson.

Mikofsky, Bernard: "1945," published in *Blood to Remember: American*

Poets on the Holocaust (Lubbock: Texas Tech University Press, 1991). "Cambodian Holocaust." Both poems reprinted by permission of Bernard Mikofsky.

Miller, E. Ethelbert: "The Fifties," reprinted by permission of E. Ethelbert Miller.

Mills, Jim Ignatius: "Raoul Wallenberg Slept Well Last Night," reprinted by permission of Jim Ignatius Mills.

Miłosz, Czesław: "Campo Dei Fiori" (excerpt) and "Dedication," from *The Collected Poems, 1931–1987* (New York: Ecco Press, 1988). Reprinted by permission of Ecco Press.

Mingovits, Victor: "Mystery My History," from a collection of the poet's work published by Watershed Press. Reprinted by permission of Victor Mingovits.

Mitchell, Stephen: Translations of three poems by Dan Pagis: "Testimony," "Scrawled in Pencil in a Sealed Railway Car," and "Draft of a Reparations Agreement," from *Modern Poems on the Bible: An Anthology,* ed. and with an introduction by David Curzon (Philadelphia: Jewish Publication Society, 1994). Reprinted by permission of Stephen Mitchell.

Moore, Janice Townley: "Lettuce for Anne Frank," published in the *Georgia Journal* (1984). Reprinted by permission of Janice Townley Moore.

Natt, Rochelle: "Oma's Opera Fan," reprinted by permission of Rochelle Natt.

Nelson, Jo: "At Babi Yar" and "A New Command," published in the *San Fernando Poetry Journal* (1992). Reprinted by permission of Jo Nelson.

Nelson, Stanley: "Celia Dances," reprinted by permission of Stanley Nelson.

Newman, Richard: Sonnets 25, 29, 30, 33, reprinted by permission of Richard Newman.

Niditch, B. Z.: "An Old Story," originally published in *Response* (Fall 1992). Reprinted by permission of Ben-Zion Niditch.

Ostriker, Alicia: "Poem Beginning with a Line by Fitzgerald/Hemingway," from *The Imaginary Lover* (Pittsburgh: University of Pittsburgh Press, 1986). Reprinted by permission of University of Pittsburgh Press.

Pacosz, Christina: "A Message from the Past for the Present" and "On the Propensity of the Human Species to Repeat Error," from Pacosz's *This Is Not a Place to Sing* (Albuquerque: West End Press, 1987). Reprinted by permission of Christina Pacosz.

Pagis, Dan: "Testimony," "Scrawled in Pencil in a Sealed Railway Car," and "Draft of a Reparations Agreement," translated by Stephen Mitchell, from *Modern Poems on the Bible: An Anthology,* ed. and with an introduction by David Curzon (Philadelphia: Jewish Publication Society, 1994). Reprinted by permission of Stephen Mitchell.

Pastan, Linda: "It Is Raining on the House of Anne Frank," reprinted from Pastan's *The Five Stages of Grief Poems,* by permission of the author and W. W. Norton and Company, Inc. Copyright © 1978 by Linda Pastan. "Response" is reprinted from *Waiting for My Life: Poems by Linda Pastan,* by permission of the author and W. W. Norton and Company, Inc. Copyright © 1981 by Linda Pastan.

Pawlak, Mark: "Processing" and "Like Butterflies," from *Special Handling: Newspaper Poems New and Selected* (Hanging Loose Press, 1993). Reprinted by permission of Mark Pawlak.

Perkins, T. W.: "Treblinka, 1944." Copyright © 1983 by T. W. Perkins. "At Birkenau." Copyright © 1984 by T. W. Perkins. Reprinted by permission of T. W. Perkins.

Phillips, Louis: "God Teaches Us to Forgive, But We Forget," from *Blood to Remember: American Poets on the Holocaust* (Lubbock: Texas Tech University Press, 1991). "Perhaps You Wish to Learn Another Language." Reprinted by permission of Louis Phillips.

Pinsky, Robert: "The Unseen," published in *Ironwood 20*, 11, no.1 (Spring 1983), and in *History of My Heart* (New York: Ecco Press, 1984). Reprinted by permission of Robert Pinsky.

Plank, Karl: "Malediction," reprinted by permission of Karl Plank. "Ash Wednesday," published in the *Anglican Theological Review* 74, no. 1 (Winter 1992). Reprinted by permission of *Anglican Theological Review.*

Pybus, Rodney: "October Flowers in Prague," reprinted by permission of Rodney Pybus.

Radzyner, Tamar: "Again," from *If the Walls Between Us Were Made of Glass*, ed. Daniel, Diethart, and Kuhner, trans. Herbert Kuhner (Vienna: Verlag Der Apfel, 1992). Reprinted by permission of Herbert Kuhner.

Ravikovitch, Dahlia: "Abuse," from *The Window: New and Selected Poems*, ed. and trans. Chana and Ariel Bloch. Reprinted by permission of Chana Bloch.

Rees, Elizabeth: "Martyr" and "Survivor," reprinted by permission of Elizabeth Rees.

Reis, Donna: "Photo, Kraków 1939," published in *Art Times* (August 1993). Reprinted by permission of Donna Reis.

Renshaw, Betty: "Recognition, On My Child's Face," from *To Audre and Alice* (Springhouse Press, 1985). Reprinted by permission of Betty Renshaw.

Ress, Lisa: "Household Rules," from *Flight Patterns* (Charlottesville: University Press of Virginia, 1985). "Household Rules" also appeared in *Ghosts of the Holocaust,* ed. Stewart Florsheim (Detroit: Wayne State University Press, 1988). Reprinted by permission of University Press of Virginia.

Richman, Elliot: "The Shop," first published in *Blastin' Out of Abilene* (Fort Wayne, Ind.: The Windless Orchard Press, 1988). Also published in *The World Dancer* (Santa Maria, Calif.: Asylum Arts, 1993). Reprinted by permission of Elliot Richman. "One More Holocaust Poem," reprinted by permission of Elliot Richman.

Ritchie, Elisavietta: "The German Officer Writes a Letter," published in *Salmon and Passager* (1992) and in *The Arc of the Storm* (Carrboro, N.C.: Signal Books, 1995). Reprinted by permission of Signal Books.

Robbins, Curtis: "*In Der Nacht,*" reprinted by permission of Curtis Robbins.

Rotenberg, Stella: "Biography," from *If The Walls Between Us Were Made of Glass,* ed. Daniel, Diethart, and Kuhner, trans. Herbert Kuhner (Vienna: Verlag Der Apfel, 1992). Reprinted by permission of Herbert Kuhner.

Rubin, Diana K.: "The Beginning of the Lies," published in *Response: A Contemporary Jewish Review* (Winter 1990) and in *Prophetic Voices: An International Literary Journal* 20 (1994). Reprinted by permission of Diana K. Rubin.

Rubin, Larry: "A Ballad for Tourists," first published in *Shenandoah*. Reprinted by permission of Larry Rubin.

Russell, Cynthia Pinkus: "Memorial Day: The Viet Nam Memorial," reprinted by permission of Cynthia Pinkus Russell.

Sachs, Nelly: "Even the Old Men's Last Breath" and "O the Chimneys," from *O the Chimneys*, trans. Michael Roloff. Copyright © 1967 by Farrar, Straus and Giroux, Inc. Reprinted by permission of Farrar, Straus and Giroux, Inc.

Schapiro, Jane: "After Poetry," from *Tapping This Stone* (Washington, D.C.: Writers' Publishing House, 1995). Reprinted by permission of Jane Schapiro.

Schmookler, Pauline K.: "I Mourn My Death," published in *Identity Magazine* 19, no. 1 (1984). Reprinted by permission of Pauline K. Schmookler.

Schneberg, Willa: "Kaddish for Felix Nussbaum (1904–1944)," published in *Bridges: A Journal for Jewish Feminists and Our Friends* (1990). Reprinted by permission of Willa Schneberg.

Scott, Neil C.: "Free from Shame," reprinted by permission of Neil C. Scott.

Sea, Gary: "Ursula Goetze," "Erika von Brockdorff," and "Ottilie Pohl," reprinted by permission of Gary Sea.

Seltzer, Joanne: "The Children's Museum at the Holocaust Memorial, Jerusalem," published in the *Glen Falls Review* (1984). "Ronald Reagan in Germany." Reprinted by permission of Joanne Seltzer.

Shapiro, Gregg: "Tattoo," from *Troika II* (Winnetka, Ill.: Thorntree Press, 1991). Reprinted by permission of Thorntree Press.

Sharon, Reva: "Unanswerable Questions" and "In the Absence of Yellow" included in *Blood to Remember: American Poets on the Holocaust* (Lubbock: Texas Tech University Press, 1991). "*Arbeit Macht Frei*" from *Pool of the Morning Wind* (Jerusalem: Shemish, 1989). "Shoshana" from *English Poetry in Israel* (Zurich: University of Zurich, 1990). All poems reprinted by permission of Reva Sharon.

Shomer, Enid: "The Distance between Two Towns" appeared in *Stalking the Florida Panther* (Washington, D.C.: Word Works, 1987). "Remembering" appeared in *Shirim* (1985). "The Document Room at Nuremberg" excerpted from "Datelines" in *Apalachee Quarterly.* Reprinted by permission of Enid Shomer.

Sidney, Joan Seliger: "Forging Links," from *The Way the Past Comes Back* (Willington, Conn.: Kutenai Press, 1991). Reprinted by permission of Joan Seliger Sidney.

Siegel, Bill: "Waiting to Go Home," reprinted by permission of Bill Siegel.

Siegel, Joan I.: "Dachau, 1968," reprinted by permission of Joan I. Siegel.

Silbert, Layle: "The Man with the Monocle," published in *Poet Lore* (1982), and in *Ten Jewish American Poets* (Downtown Poets, 1982). Reprinted by permission of Layle Silbert.

Silkin, Jon: "Trying to Hide Treblinka," from *The Lens Breakers* (London: Reed Consumer Books, 1992). Reprinted by permission of Reed Consumer Books.

Sklarew, Myra: *Lithuania,* part 1, published in *Forward,* 21 January 1994; parts 3 and 6 in *Sifrut Literary and Arts Review* (Winter 1994). The full poem appears in *Lithuania: New and Selected Poems,* 2d ed. (Azul Editions, 1997). Reprinted by permission of Myra Sklarew.

Smith, Dean: "Vigil in the Darkness," reprinted by permission of Dean Smith.

Solonche, J. R.: "There Are Times You Must Wonder," reprinted by permission of J. R. Solonche.

Speiser, Lester: "Motele the Incongruous," from *They Chose Life: Jewish Resistance in the Holocaust,* ed. Yehuda Bauer (Jerusalem: Hebrew University). Reprinted by permission of Lester Speiser.

Starkman, Elaine: "In the Kibbutz Laundry," from *Without a Single Answer: Poems on Contemporary Israel,* ed. Elaine Starkman (Berkeley, Calif.: Judah Magnes Museum Press, 1990). Reprinted by permission of Elaine Starkman.

Stein, Julia: "I'm Chugging into France," published in *Mosaic: A Jewish Literary Magazine* (1994). Reprinted by permission of Julia Stein.

Strahan, Bradley R.: "Martyrs of Israel," reprinted by permission of Bradley R. Strahan.

Streckfus, Charles F.: "The Last Letter," reprinted by permission of Charles F. Streckfus.

Striar, Marguerite M.: "Rage Before Pardon: An Interview with Elie Wiesel," "These Ultimate Survivors," "Hate Shall Not Impale Me," and "Like the Flash of a Bird's Wing" reprinted by permission of Marguerite M. Striar.

Sutzkever, Abraham: Poems from *Faces in Swamps* and note introducing this cycle from *Sutzkever Selected Poetry and Prose,* transcribed and edited by Harshav. Copyright © 1991, The Regents of the University of California. Published by and reprint permission granted by the University of California Press. "I Am Lying in This Coffin," "For a Comrade," "I Feel Like Saying a Prayer," "Burnt Pearls," "To the Thin Vein in My Head," "On the Subject of Roses," and "A Voice from the Heart," from *Burnt Pearls: Ghetto Poems,* trans. Seymour Mayne (Ottawa: Mosaic Press, 1981). Reprinted by permission of Seymour Mayne.

Taube, Herman: "Letter to a Poet," "Insects Won the Battle," and "Berlin: Savoy Hotel," published in *Between the Shadows* (Tacoma Park, Md.: Dryad Press, 1986). Reprinted by permission of Herman Taube and Dryad Press.

Tham (Goldberg), Hilary: "The Daughter of Survivors," previously published in *Bad Names for Women* (Washington, D.C.: Word Works Press, 1989). "Our Holocaust Dead," previously published in *Arlington-Fairfax Jewish Congregational Chronicle* (1989) and *Tigerbone Wine* (Three Continents Press, 1991). Reprinted by permission of Three Continents Press, now known as Lynn Riemer Publishers.

Torren, Asher: "Choni, The Circle Man," and "El Tango Fabuloso," reprinted by permission of Asher Torren.

Van Houten, Lois: "Last Train to Auschwitz," reprinted by permission of Lois Van Houten.

Verkauf-Verlon, Willy: "Walls," from *If the Walls Between Us Were Made of Glass,* ed. Daniel, Diethart, and Kuhner, trans. Herbert Kuhner (Vienna: Verlag Der Apfel, 1992). Reprinted by permission of Herbert Kuhner.

Verny, Sandra Collier: "My Jewish Husband," published in *Newsletter of the International Study of Organized Persecution of Children* 8, no. 2 (Fall/Winter 1991). Reprinted by permission of Sandra Collier Verny.

Verny, Thomas R.: "Where Jackals Run and Vultures Fly," first published in

The Hidden Child (The Hidden Child Foundation/ADL, 1992). Reprinted by permission of Thomas R. Verny.

Vinokurov, Yevgeny: "Adam," translated by Daniel Weissbort, from *Modern Poems on the Bible: An Anthology*, ed. and with an introduction by David Curzon (Philadelphia: Jewish Publication Society, 1994). Reprinted by permission of Daniel Weissbort.

Walders, Davi: "Born in Safety, 1941" and "Heading East," reprinted by permission of Davi Walders.

Waldman, Mitchell: "Hello," previously published in *Innisfree Magazine*. Reprinted by permission of Mitchell Waldman.

Warshawski, Morrie: "Gypsy Soup," first published in *Willamette Week's Fresh Weekly*, 29 June 1981. Reprinted by permission of Morrie Warshawski.

Waters, Michael: "Yellow Stars," published in *The Burden Lifters* (Pittsburgh: Carnegie-Mellon University Press, 1989). "In Memory of Smoke" appeared in *Green House* and *Not Just Any Death* (Rochester, N.Y.: BOA Editions, 1979). Both poems reprinted by permission of Michael Waters.

Wayman, Tom: "The Death of the Partisan Girl," from *Essential Words: An Anthology of Jewish Canadian Poetry*, ed. Seymour Mayne (Ottawa: Oberon Press, 1985). Reprinted by permission of Tom Wayman.

Weislitz, Vera: "Sweet Sixteen" and "Circus" from *The Daughter of Olga and Leo*, published in Prague in English and Czech by UNITISK in 1994. Reprinted by permission of Vera Weislitz.

Weissbort, Daniel: "Poland," reprinted by permission of Daniel Weissbort.

West, John Foster: "Anne Frank," reprinted by permission of John Foster West.

Weston, Joanna M.: "Gas Ovens," reprinted by permission of Joanna M. Weston.

Wexler, Evelyn: "The Suitcase" appeared in the *Dominion Review* (June 1991). "Tourist at Dachau" published in *Poets On: Arrivals* (Summer 1990). Reprinted by permission of Evelyn Wexler.

PERMISSIONS

What, Leslie: "Portraits of the Shadows in the Flames," reprinted by permission of Leslie What.

Wolf, Michele: "Badge," appeared in *The Keeper of Light* by Michele Wolf. Copyright © 1995 by Painted Bird Quarterly. Reprinted by permission of Michele Wolf.

Author Index

Translator Index